Advance Praise for
Stops Along the Way

"No conservative leader has ever written a book like this. No conservative leader has ever lived a life like Brent Bozell's. These are amazing tales."

—**Sen. Mike Lee (R-UT)**

"America is—or was—a storytelling nation. It is one of the reasons Paul Harvey's *The Rest of the Story* was so popular. Now comes Brent Bozell with a series of stories that revives the tradition of storytelling. In an age of extreme partisanship, conflict, negativity, corruption, and distrust, these stories will bless your heart as they have mine."

—**Cal Thomas, Syndicated Columnist**

"Brent Bozell is a true conservative who has dedicated his life to fighting for the American people. I'm proud to call him not just a steadfast ally in this fight, but also a friend. This book is an enlightening collection of stories about Brent's life and the Bozell family."

—**Sen. Ted Cruz (R-TX)**

"Having known his beloved mom, having read the wondrous biography of his heralded dad, I acquired a genuine curiosity—what in the heck was it like for Brent Bozell to grow up amidst the sweeping drama and smoky chaos, the menagerie of pets and siblings, of this nomadic family of amazing consequence? The answer is in this engrossing and beautiful and utterly charming book, about the bedlamic joys of Casa Bozell, familial affection, the travails of Conservatism Inc., and so much more. Brent is a marvelous writer and storyteller, wielding the pen of an infectiously happy warrior. What a kindness he has done to share this gift, and this memoir."

—**Jack Fowler, Former Publisher,** *National Review*

"We all know Brent for his work combating media bias for decades. Now we find out the extraordinary stories that led Brent to where he is today. What a captivating read!"

—**Hon. Mark Meadows, Former White House Chief of Staff**

"Life is full of surprises; ups and downs. This charming collection is sure to inspire us to dream again."

—**Dr. Alveda King, Pastoral Associate at Priests for Life**

"Brent Bozell is one of those people who never seems to close his eyes—and even if he does, he still soaks in everything going on around him. His recollections of just a smidgeon of what he's seen in his fuller-than-imaginable life in *Stops Along the Way* will fascinate his readers, whoever and wherever they are."

—Alfred Regnery, President, Regnery Publishing

"You need to read this book with a good stiff drink. Rarely do I suggest reading a biography, but this is one you don't want to miss."

—Corey Lewandowski, Former Campaign Manager, Donald J. Trump for President

"Brent Bozell's *Stops Along the Way* offers a rare glimpse into what shaped this incredible patriot's worldview."

—Larry Solov, Co-Founder and CEO, Breitbart

"Brent is a proud American who has dedicated his life to holding onto the values that really matter. His new book chronicling his life lessons from his many battles comes at the perfect time to inspire us to keep going."

—Matt Schlapp, Chair of CPAC

"Brent takes storytelling to a level I haven't seen in years. Tales of adventure that take you from Virginia to Spain to Europe to Nicaragua to DC back to Virginia to being on a plane that may be getting hijacked! A thoroughly entertaining read!"

—Hon. Jim DeMint, Chairman, Conservative Partnership Institute

"Given Brent's pedigree, I always assumed he had an interesting life, but I didn't imagine this. Great stories about his big Catholic family, school in Spain, work in Nicaragua, and, of course, politics make this an enjoyable romp."

—Hon. Rick Santorum, Chairman, Patriot Voices

"Need an antidote to the chaos going on? This is it. You'll escape to a world of wonder as only Brent can describe because he lived it! Get ready to smile, laugh out loud, and be absolutely mesmerized by these true tales and the incredible style in which they are told."

—Adam Brandon, President, FreedomWorks

"Brent Bozell's *Stops Along the Way* doesn't hold back. His youthful adventures make for great stories and explain a lot about this fascinating man."

—**Sean Spicer, Former White House Press Secretary**

"What's that old truism…the apple doesn't fall far from the tree? Well, one of my favorite authors, political activists, writers, and 'tree shakers' is Brent Bozell. His father wrote for the redoubtable Senator Barry Goldwater and is himself the nephew of the inimitable William F. Buckley Jr. So Brent, the creator and soul of the watchdog Media Research Center, has chosen some of the juiciest fruit he has collected from his many years right in the middle of the political garden—but added lots of enjoyable seasoning from his personal true adventures in many other facets of his life. I promise you'll not want to put it down and return to the sad, troubling, and harsh realities around us—Take a Bozell Break. You'll thank me for it."

—**Pat Boone, Singer and Conservative Commentator**

"Americans love stories; that is why great Americans such as Mark Twain, Will Rogers, Abraham Lincoln, and Ronald Reagan hold a special place in our hearts. And just now, the American people are in dire need of stories that make us reflect on a time of innocence, and daring. My dear friend L. Brent Bozell III has endeavored to bring us stories from his life experiences in *Stops Along the Way*. Perhaps the healing for America will come from a collection of stories that cause us to remember, dream, of those days once again."

—**Lt. Col. Allen B. West, Former Congressman and Chairman, Republican Party of Texas**

"This isn't a book—it's a raucous adventure, written in an effortless style that masterfully paints a picture of a life lived to its absolute, no-holds-barred, every-minute-like-it's-your-last, fullest."

—**Craig Shirley, Bestselling Author**

"Do not believe my brother. I did not do those things."

—**Father Michael Bozell**

STOPS ALONG
THE WAY

STOPS ALONG THE WAY

A Catholic Soul, a Conservative Heart, an Irish Temper, and a Love of Life

L. Brent Bozell III

A POST HILL PRESS BOOK

Stops Along the Way:
A Catholic Soul, a Conservative Heart, an Irish Temper, and a Love of Life
© 2021 by L. Brent Bozell III
All Rights Reserved

ISBN: 978-1-64293-924-8
ISBN (eBook): 978-1-64293-925-5

Cover photography and art by Corwin Parks

This is a work of nonfiction. All people, locations, events, and situations are portrayed to the best of the author's memory.

Post Hill Press
New York • Nashville
posthillpress.com

Published in the United States of America
1 2 3 4 5 6 7 8 9 10

For Douglas and Miss Gracie

CONTENTS

FOREWORD

BY JACK CASHILL

"What we've got here," says the captain of the guard after slugging a chained "Cool Hand" Luke, "is a failure to communicate." If there is a fundamental problem in America today, it is that very failure: we know what they know, but they don't know what we know. Like the captain, our friends on the left try to threaten those with real knowledge into silence, but like Luke, Brent Bozell won't be silenced. Like Luke, too, Brent can take a shot and remain defiant.

What I have particularly appreciated about Brent's work with the Media Research Center is that he enables us to know at least what they think they know. It is that unflinching knowledge of both sides of any issue that makes a conservative out of a liberal, and it is the reason why conservatives *always* outscore liberals on political knowledge tests.

Many of us started on the left. A baby boomer like Brent, I was the unofficial block captain of the preteens for JFK club in my vestigial Irish Catholic neighborhood. Like many conservatives, I had to *learn* my way out of a liberal ghetto. Virtually all the voices around me in the turbulent sixties were telling me, "Go left, young man."

Perhaps foremost among those telling me to go right was William Buckley. I watched Buckley on TV with my siblings and widowed mother in our Newark, New Jersey, housing project. Brent had a closer view. "Uncle Bill" was his mother's brother. Only in America could two people of such seemingly different backgrounds end up not only sharing a worldview but also participating in a book like this.

For all our differences, Brent and I have two powerful influences in common, both of which, as the reader will see, have shaped Brent's character: one is our shared Americanism; the other is our shared Catholicism. Historically, each reinforced the other.

When I started graduate school, I cited as my goal "to write books explaining America to Americans." I went on to get a Ph.D. in American studies and have written a dozen or so such books. I think I know America—not because of my degree, but in spite of it. For me, as for Brent, reality has been a much better teacher.

What I have learned over time is that we have plenty of spiritual firepower left, if only we seek to find it. We're not living in a healthy cultural world, to be sure, but we know that is so, and most of us can remember what it once was like.

Once upon a time Ronald Reagan could engage in political warfare with his nemesis Tip O'Neill but at the end of the day the two Irishmen could meet to share a beer. Don Rickles could (and did) insult anyone in sight, and we roared with laughter, no one more loudly than the object of his scorn. We can remember how this nation seamlessly put all internal discord aside on 9/11 to yet again show the world her best, once more leading the way, this time to confront international terror.

But we can also remember Christmas, when we put everything aside again, this time to joyfully proclaim to the world His birth. But shhh… the child sleeps! Away in a manger, no crib for a bed. Peace on Earth, good will to all men.

If it can be reimagined, why can't it be reborn?

That's why I like this book. Don't read these tales as stories of a bygone past. How depressing can that be! Read them as templates. Read them and reimagine a world once more filled with childhood wonderment, youthful aspiration, and adult certainty. We are in desperate need of all three today. Reimagine a world with faith as its cornerstone and family as its glue. Reimagine a time when virtue, although not easily attained, was always an aspiration. Reimagine an ordered society filled with adventures without safety nets. Reimagine freedom. Reimagine laughter.

Reimagine a love for living.

—*Jack Cashill*

INTRODUCTION

"Daddy, what did you do during COVID-19?"

I finished this book.

Some years ago I met a fellow over lunch who told me he'd recently published his memoirs to share his experiences in World War II. He had been everywhere in the Pacific Theater. He offered to send me a copy, and I told him I'd be delighted to read it. A week later the book arrived. Truth be told, I never finished it. This man wasn't exactly Audie Murphy. He was a cook. Presumably, he cooked well. It's in his memory that I stipulate what you hold in your hands is not an autobiography.

By the age of forty-five Barack Obama felt he was so accomplished he'd written not one, but two autobiographies about his accomplishments, the singular greatest accomplishment being escaping ridicule for the hubris that led him to think he was worthy of two autobiographies by the age of forty-five. You'll find nothing like that here.

These are just stories—stories of my sojourns to places that no longer exist, at least as I remember them. "The past is a foreign country," L.P. Hartley wrote in the opening of his classic novel, *The Go-Between*. "They do things differently there." Several of the places I dwelled were doing things "differently" even upon our arrival there. The inhabitants of these places deserve our understanding.

When you reach the age where AARP recruiters are becoming impatient, you've probably accumulated lots of mental memorabilia, but as with trinkets on a shelf, they become dusty over time. I endeavor to be as accurate as possible here. Where I've been able to do so, I've shared anecdotes with co-conspirators and asked for fact-checking. But here's the thing. Their memories also play games. Based on their feedback, I've removed pieces in which I lost confidence, changed others to straighten out the facts, and kept those intact whose accuracy they verified, or about which I remain convinced are accurate.

I borrow Bob Woodward's style with certain quotations, which is to say, I make them up. For the most part, though, I use quotes to accurately reflect what was said. In some instances they were memorable enough I can state them verbatim. Some fact-checkers responded to my requests with particularly salient observations of their own. I chose to include their comments as well.

There's another reason this book is not an autobiography. While these stories are true, they are not what I'd point to if asked to identify what's most important to me. That I reserve entirely for my family, a life lived with a wife for more than four decades raising five children and watching fourteen grandchildren introduce themselves to the world (and, in a couple of cases, put the world on notice). There are many, many stories here, but I assert executive privilege and declare them too personal to share.

This isn't a comprehensive look either. There is no discussion of my college years spent at the University of Dallas. They were glorious with enough anecdotes to fill their own book. The problem is that I worry about statutes of limitations. I suppose that there's a half-century cutoff, but why take the chance? Much of what would go into that book might qualify as state's evidence at trial.

And then there's the biggest hole: the past thirty-three years devoted primarily to the Media Research Center but also to other endeavors I've launched or in which I've participated. That chapter is not yet complete.

Someday I may choose to put pen to paper to document this period. Oh, there will be some fun stuff to recount, but by necessity this project would need to be more serious because on the whole it was a far more consequential period. The challenges facing this nation are grave, and some would say, on many fronts, existential. This is not the path I choose to travel right now.

No, these are just stories selected with the intention to entertain. They are stops along the way in a journey not yet complete. If from time to time the reader thinks the stories are too good to be true, that is actually a good thing. It will mean I succeeded in defeating the cliché.

LBB III
Great Falls, VA
January 4, 2021

STOPS ALONG
THE WAY

MONTEJURRA

1. The Invasion

The State of Maryland sighed with relief while the State of Virginia, had it known what was coming, would have prepared for invasion. Grant's army could not have been a whole lot scarier than the Bozells'. The army was leaving suburbia, the Washington, DC, bedroom community of Chevy Chase, and headed for the country, specifically the little hamlet of Huntly, some seventy miles to the southwest, nestled in the foothills of the Blue Ridge Mountains. It was the fall of 1964, and everything was about to change.

Let's get the vitals out of the way. There were our parents, Brent Jr. and Patricia (Trish, sometimes Tish), young and vibrant, deeply immersed in the emerging conservative movement. Among other things, Papa was a master orator and speechwriter and served on the defense team of Senator Joe McCarthy. He was the first Washington editor for the *National Review*, a failed candidate for Congress—unsurprisingly, as it was a planned suicide mission for an upstart cause—and the ghost author of Barry Goldwater's game-changing bestseller, *The Conscience of a Conservative*. Mom was the closest sibling to William F. Buckley Jr., a firecracker in her own right, and a charming hostess with a towering intellect to match her husband's. They were redheads, as were all nine of their children as well as a tenth who would arrive in 1967. I was in the middle of the pack, age nine. Add our Spanish maid, Mercedes Bravo, who had been with us since 1961 when she was nineteen and today is retired in Spain; our Ecuadoran cook, Luz Lozada, bronzed, older, stout, and with a menacing look and the heart of a lamb; a very spoiled cat, Kiki, assorted parakeets, little turtles, and who knows what else, and we were an army on the march.

Why were we leaving the exciting world of Washington, DC, for the tranquility of the mountains? Three reasons I can think of. There were financial realities. Although some think of the Buckleys as the conservative equivalent of the Kennedys, they never had Joe's money, preferring, as they did, to make their money honestly. Truth is, we were constantly struggling, primarily because money was never my father's focus—making it, keeping it, even understanding it. While running for Congress in 1962, he regularly hammered his GOP primary opponent, Charles Mathias, for economic policies that would lead to a national depression. One day a reporter pushed back. "Don't you mean 'recession' and not 'depression'?" To which my father answered, "'Depression,' 'recession.' What's the difference?" Anyone who knew Papa would understand he had no earthly idea and could care even less.

Papa eschewed what would have been a lucrative career practicing law in the pursuit of more intellectual activities such as writing for *National Review*, giving the occasional speech, and ghostwriting *The Conscience of a Conservative* for Senator Barry Goldwater. Given that he completed the book in nineteen days believing it a terrible intellectual product that no one would bother to read, he didn't fight for royalties. Too bad. The book went on to sell *millions* of copies.

Papa had a gift for misjudging the book market. He spent seven years writing his next book, *The Warren Revolution*, which this time no one read or bought. Well, almost no one. Henry Kissinger thought the book's defense of originalism provided the groundwork for Nixon's Watergate legal defense, and invited Papa to the White House to solicit his advice. In a twist of fate, Nixon's chief Senate inquisitor, Sam Ervin, shared Papa's views on originalism, which, had Nixon been impeached, might well have been gleefully exploited by Team Nixon at trial.

So Papa's income was always meager, but with an occasional infusion of Buckley family cash, he made ends meet. There was the home in Chevy Chase, then an exclusive residential area but not nearly as opulent as it is today. Located just across the Maryland border, our home allowed for easy trips to downtown DC. It also worked well in reverse. It was a good spot for cocktail parties with the men and women who constituted the early leadership of the conservative movement.

The house was necessarily large enough to fit eight children, a maid, and a cook. A swimming pool was built into the backyard, and it was constantly filled with children, ours and the neighbors', laughing, yelling, squealing, zipping down the slide (horrors!), and bouncing off the diving board (double horrors!).

The appearance was one of wealth, but wealth never interested Papa. His Old Crow bourbon was bottom shelf. His suits were simple. I doubt he owned five ties. Mom drove one of those circa 1960 Chevy half-tanks large enough to pack in her children for the trip to Mass.

Papa, on the other hand, drove a VW Beetle, then probably the cheapest car on the market. I remember the day he drove up in a brand new, shiny Bug, and we saw the price tag still on the window—one thousand dollars! Just saying that amount out loud made us jump in awe.

My father's second reason for leaving the nation's capital was his growing disenchantment with the conservative movement, or—perhaps it would be more accurate to say—his growing attraction to the Catholic Church. Life in Washington no longer excited him. Born and raised in Omaha, Papa was as middle America as you could get, so the idea of moving from the hubbub of Washington to what certainly seemed like the middle of America held real attraction. My more sophisticated mother may have been less keen on the move, but she, too, was losing interest in the world of politics and was always up for an adventure. My parents had just launched a new Catholic magazine, *Triumph*. Its offices were located at 1520 K Street in the middle of Washington, but their heart was never there.

The final and most important reason for leaving was *us*. There's no magic dust I can sprinkle here. We were monsters, out of control, and becoming more dangerous by the day. The gentle Chevy Chase community, with its idyllic cherry-blossomed streets in the spring and storied Christmas light displays in the winter, was supposed to be a bastion of serenity. With us roaming free, it was anything but.

We dominated. Chris at fourteen, Kathy at thirteen, Michael at eleven, Maureen at ten, and me at nine—we were veterans of misrule. Johnny at seven was almost old enough to join his siblings in mayhem. Aloise at five and Patricia at four were in training, and Willie, just out of diapers at three, was showing promise. We entered into a strategic alliance with the Rizzoli kids, three boys and a girl in our age range. Combined there were enough of us to ravage the neighborhood, which we did like jackals. After any escapade you'd find us racing our bicycles through the streets as unsubtle as the Hells Angels, the racket from the inevitable playing cards attached to our bicycle spokes louder than an AK-47. We'd be high-tailing it in numerous directions, some racing across front lawns, others flying bikes down hills, but all headed toward a prearranged destination, at which point—zap!

We vanished.

Gone underground. We were intimately familiar with the water drain tunnel systems crisscrossing our neighborhood and beyond. At various points there were entrances to these cement culverts big enough for children to run into, and run we did, deep into familiar tunnels, dimly lit by street drain openings above. While others above ground might be searching frantically, we were laughing down below, merrily making our way to an exit blocks away, planning our next misadventure.

Although rarely caught, we were always suspects. Our pranks were becoming more devious by the moment, and the future was looking grim for homeowners in Chevy Chase. Except for Chris and Kathy, none of us was even a teenager yet. Our parents knew we were, if not a national catastrophe in the making, certainly a local one. Something had to give, and it did. Our parents fled to the country where, presumably, we could wreak less havoc (wrong). Looking back on those adventures I suspect the neighbors were popping the bubbly before the moving trucks even left the block.

We had looked at three properties. One in Maryland was an old farmhouse that clearly didn't work. The second I can't recall. The third property was the one in Huntly. As soon as we arrived to inspect, the children poured out of the station wagon, and, monkeys that we were, ran straight for the seductive low-hanging limbs of the two massive birch trees nearby. We quickly scaled them and from the highest perch looked out to view the property.

Papa and Mom were inside inspecting things. When they emerged, and we clambered down, we squealed as one that we just had to have this place. Papa attempted to temper the enthusiasm, but I suspect he was having a dickens of a time restraining his own. A couple of weeks or so later our parents made the announcement. She was ours.

* * *

Today it's the stately and expensive Glen Gordon Manor Bed and Breakfast with lush rolling lawns, lavish bedrooms, gourmet meals, and Jaguars in the parking lot. In 1964, it was a working farm with lawns constantly at war with dandelions, bushes battling and succumbing to poison ivy, a long driveway with the gravel in full retreat, and old stone walls coated by honeysuckle. It was far nicer then. It was a home. In late October, under a driving rain, a station wagon and a VW Beetle led moving vans up the driveway. A mass of humanity poured out.

It was then called Kenmore Manor and had been owned by the Gordon family for generations. Ever the romantic, Papa immediately renamed it Montejurra, site of the annual mountainside rally of the Spanish Carlist movement where Catholic die-hards gathered to celebrate their faith. At the Battle of Montejurra during the Third Carlist War in 1873 the outnumbered Carlist forces repelled the anti-Catholic Republican army after a ferocious engagement. Three years later the Carlists again mounted a spirited defense, but this time they had only sixteen hundred men and could not withstand the assault. In retreat, they surrendered their final stronghold. Papa knew these kinds of things. No one else did.

You can just imagine the head-scratching from the hillbilly locals when the "Montejurra" sign went up.

Montejurra was one of the finest properties in quiet, pastoral Rappahannock County, nestled in the foothills of the Blue Ridge Mountains. There is a debate over its date of origin. Above the entrance hall fireplace there's one date, 1827. In another it says 1919, when a large addition was added, and it was turned into a swank hunting lodge. Other records have Montejurra's origins dating to 1834 as a Wells Fargo stagecoach stop. Some believe the earliest part can be traced to the 1780s. No matter; it's old.

Constructed of stone and stucco, the house stretches effortlessly from the kitchen and children's dining room on the one end to the master bedroom on the other. In between are eight bedrooms, an exquisite formal dining room, and an imposing entryway. The impressively wide hallway, lined with bookshelves made of black walnut, leads into the massive Great Room, whose dark paneled walls, two-story ceiling, and exposed beams made "great" seem like an entirely appropriate descriptive.

On one side of this immense room, three large glass doors open to a stone patio flanked by stately boxwoods and face the sprawling front yard several acres in dimension. The doors on the other end of the Great Room open to the enclosed patio facing the backyard. Stand in the Great Room, turn around and look up, and, yes, that's an orchestra pit up there, and why not? Across the room there is another door, this one leading down a more private hallway with four stately bedrooms, each with its own fireplace, antique sconces on the walls, and large porcelain tubs in the bathrooms. The master bedroom at the back of the house, with its attached screen porch and outdoor stone patio, was our parents' Fortress of Solitude. They needed one.

There was charm everywhere. Eight working fireplaces. Hiding places galore. There was so much to explore, a gateway to a mysterious past—bedroom halls, creaky old staircases leading to small rooms, doors leading to rooms with doors attached to creaky old staircases leading to—*Oh, yes! Now I get it! This is the way I came up before, from the other side!*

At the top of one staircase there was a closet, large, dark, and dusty from years of nonuse. At the back of it there was a door opening to yet another closet, this one ringed by wooden benches with seats that opened to the squeaks of some annoyed mouse scampering away. (Narnia, anyone?)

As a reminder that this place had once been used as a hunting lodge, there was a box hanging on the wall in the kitchen with a dirty glass panel through which you could see room numbers dangling from hooks. Each identified a bedroom. They'd jiggle and ring when the bedroom buzzers were pushed to summon staff.

The first order of business was bedroom assignments. There were two bedrooms upstairs. Mercedes and Willie were assigned one room, Patricia and I the other. We felt we'd hit the jackpot (but who didn't?). The room was large enough to fit at least three beds. The shared bathroom had a self-standing porcelain tub big enough to fit Mussolini. "Patricia, look! A porch! Brent, over here! A sitting room with a TV!" It was more condo than bedroom.

Then it was off to explore. We excitedly burst into each other's bedrooms with squeals of "Neat!" "Cool!" "I want yours!" "Mine's nicer!" "How come you get a fireplace?" "Get out!" What glorious pandemonium—nine redheaded children out of control, a maid and cook attempting to bring a semblance of order, and parents guiding the movers. I can still hear Mom: "Honey, for the last time. Get. Out. Of. The. Way!"

But none of us expected what was under the house. From the outside you could enter the basement using steps by the kitchen on one end, or by our parents' porch on the other. From the inside you could descend an old staircase behind the kitchen pantry, or on the other side of the house, use the one next to the Great Room. You had to duck going down both sets of stairs. You smelled the dimly lit basement before you saw it: dank, raw, old mildew, the stuff that might give instant pneumonia or carry COVID-19, but for Bozell children it smelled like adventure.

Taking the pantry steps, you reached a dusty low-ceilinged cellar the size of the kitchen above it, with little in it. The floors were cement, the walls cinder block and plasterboard. It was empty raw bones, and we could engage in endless kickball contests down there without causing damage. At the far end and to the left of this room there was a smaller storage room with shelves that would hold potatoes over the winter and freezers for frozen vegetables and meat. But on the far end and to the right was the long, dark passageway that spanned the length of the house, following the contours of the hallways above. It was perhaps three feet wide, and low enough that adults needed to duck, especially as they came across the occasional lonely light bulb challenging unwary heads. The walls were hewed out of rough limestone, and it was far dustier—wait, is that a tunnel?

Indeed it was. Just a few feet down the passageway there was an opening on the left side of the wall, a dark, unlit tunnel carved into the foundation, perhaps three feet high and two feet wide, once used for pipes and wiring.

Flashlights in hand, we crawled on the loose dirt, dirtying our clothes as the tunnel meandered under the house, finally emptying out further down the passageway. Leading off from this tunnel we found two more passages, both smaller, one so little it required you to crawl on your stomach. Both reached their exits out other walls. Down the hall there was another, smaller opening about four feet above the ground, cut out of the stone. There was no independent lighting in the hole, and after your eyes adjusted to the indirect lighting from window wells you'd find yourself in some sort of a room carved out of the stone, serving no discernible purpose.

You continued down the passageway until it opened into another cellar of sorts, as rough-cut as the hallway, with dim light from a couple dirtier window wells across the room shooting beams of dust. You were now underneath the Great Room. Here lived the massive, ancient, and impossibly inefficient propane heating system. Off to the side there was a heavy metal vault door, open but inoperable, with shelving inside.

You could just imagine a bygone era with the shelves filled with silver and other valuables stored there when the Gordon family returned to their primary home in Baltimore. As before in the hallway, there was another hole in the far wall, this one high enough that a child would need a leg up to enter, again opening to another stone-walled, dirt-floored room. The Viet Cong would have found themselves right at home under this house.

An old house like this has her stories, much of it folklore, but even folklore can have a basis in fact. We heard that slaves were hidden in these tunnels during the Civil War, but the story was too noble by half. A second story about a Yankee soldier hidden under that house made more sense.

Huntly was a veritable hot spot during the war. During his famous 1862 campaign the legendary Stonewall Jackson marched his "foot cavalry" up and down the Shenandoah Valley just a few miles west. Closer still, famed Rebel cavalry commander General Jeb Stuart patrolled the area and his deputy, Colonel John Mosby, dueled Union forces throughout the countryside.

Stuart and Northern Cavalry General Armstrong Custer despised each other and dispensed with the rules of warfare by regularly lynching each other's prisoners. One Southern partisan, Albert Gallatin Willis, was hanged from a tree about a mile away from Montejurra in retaliation for the execution of a Yankee a few miles to the north. And then there were the twenty-eight thousand Rebel soldiers under the command of General James Longstreet who marched through our property on their way to Gettysburg. Then, too, the battered remnants of Lee's army retreated to safety via Chester Gap, just three miles away, and all of this just a century before the Bozells invaded.

Now to the outdoors. This would take longer to explore, years really, if you included the surrounding hills beyond our forty-eight acres.

There was the stone and stucco guesthouse. Occasionally it would serve as Papa's office, and, toward the end of our stay, it was used for a short while by Cy and Kathy after their wedding, then by Chris and his wife, Mary, after theirs. Other than that, the four-bedroom abode was empty except for the living room, which we used as a playroom with endless ping pong and pool games. Under that house was the old sooty garage where old, rusting tools were left behind including axes, rusty saws, small sickles and large scythes, primitive handheld tools, and the like.

Outside the kitchen there were the two formal gardens, English boxwoods in delicate, manicured designs with their American boxwood counterparts taller and untouched, protecting the edges. To the east of the formal gardens, under those massive old beech trees we'd climbed the first day, you could see remnants of a small slate patio used for summertime dancing, lit by floodlights set in the trees. To the west of the gardens there was the hillside that would serve as our vegetable garden.

Behind the house the yard backed into a three-foot stone wall built by our self-indulged idea of slave labor, by which I mean Kathy, Michael, and Maureen in the summer of '68 when I was away at camp and spared. On the other side of that wall, up a little rise, was the Pool from Hell. In all the years we were there, it never stopped leaking. We had no idea how to fix it, and everything we tried only made matters worse. One time Papa figured out how to replaster the entire thing, and I swear it looked absolutely beautiful. It looked beautiful, that is, until we filled the pool with water, and all the plaster cracked off. We spent all summer taking pieces of cracked mortar out of the pool. One year, Papa used some sort of red compound as an adhesive that never quite adhered, so when the plaster came off (again) we were left with the world's first red pool. That was Papa. That was us. And that was Montejurra.

There was the seven-stall horse stable, rather new and with a well-appointed tack room. Except for Patricia and Mom, who once was a champion rider, we weren't particularly a horse family, so Papa allowed our neighbor Butch Eastham to use the stables for his horses provided he mowed our fields and gave Patricia the occasional use of a horse to take into them. We had another horse there, just for a moment, but that episode will have to wait a bit.

We need to return to the day we moved in.

2. Douglas

As we raced around the house in full exploration mode we came across a small black man in the Great Room sweeping the dusty floor. He was in his late forties, standing slightly taller than five feet, donning an old pair of glasses on a face marked by deep crevices from a lifetime working outdoors. He wore a dirty farmer's cap, an old flannel shirt, well-seasoned jean overalls, and equally seasoned boots. We would never see him attired in anything else.

Papa approached this stranger and asked him to identify himself.

The man doffed his hat, exposing his salt and pepper hair. "Mah name's Douglas, and Ahs comes with the place." Yes, he spoke that way. Remember, the past is a different country.

We had met Douglas Russell.

Douglas Gordon Russell was born on August 11, 1916, and he really did come with the place. He was born on the property and was raised by

Mrs. Elizabeth Gordon, who changed his name from Charles to Douglas Gordon in memory of her deceased husband. Mrs. Gordon was fabulously wealthy. Her second husband Basil was reputedly the first man in America to accumulate a million dollars in cash and owned miles of land surrounding Montejurra.

Folklore has it she eventually sold most of it for fifty cents per acre to provide homesteads for poor families living in the hills. Douglas clearly revered this woman. By his account, she was a kind lady who taught him all the essentials of farming. She also trained him to be a proper footman. He would tend to her friends when they came to dance on a patio illuminated by a spotlight strategically placed in the trees. A different country.

To our knowledge Douglas rarely roamed farther than Flint Hill, four miles southeast, or Front Royal, eight miles in the opposite direction. Oh there must have been an outing here and there throughout the course of his life, but the only exception he spoke of was the time Mrs. Gordon took him to her primary estate in Baltimore. While there he somehow participated in an amateur fight with a young boxer named Joe Louis. Douglas giggled later recounting how he was flattened in two rounds. Good story. I like to believe it was true.

After Mrs. Gordon died, the property passed to her nephew Bernie Dahlgren, a haughty man whom we knew slightly but disliked immensely. The house had lost its luster allegedly because he'd accumulated large gambling debts and was unable to maintain it. If Mrs. Gordon lived her life as a benign stereotype of the Old South, Dahlgren represented all that was wrong with that not-so-distant past. He had kept Douglas as something of a serf—uneducated, penniless, and unaware of any life other than that of "Massah Dahlgren's" servant. Douglas, who was incapable of uttering a cross word about anyone, managed to extend that courtesy to the Dahlgren family, more, I believe, out of fear than respect.

Douglas was our bridge to a time gone by. My brother Michael quotes Chaucer and speaks for his family when he describes him as "a perfect gentle knight." He had a constant smile when he was around us, a chuckle when we made him laugh, and a visage soft and wise when we approached him privately to confide in him. He was prematurely long in the tooth from a lack of dental care and decades of rolling and smoking cigarettes from the inevitable red can of Prince Edward tobacco tucked in his back pocket.

His arms might have looked thin and pale, but they were sinewy and unexpectedly strong. Although just 120 or so pounds, Douglas effortlessly carried loads of trash a third or more of his body weight down the drive and over the hill to a burning pit a quarter of a mile away. He managed heavy machinery. He hoed fields for hours on end in the hot, sticky summer sun. Working like this since his boyhood, he developed arm muscles so taut he could not touch his shoulder with his hand, the reason, he smiled, that the army had rejected him for service. But his most distinguished feature was those hands, so powerful for such a little man, with calluses so thick he could extinguish cigarettes between his fingers and not feel a thing, or if he sliced one accidentally, causing gashes and enough bleeding to make you cringe, he'd barely notice. They were that tough, and so was he. Maybe he did fight Joe Louis.

But where did Douglas live?

It turns out that over the hill from the vegetable garden there were two aging clapboard tenant houses Papa had not been told he owned. In one house resided a black family headed by Carl Fry, a handsome man in his late twenties who looked just like a young Cassius Clay and who handled odd jobs around the property in return for free room and board, unless he was in jail for petty crimes. Since the jail had ground floor windows, we could go talk to him when he was in the slammer.

His wife and their small children kept to themselves (I don't know if I ever knew how many there were). They would live in that house for a few years until we learned the children were stealing our chickens under orders from their mother. Papa finally and reluctantly asked them to leave, which they did, but not before they thoroughly gutted the house from within. A different place.

Douglas lived in the smaller house. Built on the slope of a hill, the front door was on the second floor. The first floor was accessed from the back, on the lower side of the hill. One larger room was the primary living area, always dark, warm, and cozy, with its low-ceilinged roof and sweet aroma of age and firewood from the large potbelly stove in the middle of the room. On one side was the kitchen with its primitive cooking accessories. On the other was the old iron bed where Douglas slept when nursing a hangover. In short order the house, especially this room, would regularly host Bozell children who came to visit. Wintertime in the house was special. After a morning sledding down the snowy hills, we'd burst into the house, cold and hungry, and sit by the warmth of the fire drinking hot chocolate. More than once, Miss Gracie cooked us her delicious fried eggs using old bacon grease.

Did I not mention Miss Gracie? Well not to worry. We didn't know about her at first either. When Douglas told us where he lived, a number of us raced up the driveway and over the hill to see what else we'd purchased. We knocked on the door loudly, making a racket. The curtain from the window on the right side of the door parted, and we peered in. We were looking right into the face of a diminutive old black lady who could not have looked less threatening, except for the massive pistol pointed at our faces. We'd just met Douglas's mother, Miss Gracie. Douglas soon joined us at the house, assuring his mother that these little redheaded scamps meant no harm. She unlocked the door and let us in.

Ah, Miss Gracie. She was four foot nothing, perhaps eighty pounds, looking impossibly old and timeless from a life of hard work. Miss Gracie wore a simple peasant's frock, house slippers, and a headband to control her unruly hair. Continuously chomping on her gums, with only a couple of old teeth to get in the way, she would sway softly in her rocker as she nodded and mumbled, "Uh-huh," to whatever we said, no longer able to hear much of anything and indifferent to what she missed. We instantly fell in love with her, and she with us.

We had free reign of the cozy Russell house—except the room from which Miss Gracie had appeared through the window. That room was always locked. Not even Douglas could enter. I recall being in there only once after begging her incessantly when we were alone one day. She reached into her frock pocket and pulled out an old key to open it for me reluctantly. This is where she kept her little special things, her only special things, including pictures of her departed husband and, of course, that massive revolver.

She told us she had multiple suitors and chose as her husband whoever was first to buy her a new dress, and there it was. She had other heirlooms collected and preserved over generations. It was all there, on display, her life's treasures. It was her private sanctuary, and one we honored with childhood awe. But let's dispense with sentimentalities and grant the truth. It was probably the only locked door we ever honored.

Papa hired Douglas because what else was Papa going to do? Fact is, Douglas was a gift from heaven, the hired hand Papa desperately needed to help maintain this large estate. Papa quickly understood the simplicity of Douglas's existence. He had even less understanding of money than my father did—none whatsoever. Money mattered little to a man who had almost no desire to leave his property, the exception being his Saturday sorties into Flint Hill or Front Royal for his treasured bottle of Boone's Farm, which outings always resulted in a killer hangover Sunday. So Papa offered him fifty dollars weekly for that outing and promised to care for all other needs for him as well as for his mother, and did.

Douglas spoke and acted as he was taught. All the boys were "Massah" and the girls "Miz." He couldn't quite master some names. Patricia was "Miz Treecia." Aloise was "Miz Loueesah." Mercedes was "Miz Feathers." Luz was "Miz Luther." So it went. It was what it was, and we were all comfortable with this solicitous behavior—except once. Several of us were with Douglas raking gravel into the middle of the driveway when an unexpected Dahlgren, with his daughter in tow, slowly ambled up the drive on horseback, looking as haughty as we knew him to be. We looked at them without interest. Douglas, on the other hand, straightened his body, stood at attention, tilted his head down, and just as they passed, removed his hat and ceremoniously…bowed.

We were young, but we knew better. As soon as that man rode by we erupted in outrage and pleaded with Douglas never, ever to bow to that man, or any man, ever again. Douglas was confused and though he listened to our pleas, you could tell he was not prepared to heed them. It was then that I came to believe that while Mrs. Gordon had been so kind to him, her nephew had treated him as chattel. It was horrifying to consider.

Douglas was known to and liked by all the farmers and families in the area. It was amazing to watch him travel to Flint Hill or Front Royal. He'd never learned to drive, but he didn't need to. He'd just walk to the end of the long driveway, and stick out his thumb at the sight of the first car, which seemingly always stopped and ferried him away. The same would happen with the return.

Now, in the interest of full disclosure, I'm required to shock you and unpack an uncomfortable truth, but it's important to put things in their proper perspective. Most of those farmers and their families who knew and were so fond of Douglas, instantly providing him with that transportation, had a nickname for him: "Little Nigger." Such were the realities of that time. Blacks and whites could coexist easily, and happily, provided blacks maintained their position in the area's ancient caste system. I wonder how Mrs. Gordon approached the race issue. It is inconceivable she would use this epithet, and her admirers would point to her care of Douglas and his reverence for her, as all the evidence needed to vindicate her, but she was as trapped in time as Douglas was.

There is an interesting corollary here with my grandmother Aloise Steiner Buckley, as lovely and Catholic and charitable as anyone you would ever meet, and, like Mrs. Gordon, wealthy, aristocratic, graceful, and gracious, a Southern belle (in her case New Orleans) surrounded by black servants living on her estates. But was she also a racist? Her son Reid tackled that sensitive subject head-on in his biography, *An American Family: The Buckleys*:

> Mother was a racist, if that term is to be applied in today's usage, with no discrimination—as a compact statement permitting no "differentiation," no "unpacking." Aloise Josephine Steiner [Buckley] assumed white people were intellectually superior to black people. She had been raised surrounded by Uncle Toms and Aunt Belles—by former slaves. She was by no means a racist if by the term one suggests fear and hatred of, and disdain for, the Negro. She truly loved black people and felt securely comfortable with them from the assumption of her superiority in intellect, character, and station. They were dear, kind, simple

people. Their goodness was a reproach to many white people. But they had their place and she and her kind had their place. The duty of her kind was to care for black people, to extend affection and loyalty to them, from whom she and Southerners of her day and class expected loyalty and affection in return…

Mother was surrounded by servants who had been in her employ twenty, thirty, forty years. They were loyal, their affection was great, and only decrepitude retired them. …After Father died, and when Mother became old and senile, we kept getting letters from black people expressing their gratitude and also their affection. I don't know how many mortgages my parents paid up…or how many children of those servants, and others, they financed through college and law school… It was noblesse oblige, which was part of the deal. But the basis of it was mutual affection and respect that arose out of human interaction…

The unpardonable aspect of that relationship, and in this peculiar to white-black relations, was Jim Crow. Jim Crow was a social fact of life that my parents did not question. Its quotidian cruelty and humiliation did not occur to them… I grew up at a time when there were two water fountains, one shiny and enameled, for whites, the other a rusty spigot, for blacks. I grew up when—of all imbecilic things—there were two sets of gas pumps, one for lily-white hands, the other for the black hands that swabbed your bottom when you were an infant, washed your clothes, cared for you when you were sick, cooked and served your food, but which—my, no!—were not to touch the same gas pumps.

I have no recollections of segregated water fountains and gas pumps. On the other hand, that isn't to say there were no hard-core vestigial racists in the neighborhood. They were there, and that included the nameless, faceless members of the KKK. We got our own taste of their ways within weeks of our arrival. As we were gathered in the Great Room one evening playing board games, someone cried out that there were flames outside.

We opened the curtains and looked through the three double-paneled glass doors. There in the middle of our expansive front yard was a large burning cross. Welcome to the neighborhood, Catholics. If my parents were alarmed, or even just concerned, they didn't show it. I suspect Papa worried for his family, but he was never going to say so. He explained to us that the KKK weren't just racists, but they were also anti-Catholics, and they were cowards for not showing their faces. So don't worry. For the record, Mom despised cowards, and I suspect she harbored secret hopes that one would show his face so she could blast it off with her twenty-gauge shotgun.

The older children could understand the horror of a burning cross in our front lawn, and yet no one was terribly upset. We were invincible. Nothing, but nothing, could ever affect us, not even this nuisance. We were Papa's children, and if he wasn't worried, then neither were we. Or, to put it another way, for the KKK to get us they'd first have to go through Papa and Mom, and good luck with that.

We would never know who was responsible, or how many Klan members participated, but we had some suspicions, which included some farmers who eventually did work for us and who gave Douglas those rides into town. Such was life in Rappahannock County, Virginia, in 1964, seventy miles from our nation's capital.

3. All Work and All Play

As you might imagine, our arrival immediately disrupted the town. Town? Huntly consisted of an old house that doubled as a post office that doubled as a minimalist general store that sold tobacco, soda, bread, candy, and little else. Outside there were a couple of inoperable gas pumps. You knew you were in town when you saw the little green "Huntly" sign on the side of the road. You knew you'd left town when you saw the reverse of that sign, also marked "Huntly."

At some point Richard Nixon proposed to shut down a number of local post offices as a cost-saving measure. The Huntly post office was on the list, but it was taken off the list when someone realized that in shutting down the post office, Nixon would be killing the hamlet.

Huntly had 150 residents max, mostly poor white families and poorer black families in rickety farmhouses along the road and in the hills. They scraped by on welfare or as farmhands. Huntly also had a dentist living in one house, a carpenter in another, and us, and that was pretty much it for demographics.

We were virtually alone in the country. We were a community of farms, and most didn't have children our age. But there were nine of us and, in 1967 with the birth of Jamie, an even ten. We made our own fun.

The thirteen years the Bozells spent living at Montejurra would seem to blend as one except that the family was in constant flux. During the school season we came and went. At different times five of us went off as high school boarders, and eight of us eventually went off to college. A few returned for a short stint after college; others were permanently gone. And so it went.

To best give a flavor of our life, let's place ourselves in the earliest years, the midsixties, when we were together.

Summers could be sweltering in Virginia with the three Hs—hazy, hot, and humid—endemic to the area. The swarms of gnats swirling endlessly in our faces only made matters more uncomfortable. If we stepped outside after breakfast, and it was already warm and sticky, we knew the day would be brutal, and so we dressed accordingly. We wore T-shirts, cut off shorts, and nothing else, including shoes. Often we boys went shirtless too. Old family friend Mike Lawrence once told me that guests to Montejurra were often alarmed at the sight of these ten redheaded children running wild and with calloused feet, effortlessly skipping over jagged limestone chipped gravel, looking unattended, and utterly oblivious to their disheveled appearance, which was probably true. Huckleberry Finn would have approved.

There were several protocols designed to maintain a semblance of order. Breakfast was served at 9:00 a.m. Anyone a minute late supposedly lost that privilege, except we never did. On weekdays our parents were long gone to work (she as early as 4:30 a.m., he by 7:00 a.m., with a seventy-mile commute each way), and with enough puppy- dog begging we could manipulate Luz into serving our breakfast of choice. After breakfast it was two hours of work outdoors normally supervised by an older sibling who would ruthlessly ensure we actually performed that work. If our chores were completed on time, we might head for the pool for a refreshing cannonball. At noon we returned to the house for lunch and sandwiches, after which, with the sun at its most oppressive, we'd repair to our rooms for a couple of hours of mandatory reading. Writers and editors both, our parents were militant about reading, and thank God for that.

By 3:00 p.m. we were back outside for another hour or two of work, after which we headed back to the pool for extended swimming or to play games of pitch and catch or enjoy whatever other fun we might have in mind. At about 6:15 p.m. we'd hear the clanging of the vintage old cowbell, a sound which resonated throughout the property signaling that we had fifteen minutes to make it to dinner. Douglas would head for his house as well. His day, too, was complete.

On many a particularly humid day, the skies opened in the late afternoon and delivered a short downpour. Afterwards, the climate might change deliciously—blue skies, dry air, a soft breeze, and most glorious of all, temperatures dipping down to the high seventies. Many a time we couldn't wait for dinner to end so we could blast outside and enjoy the evening.

That meant games. Teams would be chosen, and the fun would begin. There was nothing more amusing than football. The highlight was making eleven-year-old Johnny our wide receiver on a deep crossing pattern. It didn't matter who the quarterback was. The QB would deliberately sail the ball toward the big boxwood by the house, and Johnny would fearlessly hurl himself into the middle of it to catch the ball. He never failed to make the reception with his siblings rolling in laughter.

Better yet were the ruthless games of croquet. In more polite circles, the primary strategy is to tap your opponent's ball so you have two more taps to make it through the hoop and continue your journey. In Bozell world, you tapped your opponent's ball and immediately took the one slam option to send his or her ball crashing down the hill and into oblivion. Winning was rewarding only if you adequately punished the opposition.

The favorite sport for all of us was badminton, which we played for hours, until it was too dark to locate the birdie once it dipped below the horizon and camouflaged itself against the blackened mountains. Once darkness enveloped us, we were back inside for baths, perhaps a game of chess, a bit of reading, and lights out.

Notice something missing here? Electrical entertainment was minimal in our lives. There were only three TV stations whose signals reached Montejurra. Worse (for us), we were allowed only two hours' viewing weekly, and even then the choices were limited. On Sunday evening each of us would declare which two hours we'd chosen for the following week—*Bonanza, Hogan's Heroes, Get Smart, I Dream of Jeannie,* and the like—and for those two hours the TV room would be our private Valhalla.

We had a lovely stereo record player in the living room, but woe to the person who played anything but classical music on it. Guaranteed: if Mom caught us playing anything composed in the twentieth century, she would smash our record over her knee. Several of us had little record players in our room, and it was only there that we could listen to our stack of 45s.

Radio? Chris and I became addicted to Cincinnati Reds baseball games. At about 7:30 p.m., around the second inning, the signal for WLW Cincinnati would push its way into the dial, steadily strengthening so that by the fifth inning Al Michaels and Joe Nuxhall (with his trademark sign-off, "The old lefthander rounding third and headed for home") were heard crystal clear. A favorite listening spot was on the top of the roof. Just Chris, who hated the Reds, and I, who loved them, under the stars, pulling for different outcomes.

We played constantly. Given that we were alone we had to create our own enjoyment. We had bikes, but other than that and some standard sports equipment, we made our own games. A favorite pastime was the creation of characters and the mandate to remain in character so long as the game lasted. Different children had different games, though it seems there was one common denominator: Michael, who originated most of them. A few of us had our singular personalities bestowed by others. As the oldest, Chris saw himself as separate and certainly not equal to his siblings. Papa ceremoniously bestowed on him the title of "Sun King," which stuck with all of us, especially Chris. Aloise sported shorter hair than her sisters, and it was always, always a disheveled mess, no matter how many times she washed and attempted to brush it. She became "Bruja," the family witch.

If it was particularly hot and oppressive, we'd turn to Johnny for relief. He'd oblige, transforming himself instantly into an Indian, slowly dancing in circles, arms outstretched, one high, one low, body tilted forward, oblivious to all around him, grunting incantations to the gods in a plea for rain. (Occasionally it worked.) Sometimes this play-acting was spontaneous, intended to delight brothers and sisters while confusing everyone else. Maureen topped us all. With a perfectly straight face she would approach people and, extending her hand, would issue her patented greeting: "Hi, I'm the Virgin Mary's sister. Just call me Ann."

Montejurra wasn't a working farm, but that didn't mean we weren't farmhands doing a whole lot of work. From the start, all of us were put to work outside. Jamie was exempt because he wasn't yet born, and, for a while, Willie was too because he'd just recently learned how to walk. For the rest of us it was constant mowing, or weeding, or raking, or pruning, or whatever other work was necessary to complete a project devised by Papa. Papa wanted vegetables, an endless supply of them. Close to the house we maintained the primary garden where virtually every vegetable imaginable was harvested—corn, spinach, beets, beans, peas, tomatoes, squash, carrots, watermelon, cantaloupe, and enough potatoes to have ended the famine in Ireland.

When we were compensated—if we were compensated—Boss Man paid on the order of thirty-five cents an hour but only after twenty hours of free labor. He considered chores our mandatory contribution to the well-being of our family enterprise. Indentured servitude though it may have been, the work was understandable. It was the price for living on this magnificent property and for learning our parents' work ethic. There were different chores year round, and we performed them all.

As Mrs. Gordon taught Douglas, now he taught us. We learned how to best use the push mowers and, more importantly, how to fix them after abusing them mercilessly. We learned shortcuts too, like putting gasoline on spark plugs to ignite engines, an action that surely violates every safety standard on the books today. We learned how to maintain the vegetable gardens, from seeding to cultivating to picking the vegetables. We learned how to use sickles without chopping off our legs.

From the moment he arrived at the house around 8:00 a.m. to sweep the front patio and take out the trash until the moment he retired to his house before dinner, Douglas worked, breaking only for lunch and to roll and smoke the occasional cigarette. The one thing that threw him off was…us. He was a joy to spend time with, to listen to as he told us stories, or to lend us an ear when we needed to get something off our chests.

One afternoon he and I were chatting about baseball, and I asked what was his favorite team. To my surprise he answered the Cincinnati Reds. Even more amazing, he told me he listened to them on his radio at night just as I did. That led to numerous evening escapes to go over the hill and sit with him on the upstairs couch, in the dim light, with Miss Gracie pitter-pattering below while the game crackled through the speaker of his little transistor radio.

Douglas was a marvel to watch as he planted the seeds for the coming summer's crops. Johnny takes the story now:

Douglas was a consummate teacher. I distinctly remember the first time I was told to work with him in the vegetable garden bordering the dirt road to his house behind the hill. I wandered down (probably in a T-shirt and shorts and NO suntan lotion). There he was, surveying the landscape, alongside a wheelbarrow loaded with a hoe, a steel rake, a set of short clippers, a shovel, an array of bags of vegetable seeds, and two short, pointed wooden posts tied together by some eighty yards of coarse hemp string.

I suppose I asked, "How can I help?" or something to that effect. I suppose he answered something like, "Massah Johnny, take this post out to the end of the field—I'll let you know how far." So I took it and walked, all the while unravelling the string, until he told me to stop and stick it into the ground, which I did. At his end, he moved right or left until his excellent eyesight told him the lay of the string was exactly perpendicular to the width of the field and dug his post into the ground. He then took the shovel out of the wheelbarrow, smacked the post two or three times to make sure it wouldn't move, walked over to my post, and did the same.

That done, we went back, and he handed me a bag of seed and grabbed the hoe. "These [insert any vegetable you like] seeds, Massah Johnny, we gonna plant 'em right. These gotta be 'bout [insert a number] inches down and 'bout [insert a number] inches apart. So Ah do the hoein' and you place the seed like Ah say." Since Dougie also had a genius for logistics. We always started at the far end. That way we would be closer to the garage when we finished.

He started hoeing, and I started planting in the not-so-amiable Virginia summer heat and humidity. When I looked back every so often to see how far we'd gotten, I saw him, a bit bent over on one side of the string, hoeing away backwards, non-stop. To my amazement, then and now, though he never stood straight up to check it, the row was as straight as an arrow and exactly the same depth all along those eighty yards of land.

How he could pull that off each and every time, no matter what the distance, the depth, the composition of the soil, whether uphill or not, on the seemingly thousands of rows he completed still fills me with awe at the man's skill and brotherhood with the land.

As time went on Douglas's drinking increased. It was no longer just Saturday and somewhere else. Increasingly, we found him imbibing on the property, but somehow his work continued. There are several who will serve as witnesses to a scene of Douglas so dead drunk he could barely stand while hoeing and planting his seeds as Johnny described. We'd giggle watching, wondering how the hell those lines were going to turn out, imagining a field looking like an LA highway interchange. It was amazing. Once the crops appeared they were in perfect lines, arranged no differently than when he was dead sober. To this day no one can explain it.

For a diminutive man, Douglas was strong as an ox. We'd watch him effortlessly manage the heavy rototiller all day long, up one side of the hill and down the other, barely breaking a sweat in the hot summer heat. One afternoon when I realized I'd grown to his size, I asked him to teach me how to use that machine. He was reluctant, but I insisted, and so he showed me the essentials and yanked the chord to bring it to life. He stood back as I positioned myself behind the rototiller that was idling and waiting for me to squeeze the handle. It would engage the tillers, requiring only that the operator press the metal bar down and into the hard soil to carve out the rows for the seeds while the tillers moved him forward. Well, I didn't have the strength to break the soil, nor to control the blasted machine after I squeezed the handle, and in a flash it got away from me. Holding on for dear life while maintaining a death grip on the handle that would have stopped this infernal beast instantly had I just let go, I raced down the hill, out of control, while Douglas roared in laughter.

Douglas was a man of the earth and knew its secrets. One autumn afternoon I accompanied him as he took a ham shoulder, coated it with brown sugar, and placed it in a plastic lawn bag with punctured holes. We then inserted it into an old metal trashcan, also punctured at the bottom with little holes to drain the blood. We took the final product down to an abandoned pump well, clotted with years' worth of leaves that had blown through the entrance and were now decomposing below. He placed a lid atop the can, pushed it down into the leaves, and placed a stout rock on top to keep any animals from getting in. He left it in its damp environs for two months, after which we brought it out of its prison, opened the bag, and cut off a piece. Sweet ham never tasted so good. It was the perfect country recipe.

Papa, too, had ideas. Some were terrible, as in the time he planted seeds for a hundred pine trees, knowing many wouldn't make it, hence the number, but never understanding why not a single tree ever sprouted. But he did know how to seed our massive front lawn. Much to our delight one summer, he declared the lawn was not to be cut until further notice. Higher and higher the grass grew, so high that as children we could run inside and play hide and seek within it. So tall that one day an elderly man who lived in a house down the road marched up our driveway, cursing loudly for all to hear, preparing to confront Papa about the terrible abuse he was heaping on this wonderful property by letting it go to pot. Papa was letting her seed herself. In time, nature took her course, the seeds fell, a man was brought in to cut and bundle the hay, we were brought in to mow and rake her back in shape, and in short order the new lawn appeared, stronger and healthier than ever.

4. Life on the Farm

We had animals, lots of animals, too many animals.

We had the cats which we named after breakfast cereals. We had Cheerios, Froot Loops, Cocoa Puffs, Corn Flakes, Frosted Flakes, Wheaties, Mini-Wheats, and so many others. I suspect we concluded we had one cat too many when we began running out of brands. So one morning we gathered up a number of them, put them in a car, and drove them a few miles on a winding trail deep into the hills, finally letting them out to fend for themselves (country, folks, country). At the 6:00 p.m. evening feeding, they were all back. This time they remained.

We had lovely dogs, but from time to time mongrels would join the pack. That's because Papa seemed to love teasing Mom by arriving at the house with emaciated creatures to which he'd attach grandiose names like Caesar. We had three real pets: Crancy the ever-loyal black Lab belonging to Chris, and the two sister Beagles, Abby (Michael's and mine) and Mo (for Kathy and Maureen). Under no condition was any dog ever to enter the house, so proclaimed Mom who, years later, admitted she'd slip Crancy into her room at night to keep her company. In the summertime the dogs slept under the stars. In the winter they had a different abode. We tucked straw and old discarded rags around the guesthouse furnace making for the snuggest of beds for the dogs. How we didn't burn down that house I'll never know. God cares for children, fools, and drunks, but most especially Bozells.

Poor Mo reacted poorly to her spaying, mysteriously exploding in weight, at all times desperate for her next canned meal because there was nothing she could catch on her own. One winter day when it was terribly cold, she failed to appear at her feeding time. We knew something had to be terribly amiss. Children set off in different directions calling and looking for Mo but to no avail. Michael finally solved the puzzle. He led us to the pool and pointed down. She must have fallen in, and because of her weight, she cracked through the ice. Poor Mo was frozen in the water, where she remained for a couple of months until warmer weather thawed her out.

Abby had another problem. No dog was ever more fearful than this beautiful, lovable, constantly trembling coward.

We had an endless supply of rabbits. Our resident rabbit meister was Aloise. She made no effort to contain the population. In fact, she actually brought them down to the basement to live and multiply in the tunnels. I was reading in my bedroom one afternoon when I heard a violent commotion through the floorboards. Someone had left the cellar door open, and the dogs had entered. Minutes later the dogs were all out of the tunnels and racing across the backyard. In the back of the pack, way back, was poor Mo. Crancy was in front of her, charging full throttle. In front of Crancy was a pack of some fifty rabbits running for their lives. In front of them was Abby, running for her own.

We owned three pigs, Hector, Herman, and Harry. They were primarily my responsibility. We took possession of them in the summer of 1967. For the next year my job was to trudge over the hill to their pen to feed them twice a day, rain, sleet, or snow. At the start of the following summer I was sent to camp in New Hampshire. In a letter to Papa discussing this and that, I closed with a postscript to the effect of, "How are my pigs?" Papa responded a few days later addressing this and that and a few things more. He, too, closed with a PS: "How are your pigs? Breakfast was grand." So ended the tale of Hector, Herman, and Harry.

We inherited a chicken coop and later built ourselves a new one. We had several dozen birds that produced the most delicious eggs, deep orange and so fresh they were warm to the touch. Michael had a favorite, Blackie, but Blackie got sick and, unbeknownst to us, Luz killed and cooked her. The younger children were not happy to learn they'd dined on their pet chicken. I had my three favorites: Marlboro, Winston, and especially Tareyton, who perched on my shoulder while I sprinkled scratch for the rest.

Goats? Why the hell not. Our first two goats were Napoleon and Josephina. We bought them to eat the dreaded poison ivy on the stone walls around the property, but they preferred to dine on the ropes that bound them, quickly chewing through them to make their escapes.

Aloise was in charge of these as well and ultimately will have to answer for Napoleon's death. A makeshift coke bottle and black rubber nipple for suckling didn't work for him, it appears. Something about an air bubble. Cleo and Rebecca joined our goat family later. They produced milk no one liked, except in hot chocolate. The cream was delicious. Eventually they were given away.

We had several geese. I don't know how they got there or what purpose they served. It's safe to declare they were utterly useless to the health and well-being of our existence. I hated them, and I was not alone in that opinion. They milled around the kitchen door, and, if you got too close, they angrily and relentlessly chased you, chomping at your bare feet. They were fast too. Whatever their final hours, I hope they were painful.

What we really wanted was a horse, the "We" caucus led by Patricia. After enough pleading, Papa agreed and brought one home. Our own horse! What happened that day remains in dispute. More than one person places me at the scene of the crime. I was not and refuse to take any responsibility. Chris and Michael, on the other hand, will have to answer to Saint Peter. They took control, tying a rope to the still unnamed animal, to walk him around one of the paddocks. The bell rang for lunch so they tied him to a post and ran back for sandwiches. When they returned, our new horse was on the ground, very dead. He'd somehow gotten tangled up on the rope and strangled himself. The poor guy had lasted less than three hours with us. Imagine how his owner must have reacted. Did I mention he had not been sold, but loaned?

And then there were the sheep.

Ever the romantic, Papa wanted sheep from day one. There is little that's more soothing than the soft, hollow, lonely clang of a sheep bell off in distant fields. Papa knew that sound from Spain and had visions of dozens, hundreds of sheep in the fields fulfilling his fantasies. Ever the pragmatist, Mom wanted nothing to do with Papa's sheep dream and for a pretty good reason. We didn't know a damn thing about raising sheep. So what? We sided with Papa.

After much negotiating, a deal was finally struck. Papa would get his sheep, but only a dozen of them. We'd see how well these fared and then decide about expanding the flock. We were ecstatic. Several of us were commissioned to go into the forty-five acres of fields to ensure the wired fencing along the perimeters was secure. That proposition alone should have tipped us off. Secure? Sheep can hiccup and clear wire fencing. Or go through it. Or under it. None of these things occurred to us. Ditto the useless stone walls we didn't bother to inspect because they were intact. We reported everything was prepared when, in fact, nothing was. We gave the all clear.

Moments after the sheep arrived, we realized we (and they) were doomed. The sheep were brought by truck to the guesthouse parking area. A four-foot wall separated it from the fields. Thinking the wall too high for the sheep to jump over, we improvised a ramp down from the truck and on to a connecting ramp up over the wall. Easy down, easy up and over. The ramps were put in place, and the hatch was opened. The sheep stood at the end of the truck, looked down the one ramp, up the other ramp, and then just jumped over the wall and into the fields, not bothering with either ramp.

Once in the fields, the sheep had no intention of staying put, especially when the packs of wild dogs declared, "Buffet!" and came charging down from the hills. I've seen these dogs before. They look more like the jackals in *Lady and the Tramp*. They were as vicious as they were grungy, and they were apparently hungry.

Within twenty-four hours all of our sheep were dead. It was a slaughter. They'd been chased in every which direction that night and didn't stand a chance. Farmers around the area were on the phone with us. "Y'all the folk with 'em ship? Ah's a-gotta one dead'un my yard!" Some were still on the property, somewhere. We went into the fields in search of them, finding only cadavers. Some were mauled, others had just run themselves to death. Such was the fate of the last one discovered, appropriately not in a field but under a large bramble bush just outside our parents' bedroom. So it was fated! My father's dreams of shepherding had come to an inglorious end right outside his window.

5. Crimes and Punishments

Ten children living under one roof quarrel. When ten children are quarreling, there is chaos. When each quarrel ends with, "I'm telling!" then you've invited your parents into a discussion—into countless discussions—that neither of them wanted to arbitrate.

Enter Complaint Session. It was perhaps Papa's most ingenious creation. What made it so brilliant was its simplicity.

Sunday night we took our usual dinner, the older ones in the formal dining room, the younger ones at the kitchen dining table. After dinner the younger children would join their older siblings, and Papa would call to order Complaint Session. It would begin with the youngest, Jamie (when he became old enough to participate), then up the ranks—Willie, Patricia, Aloise, Johnny, me, Maureen, Michael, Kathy and Chris, then Mercedes, and finally Luz. When your name was called, you were invited to offer any complaint you had against anyone else (but not the grown-ups). The defendant would then be allowed to present his/her defense, after which Papa would pass judgment, and if the defendant was found guilty, Papa would declare the punishment. It was expressly understood that there would be no retaliation, or else it would be curtains.

Picture yourself in juvenile court with what would surely be a week's worth of ten children's endless lists of particulars hurled against one another, each requiring adjudication by my father. It would take forever.

Complaint Session was the antithesis of that. Let me offer a scenario. Follow closely if you can. Monday afternoon Johnny pushes a fully dressed Willie into the pool, and Willie screams, "I'm telling! Complaint Session!" On Tuesday morning Michael turns the garden hose on the back of Patricia's head, who screams furiously, "I'm telling at Complaint Session!" Wednesday morning Chris kicks Johnny's football onto the roof, on purpose. "You're such a jerk! Complaint Session!" Thursday afternoon, after having raked twenty piles of leaves and gone inside for a drink, Brent returns to find them all blasted to smithereens by Maureen, who had been dared to do this by Michael and Aloise. "Thanks, idiots. Complaint Session!" Friday morning Kathy catches Brent listening to her

Beatles albums on her record player without her permission, yet again. "I'm telling! Complaint Session!"

Saturday morning Chris learns that Kathy ate his peppermint ice cream the night before. "You're sooo dead! Complaint Session!" At the same time Patricia teases Jamie for being such a little girl. Jamie might be a toddler, but he's powerful because he's Mom's favorite and he knows it. "I'm telling! Complaint Session!" Saturday afternoon Michael bikes the mile round trip to the post office to buy an orange Nehi. When it's nice and cold in the fridge, Willie helps himself to it. Michael has run out of patience with his little brother. "This time I'm really, really telling. Complaint Session!" Saturday evening Aloise keeps running into the TV room and switching channels to disrupt Maureen, who is trying to watch *Gilligan's Island*, slamming the door as she leaves, giggling devilishly. Finally Maureen hurls a book at her screaming, "I hate you! Complaint Session!" Aloise runs into her room, locks her door and flicks the switch—nothing. Jamie has broken her lamp after bouncing the wrong way on her bed and falling off. "Way to go, stupid!" she yells through the walls into his room next door. "I'm telling! Complaint Session!"

Everyone has committed a crime against someone else.

Now it's Sunday morning, and the realization hits that in a few hours all are coming before the hanging judge. Time to negotiate. Chris approaches Johnny. "Don't tell on me for putting your football on the roof, please?" Johnny agrees, but only if Willie forgives him for chucking him into the pool. Willie complies, conditioned on Michael dropping his complaint about that soda, and good luck with that one. Michael surprises Willie by saying he'll happily facilitate—provided Patricia lets him off the hook for blasting her head with that hose.

Patricia considers and then agrees to the request, but Jamie must agree not to rat her out for teasing him. Feeling very powerful, Jamie resists, but ultimately Aloise tells him that if he pardons Patricia, she'll let him skate for vaporizing her lamp—that is, if Maureen shows her mercy for her merciless teasing. Maureen is still exposed for her transgressions against Brent, who willingly agrees to bury the hatchet provided someone first convinces Kathy that his life is more important than her *Rubber Soul*, which life she agrees to spare but only if Chris forgives her for stealing his ice cream which he summarily will not until she convinces Johnny to back off. Once Johnny agrees, the negotiations are concluded.

Chris pardons Kathy who pardons Brent who pardons Maureen who pardons Aloise who pardons Jamie who pardons Patricia who pardons Michael who pardons Willie who pardons Johnny who pardons Chris.

Come Sunday evening…

"Jamie?"

"Nofin'."

"Willie?"

"Zippo."

"Patricia?"

"A-OK!"

"Aloise?"

"All's good here."

"Johnny?"

"Never better."

"Brent?"

"What? A complaint? Be still my heart!"

"Maureen?"

"Why, I love everyone, especially Aloise!"

"Michael?"

"For me to complain unfairly would be a sin against the Holy Spirit."

"Kathy?"

"I'm sixteen. When will you ever accept that I DON'T LIKE COMPLAINT SESSIONS!"

"Chris?"

"I am Sun King. I mete out my own punishments."

Papa could silently declare victory.

Mercedes and Luz never complained, though God knows they could keep us there for hours if they wanted.

Of course, it wasn't always this way. Sometimes grievances were aired. Papa would listen, then give the accused the opportunity to respond. Given that in about 100 percent of the cases the accused was guilty, a punishment was proclaimed. "You will rake the backyard by yourself." "You must write 500 times, 'I will stop putting mud on top of my sister's head.'" "You cannot watch television for the next two weeks. Wait. Didn't I give you that punishment last week?"

The complaints adjudicated, it was time to kneel for Sunday prayers, which included a Rosary, a Hail Holy Queen, and a Prayer to Saint Michael the Archangel. With that, Complaint Session was adjourned.

Reader advisory: although there is no sex or violence in the section that follows, there is smoking, lots of it, about which there are no apologies. Different time, different place.

The most common of Papa's punishments involved our smoking. With the exception of Aloise, who exited the birth canal complaining about the stench of smoke five miles away—"Gross!"—and Chris, who smoked a pipe with cherry tobacco, we smoked cigarettes, some more than others, I more than anyone. I shall expand on this subject in our next chapter, but suffice it to say we were so seasoned that some of us developed an affection for particular brands—no, seriously—before high school.

We were caught time and again. It seems that at all times there was at least one of us either under indictment or in the hoosegow. There was no such thing as a not guilty verdict. Mercedes and Luz might choose to look the other way, but they never fibbed if our parents confronted them with a suspicion. We were just foolish: leaving packs in public, stealing cigarettes that would easily be missed by their owners, or more commonly, just smelling like an R.J. Reynolds factory. Papa had long ago killed his sense of smell, so he was not the problem. Mom, on the other hand, was a bloodhound.

Unless we saved enough money to get our own, most of us just helped ourselves to Mom's Kents or Papa's Alpines. Ah, those glorious days when we were free to bike a half mile to the country store and buy ourselves a grape Nehi and a pack of Pall Malls. I was caught more than anyone, not just because I smoked more—although that was part of it—but because I had no gift for hiding my habit from the authorities.

There are more stars in the universe than times I was caught, but not many more. I was caught so many times that after one episode, Papa had me write a paper (a Papa twofer: a punishment and a writing exercise) explaining my antics since the last time I'd been caught. Naturally (and stupidly) I lied. I proclaimed that since the date I *thought* I'd last been caught, I hadn't smoked until this very unfortunate day. Clearly disgusted, Papa refreshed my memory, reminding me that he had actually caught and punished me for smoking during my period of alleged smoking abstinence. I simply couldn't keep up with all the times I was nabbed.

Smoking demerits came in as many flavors as cigarettes, none of them good. Back in Maryland, when I was nine, we had a Saturday afternoon tradition: Mom would pack up as many children into the station wagon as possible and take us to the movie theater for the matinee. It was always such a treat. One Saturday I told her I wished to stay behind to read a book that was of particular interest. Of course, she melted with pride. What mother's nine-year-old child could be so...driven? Off they went. I was left alone in my castle.

Or so I thought. It transpired that during the movie Mom started thinking about her angelic little son all alone in that big house. You guessed it: she decided to come back to keep me company while the rest watched the movie. Imagine her reaction when she entered the family room and found me comfortably nestled on the couch, reading comic books, and, yes, smoking her cigarettes. A smile frozen solidly on her face, Mom directed me into the bathroom, handed me a pack of her Kents and a box of matches and, as she shut the door, insisted I smoke every last one of them. I think they call this "aversion therapy." If so, Mom invented it.

I sat on the john and lit one up. Good to go, I smiled to myself. This is a punishment? I finished and lit the second one. Not so nice this time, but hey, okay. The third was definitely not okay. Halfway through the fourth or fifth, Mom opened the door. She would later tell people her son had a distinct shade of green as he tumbled out of the smoke-filled hellhole. That torture kept me from smoking again—for weeks.

Turns out I wasn't the only one to suffer that punishment. Fast-forward to Montejurra a few years later, and Johnny, then age twelve, explains what happened after he was caught:

Papa called me to the living room to give the bad news.

My entire body was saying, "Oh, shit!" a few seconds later. He informed me in his no nonsense mode that I was to write a one-thousand-word report [Sound familiar? Papa's twofer, again] on why I had smoked, why it was a stupid thing to do, and some other considerations I couldn't make sense of. So I did. While doing so I started to feel grateful that I had gotten off so easily.

That was not to happen.

I handed him the paper, which he read and (I guess) approved of. He then invited me sternly into the patio, closed the doors, and told me to take a seat. Nonchalantly, he placed the report on the glass table, reached into his pocket, pulled out a pack of cigarettes, and said: "Now, I am going to light a cigarette, hand it to you and you will smoke it entirely. I will then light another one and hand it to you. Let's see how many cigarettes you can smoke in a row." I slumped in utter defeat and stupor.

After not very many cigarettes, I turned a greenish yellow [!!], stumbled to my feet, yanked the door to the back yard open, and vomited all over the nearest boxwood. Once I was done he said, "So how about a swim in the pool?" I thought, "Are you kidding me? Now you want to play nice?" I politely declined and went to my room hoping to recover my health, wounded ego, and self-respect before dinner.

We wrote hundreds of confessional lines, thousands of lines, so many goddamn carpal-tunnel-inducing lines that at night we looked like thirteenth century Benedictine monks copying the *Bible du XIIIe siècle*. During the summer we could write these lines at any time during the day so long as we met the deadline, which was usually that night. During the school year the writing commenced after homework was completed, meaning we could be up until midnight or later if the lines needed to be slipped under our parents' bedroom for review the following morning. If we focused on a specific infraction, we'd write something like, "I will stop sneaking food into my room," or, more typically, "I will stop smoking cigarettes." Then, too, there was the generic, "I will obey," when the parent issuing the punishment was either a) too tired to be imaginative, or b) too devoid of ways to address that infraction.

It wasn't the quality of the phrase that mattered. What we really cared about was quantity. One hundred lines was a cakewalk, and I don't recall cakewalks. Five hundred lines was more like it. One thousand lines was extreme but not uncommon.

Johnny hit on two characteristics that defined Papa's discipline. One was self-control. Believe or not, I cannot remember him ever raising his voice in anger. I don't mean yelling. I mean raising his voice. Never. In fact it was quite the opposite. The quieter he became, the more trouble we were in. If he was silent, one or more of us was dead. The second was his perspective. If a transgression was major, so too would be the punishment, but once it was over, it was over.

Poor Johnny. I recall another punishment he suffered, again unique. I know this because I witnessed it. Johnny, still more or less twelve, liked to play with matches and burn things as boys do everywhere. But in Johnny's case, his little bonfires were becoming, if not quite big enough to be seen by passing satellites, at least big enough to attract the authorities—and Papa.

One happy springtime Saturday afternoon, Papa went into the back-yard, began collecting leaves and branches discarded over the winter, and built them into a rather impressive mountain of brush. When it was complete, he summoned Johnny to the patio and sat him down. "So, do you like burning things?" Johnny warily nodded his head. "Good!" Papa responded. "Look at the pile I just built. Let's burn it!" With that, he handed his son a pack of matches.

I'm not sure what Johnny Pyromaniac was thinking. Probably it was that this was going to be one big flaming funfest. They went into the back-yard, and Johnny ceremoniously lit her up. In no time it was a bonfire, huge and crackling, the flames leaping ferociously into the sky.

At which point Papa walked behind a bush and returned holding two pails. Pointing to the pool some thirty yards away, he commanded sternly,

"Now put it out." My heart went out to my poor little brother whose fortunes had so immediately been reversed.

Johnny may have been an arsonist, but he was not a complainer. Without a word he picked up the buckets and began hauling water, trip after trip, until the final embers were out. His days playing with matches were over, except, of course, those necessary to keep his cigarettes lit.

Papa used weather and geography to his advantage. Aloise remembers him making us wash the cars in the dead of winter. Trust me, she does not exaggerate. Temps could be in the teens, and it did not matter. He had another curious punishment for some of his children. After misbehaving at church, Aloise recollects "having to stand on one of the hills on the property in Mass attire on another frigid and wintry January day for God knows how long." Thinking back, I find this rather hilarious. Patricia and Willie also commanded the heights from their own lonely summits. There were different settings indoors used as props for Papa's creative juices, as in the time Aloise and Patricia were made to sleep on top of the freezer in the basement. Why there? Why not?

Papa could be pragmatic too. That usually meant assigning a punishment that would simultaneously address a need, on the property or inside the house. For one forgotten infraction, I was ordered to the laundry room to iron clothes. For about an hour, I was having a blast. Then Mom came in to check on me, looked with horror at the scorched fruits of my labor, and immediately granted me parole.

Kathy, on the other hand, knew how to manage the iron. She had no choice but to learn. When caught doing something really, really egregious (no, I won't say what it was), Kathy recalls, "It was five hours of laundry duty each weekend until all damages were paid. I think it lasted all winter."

And finally there was the occasional punishment that backfired. On this occasion, our parents were so fed up with the misbehavior of Kathy, Michael, and Maureen, they exiled these impossible teens to the guest house until further notice. Out the door they went, formally banished. My parents' tough love was far too tough for Luz and Mercedes, however. They reacted by doing the unimaginable: they disobeyed my parents and snuck delicious meals to the wayward teens, including first dibs at the fresh eggs collected in the morning. What began as ostracism morphed into something entirely different and wholly unexpected.

"It got so that before long we were inviting people over for dinner," Maureen remembers. "I think that's when Mom and Papa decided that punishment wasn't working."

Why were Kathy, Michael, and Maureen banished?

Michael.

No one was more mischievous than the brother who a dozen years later would become Brother, and later, Father Michael. Michael didn't just behave badly. He orchestrated bad behavior: conceiving, recruiting, and leading those chosen for his misadventures. Smiling brilliantly and winking slyly, he'd outline his idea, and off we'd go, unable to resist the Pied Piper because it was Michael. In our next chapter we'll explore some of his legendary adventures in Spain, but let the record show that, as a young boy, he was equally troublesome.

If my family were to sit about for an evening of remembrance, we'd probably arrive at enough Michael stories to fill their own chapter. Age slowly withdraws data from all of our memory banks, but Michael's more than most. As a cloistered monk, I suspect he has more noble things to think about. So when I ask him to recall his misdeeds, he answers, "I don't remember any punishments in Montejurra other than working outside for years on end for so many misdemeanors that they blur into one Original Sin. Besides, by that point I was so perfectly demonic in my wickedness that only capital punishment would have made any sense." We relax in knowledge that Saint Augustine had a rough start too.

Allow me to give you an example of Michael's devilish humor.

Next to us was a farm owned by Bernie Dahlgren, the man who had sold us Montejurra and whom we disliked because of his awful treatment of Douglas. On that farm there was a barn, and in that barn is where we'd play. It had three levels. At the top was where the farmhands stored their bales of hay, brought in through a large door on the side of the building. On the main floor they kept the farm equipment, the machinery, tools, and such. On the far side of this open room there was a small opening in the floor with a ladder that led under the barn, down to the grimy, muddy, smelly pigpens. Michael and others, not I, had made more than one trip to that barn to cause trouble. Whatever it was they were doing, the farm-hands finally told them that if any of them ever returned, they'd be met with physical violence. Or shot. Or worse still, they'd be reported to Papa.

Whatever it was, none of us took this as a threat. To us it was a chal-lenge, and Michael conceived the caper to end all capers as a response.

While living in Maryland we'd come to know the family of E. Howard Hunt, of Watergate fame. Two of the Hunt girls had come to visit us at Montejurra. Lisa and Kevin (yes, girls) were slightly older than I, maybe fourteen or fifteen, and friends of Kathy and Maureen. Lisa wore a heavy metal brace on one leg, the result of an automobile accident. The Hunt sisters were all-in on Michael's plan of action.

Santa had been particularly generous to Patricia a number of Christ-mases before, giving her a lifelike doll, perhaps three feet tall. The toy had been left unattended in the basement for quite some time, collecting dust, waiting her turn at the dumpster. But, like *Toy Story's* Buzz and Woody, she had one final mission in her. Her hair and clothes were made thoroughly disheveled while black and red paint was strategically applied on the body. She now looked like a prototype for the zombies of *The Walking Dead*.

Off with her we went to Dahlgren's farm, making our way through its tall cornfield and up to the upper level of the empty barn. We had to be quiet; the farmhands were around. First we rearranged bales of hay in such a way to create secret tunnels that Japanese soldiers on Saipan would have envied. Once this chore was completed, we took the muti-lated doll, tied a noose around her neck, threw the rope over the rafters above, and hanged her. Peeking out the door slats, we waited until the farmers were close enough and then flung open the big barn doors with a loud commotion. They looked up to see the doll hanging from the rafters and naturally erupted in various forms of audible horror. It took only a moment to see this was a prank, but, for us, that moment was enough. We dissolved in laughter, victorious laughter. We'd not just fooled them, we'd made fools of them.

That was it. They were going to teach us a lesson. A couple of them came charging into the barn as reinforcements arrived in a jeep and piled out. We went diving into our tunnels, pulling bales over our heads. We could hear them cussing as they yanked and tossed bales apart.

My heart was in my throat. This time, maybe this time, we'd gone too far, but aided by our deep tunnels and God's mercy not one of us was nabbed. The men left the barn continuing their search. Now we had to find a way to escape the barn with them still wandering outside. There was only one route: down the ladder, through the filthy pigpens, over the fencing, and into the safety of the tall corn fields.

We would have made it easily but for Lisa. She was above me as we took our turns climbing down the ladder. Somehow she slipped and lost control. The metal brace on her leg smacked me in the head and knocked us both into the slop below, with me dazed from the blow. Two of our loyal compatriots led us rapidly through the slimy pit, out the side, and into the tall corn. Instead of returning home, we wisely headed to the pond of a neighboring farm and cleaned ourselves off.

We were caught, of course. How could we not have been? Everyone on the Dahlgren farm knew we were responsible. Like Michael's, my memory banks cannot retrieve details of the specific punishment. Whatever it was, a) we deserved it, b) it was probably a doozy, and c) it did nothing to deter us. Just a speed bump on the road to perdition.

Watching a band of kids in their everyday mischief, the observer might not suspect the deeper context in which we lived. Montejurra was brimming in the Catholic thing. It was in the art hanging on our walls, here a large painting of Spain's El Escorial, there another of Avila's medieval walls, and down the hall a brightly colored page from some piece of long-forgotten Gregorian chant expertly framed. It was an ornate crucifix hung in one public room and smaller, simpler ones hung in private bedrooms. It was coffee table books about timeless castles and monasteries. It was in the books lining the shelves, perhaps a history of the Crusades, or a children's book on favorite saints, or a treatise by Belloc, Muggeridge, or Aquinas. It was in children's personal missalettes on their dressers and rosaries hung on their bedposts, both perfunctory gifts at Confirmation. It was in the mandatory grace before meal and rosary after dinner on Sunday night. It was in the comfort that St. Anthony could be recruited to find a missing object and St. Jude to solve what would otherwise be a hopeless predicament. It was in the knowledge that any sin could be temporary if corrected by Confession, but to break your Catholic word of honor was to lose all trust forever. It was in any discussion of politics because politics was conditioned on faith. It is told that after Willie was born in Spain in 1962, friends gathered to celebrate at the house, and a good-natured argument erupted among the well-wishers as to what saint should be chosen for the baby's middle name. The discussion became so boisterous that finally Papa could take no more. He threw up his arms to quiet his guests and in resignation proclaimed his newborn son would henceforth be known as William Fergus Y Todos Los Santos Bozell.

It wasn't just the faith. It was the culture. It wasn't a backward look bemoaning lost traditionalism. Our Catholicism looked to the future with brio, toward traditionalism. We aspired to reclaim the faith in all its spirituality. Montejurra teemed with staff from Papa's *Triumph* magazine throughout the summer. They would join us for a Saturday afternoon swim, stay late into the evening, or, if too much drink was consumed, hunker down for the night. These were writers and intellectuals, some of them brilliant thinkers, most of them with engaging eccentricities. Deep conversation was the order of the day, often in the living room during the afternoon and on the candlelit porch in the cool of evening with chess games going here and there and Baroque music filling the air.

So it went through those glorious summer months: working, reading, swimming, carousing, tossing horseshoes, weeding on hands and knees with Douglas, channeling Pete Rose, swatting gnats, tending to sunburns and poison ivy, or just sitting on the dirt floor of the stables listening to the summer rain pound the tin roof above.

6. Off to School We Go

But when school began, everything changed.

Now the routine was far more structured and serious. We were up by 6:30 a.m. because we needed to be dressed and fed by 7:30 a.m.

When he wasn't in jail, Carl Fry would often drive us. Otherwise, a local Front Royal cabbie would come and take us. Our parents never did because they commuted to work in the opposite direction.

Once we arrived at Front Royal, a miniature yellow school bus would carry us to Powhatan School in Boyce, about an hour drive along meandering country roads including stops for a handful of other kids along the way. Powhatan was housed in an old antebellum mansion. The founder turned bedrooms into classrooms, all of them connected by old hallways with creaky floorboards leading down rickety stairs to larger rooms for larger gatherings, the largest of which could seat 150 or so children. School let out at 3:00, and we were home by 4:30. The sunlight, the bustle, and that airy informality of summer was gone. A quick snack, and we went directly to our rooms for homework, of which there was always plenty.

Dinner was served at 6:30, usually at the kitchen table. When we ate in the candlelit formal dining room, we dressed as our parents did, coats and ties for the boys, and robes for the girls. We didn't do much talking during dinner. Rather we listened and tried to keep up with Mom and Papa as they commanded the conversation, delving deeply into matters of the faith or politics. If there was outreach in our direction, it usually came from Papa who was naturally more talkative and had more formal matters to take up with us—school, behavior, chores, and the like.

After dinner, it was back to our rooms to complete our homework assignments and then some final camaraderie—unless, of course, one or more us was quarantined in his or her room writing, "I will not smoke again," a gazillion times.

Chores continued throughout the year. Chickens and pigs still needed caring. We would let them out and feed them early in the chilly morning before leaving for school and lead them back inside their sheds and coops as the sun set in the cold gray of early evening.

Maureen once brought Aloise for company to the chicken coop during a blizzard. Aloise, the second youngest of the girls, returned to the house with frozen hands. I still remembering her screaming when Luz and Mercedes put her in a tub to unthaw them.

On weekends we raked, and we raked some more. When it came to leaves, Papa was a perfectionist. We were instructed to remove every leaf, *every* leaf. This meant crawling on our hands and knees under bushes so thick it was impossible to even see the wet leaves that had been swept there. But we knew they were there, and though they posed no threat to anyone, or anything, ever, we picked them up, one by one, every *single* one. Nothing less could put Papa's mind to rest.

If the weather permitted, we would find some outdoor activity to distract us. For a stretch, Chris and I took to playing night football. One end zone was next to the living room bushes, and the other was down by the road some two hundred sloping yards away, the field lit by a weak flood-light at one end and, if lucky, the moon at the other. I was the Oakland Raiders. He was the Washington Redskins.

I was eleven. Chris was sixteen and twice my size. One of us would take offense, the other defense. On offense, you hiked the ball to yourself and charged forward. If you wanted to be fancy, you threw the ball to yourself. On defense, you tackled the person in front of you with the football. It was simple as that. Something or other merited a first down, and the drive would continue—endlessly—Chris being a wee bit merciful but not much more than that. Back and forth we fought, our bodies slamming each other relentlessly. We had the time of our lives—just the two of us.

Once fall turned to winter, all activity moved indoors. After home-work we'd take our baths, get into pajamas, and—given the cost of heating an old house with a wholly inefficient furnace—don our bathrobes as well. We would then congregate in the Great Room with Vivaldi's joyful "Trumpet Concerto in C Major" or maybe Brahms's softer 1st or Beetho-ven's moving 7th or Bach's solemn Masses filling one sense and a crackling fire of well-seasoned wood filling at least two others.

A half dozen or so of us would stretch out on the floor playing Monopoly or Clue or some lesser game. One of us invariably sat on the edge of the couch, hunched over a chess set, facing off against Papa in his easy chair, he blissfully lost in thought, sipping his Old Crow and taking a drag off his Alpines. On the rare occasion Papa faced defeat, we'd wait for it…wait for it…wait for it…and…pow! He'd stand up and "accidentally" knock all the pieces off the board, after which he'd solemnly apologize for his clumsiness and declare that, of course, this meant the game was a draw. His opponent, triumphantly giggling in glee, knew better.

Nothing, but nothing, beat the game of Diplomacy. That's when all of us (save Mom, who had no patience for the game but reveled in our joy) went to war on the living room rug. Those familiar with this iconic board game understand its unique ability to disrupt entire communities for days if the game drags long enough and feelings are hurt sufficiently. The setting is World War I. There are seven European powers, and the object is simple: conquer your enemies. War being war, Diplomacy includes an element that to my knowledge is unique in the world of board games: you're allowed to cheat, and you're punished only if caught. In time we all became master dissimulators. To this day people don't like playing games with us. "Bozells do nothing but cheat," or so my dear wife charges in disgust.

Norma speaks the truth. More than a half century later, seven of us were together again, this time in my mountain aerie, Tocacielos, not forty-five minutes from Montejurra. Naturally we had to play Diplomacy. Countries were chosen, alliances were made and broken, and war raged back and forth all over the continent. Ultimately, Kathy and I joined forces and together crushed our enemies, at which point I naturally turned on my sister and took her out as well for the final conquest. It's a fair guess that every one of us was cheating at some point. I was just better at it that day.

Finally, Christmas. The season began with the search for our tree. Whatever the weather, even in deep snow, we set out, driving as far we could, then trudging up the mountains in search of a tree large enough to fill the Great Room. Once one was discovered, we cut it down to some fourteen feet, dragged it whatever the distance to a pickup truck borrowed for the occasion, and hauled it back to Montejurra to be pruned and raised.

The furniture had already been moved aside, and whole bed sheets were spread on the rug. The large French doors would be opened, and the tree dragged to the opposite end of the room. There was no store-bought mount large enough to hold this beast, so every year Douglas built one. Once lifted into place, Papa would climb the ladder and furiously connect wires from the tree to nearby walls until the tree was finally stabilized.

Then Papa arranged the lights, and his work was done. Now he could sit and enjoy his Christmas specialty: spiced vanilla milkshake infused with a generous dosage of Old Crow.

The rest of us would chip in with the ornaments, finally throwing strands of tinsel, one after another, until hundreds were hanging. She was a lovely sight. Mom took control of the Christmas decorations around the house, some which exist to this day on her children's mantles.

Christmas Eve. Wearing our pajamas and bathrobes, we'd gather by the piano. Mom would bring out the tattered Christmas carol book, and together we'd sing "Silent Night," "Oh Come All Ye Faithful," "O Holy Night," "We Three Kings," "The First Noel," and all the Christian classics.

Then came the climax. With joyous abandon, led by raucous pounding on the keyboard, we sang "Jingle Bells," our voices raised loudly and in excitement to summon Santa. We'd await the signal from the one child posted by the French doors. Moments later the child would scream, "He's here! I saw him! Santa's here!" At this point we'd all dash to the window to see him. We'd wait…yes! There! In the yard, hiding behind the large boxwoods, then jumping out and waving to us, only to duck away, and then reappearing somewhere else, jumping, cajoling, dancing in the yard for us. And then he was gone. A few minutes later Papa would reappear, Clark Kent–style, with the younger ones jumping all over him to explain excitedly what he'd missed while the older ones smiled at him conspiratorially.

The lights were turned off, leaving only the glowing embers of the fireplace and the soft-colored Christmas lights. The music was turned down, and we were patted off to bed with admonitions that Santa would decide who was naughty and nice. The following morning it was pure jailbreak as ten children burst into the Great Room, body-slamming anyone in their way, making their way to the tree and around the room wherever their presents appeared. Wrapping paper would fly in every direction while children yelled in delight over a special present gifted by the magic man they'd seen the night before. A magical place in a magical time.

Our Clark Kent, however, was not Superman. Unbeknownst to us, and even to him, Papa's health was slipping, and Montejurra was slipping along with him.

Montejurra had always been a money pit, but now things were falling apart, and we could no longer afford the upkeep. The slate roof was leaking in several places and had caused more than one ceiling to collapse, including the one over Willie's head in his bedroom. The oil heating system had needed replacement for years, thousands of dollars more. The electrical system was probably installed by Thomas Edison himself and posed a real fire threat. Untold thousands here. Numerous other maladies were crippling this stately manor. The most important reason, superficially at least, was unknown to us at the time, but which once discovered almost condemned her. Asbestos.

Ever-present financial worry was becoming the stuff of crisis. *Triumph* magazine was failing, as were other ventures Papa had launched. He was operating with a demoralized, minimal staff and a shoestring budget, but debts continued to mount. We would hear him from our bedrooms late at night slowly pacing the hallways, floorboards creaking, walking from one end of the house to the other, for hours on end, stopping only occasionally to refill his glass of bourbon—we could hear the clink of new ice cubes—vainly attempting to find a solution. His eyes were bloodshot from exhaustion. The unimaginable was happening. For once we were concerned for his well-being.

Then it got worse—far worse. His behavior was becoming ever more erratic with rash and oftentimes clearly nonsensical decision-making. He was losing control. In time his conduct would become so irrational as to require hospitalization. We would learn he was suffering from manic depression, now known more kindly as bipolar disorder. For the next quarter century, he'd struggle with this horrific illness, enduring enough physical and mental torture to make you weep. While his physical agonies never abated—the illness left his body shattered—his spiritual transformation was astonishing. A new tenderness emerged. He became a man focused on a life of prayer with the poor as his singular public focus. He took vows as a Third Order Lay Carmelite. Some believe he died a saint. His wife and children saw him as that and more. He was Superman again.

But we could foresee nothing of this at the time. We knew only that our perfect world was akimbo.

In early 1975, poor Douglas was diagnosed with terminal stomach cancer. A lifetime of smoking and an adulthood of drinking had caught up with him. It was time for Douglas to retire, yet when advised of this by Papa, Douglas simply could not understand that concept. He'd never *not* worked. Now he was to stop completely? Besides, what would he do?

That's when Papa handed Douglas his bankbook. Remember bankbooks, where accounts were entered by the teller in pencil, and you carried it with you as your only evidence of cash in the bank? Papa had given him fifty dollars spending cash every week but had also regularly deposited money into a private savings account for the man. Now Douglas had thousands of dollars to his name. To Douglas, this was incomprehensible.

He had no idea what to do with it. As a testimony to this man's heart, he approached me and offered me the entire amount so I could go to law school. I declined. He then approached Johnny and offered to put him through medical school. I suppose others were targeted as well.

Each time we told our old friend that, no, he was now retired and this was his to enjoy. His time on earth was passing quickly, and we all knew it. Buy yourself as much wine as you'd like, we'd tell him. Take a trip! Buy fancy clothes! Do…something, anything you want! Douglas was at a loss. We learned later his abusive nephew stole his tiny fortune.

Only the youngest children, along with newly married Kathy and her husband Cy, were there to care for Douglas as cancer devoured his body. The rest of us were in college or had moved out. Willie, just fifteen, became his constant companion, spending long days and evenings at his side. When Willie sensed the end was near, he rushed home in tears to announce the poor man was dying. All of my family still there tore up the hill to gather at his side. Cy carried him to the waiting ambulance. "Douglas weighed only a feather," he reported to his wife. Dr. Ed Eastham, the country medic who lived nearby and cared for us all, met the family at the hospital. He told them Douglas had been sedated and administered morphine to lessen his pain. He left to tend to his patient but returned shortly thereafter. Douglas was gone.

The funeral for Douglas Russell was held at the Macedonia Baptist Church in Flint Hill, packed to the hilt with black families from the area, along with one white one. Miss Gracie wailed, "My Dougie," as she threw her arms on the coffin, refusing to accept that he had died. Mourners tried to console her while beating their makeshift paper fans in the brutal heat.

Four years after her son's death, Miss Gracie joined Douglas in heaven. Follow a back road to a dirt path deep in the hills. At one point it's virtually impassable because of the heavy brush that has enveloped it over the years. Fight your way through and on the other side you'll arrive at a clearing. It is the old Russell family cemetery. Douglas's spot had a simple black metal marker with his name. Not far away, his mother was laid with similar identification. Almost a half century after their deaths, one of us visited the cemetery and decided to have proper tombstones commissioned. Amazingly, the old lady at the Maddox Funeral Home remembered them both and with affection. And respect. She would not comply with the request until she had the formal consent of a family member. Patricia was entrusted with this assignment and found a niece who granted it. Proper tombstones now recognize their resting places.

7. The End of the Affair and a Toast

One by one we were leaving Montejurra. Kathy had married in the spring of 1972; Chris and Mary followed suit that winter. Both couples began their marriages with short stints in the guesthouse, and then they were gone. Michael had finished his studies at Providence College, and soon would be accepted by the Benedictines at their cloistered monastery in Solesmes, France. Maureen had completed her studies at the University of Dallas and was also preparing to make her own way. I was still in Dallas, studying and, for all intents and purposes, living in Texas. Johnny had completed one year at Providence and left for Spain. The four youngest remained: Aloise and Patricia in a local high school, Willie and Jamie in grade school. But they no longer had the comfort and companionship of six older siblings. Montejurra was emptying.

Did we live in Montejurra for an eternity? Of course, we did. Isn't that how children remember such things? Yet it was only thirteen years, 1964–1977. They were glorious, but it was time to bid her goodbye.

It was a gloomy, overcast day, just as mother nature would want it, while Mom and the older ones huddled in the guesthouse, planning our exit strategy. Papa was slowly self-destructing and Mom wanted desperately to leave the increasing loneliness of an isolated home and return to the safer confines of the city. We were meeting to make the decision to move. The issue was hotly debated. Kathy and Johnny fought to keep the property; the rest of us sadly took the position that the time had come. In the autumn of 1977 she was sold. It was a confusing, disorganized, and sorrowful exit. Montejurra was no more.

But this cannot be the end of our tale. Montejurra must not be remembered with decay and death. No, no, a thousand times no! Let us return to another day, the day Montejurra would choose for her own remembrance. Let us do her justice, with a toast.

When Cy and Kathy were married in 1972, their reception was held at Montejurra, with about one hundred guests in attendance. Kathy's brothers and sisters had worked literally for months preparing the property for this day, pruning, weeding, raking, picking, mowing and mulching, sweeping, hauling and stacking, plucking, moving and removing, storing, unstoring and restoring. There was not a single dead leaf from winter left under a single boxwood, not a pebble out of place on the driveway, not a bush unevenly trimmed, not a blade of grass uncut, not a particle of dust on the patio, and not one single weed alive anywhere in sight.

The weather that spring day was idyllic, with bright sunshine in the clear blue skies above and perfect springtime temperatures below, the wisteria, rhododendrons, and tulips in full bloom, their fragrance gracing the guests as they walked the property. Then Douglas arrived, escorting Miss Gracie. A lawn chair was quickly brought out for her and placed in the middle of the patio. Douglas and Gracie were our guests of honor and treated accordingly.

We have an iconic photograph of that day taken on the patio. Chris and Mary, then engaged, are standing on the left. Cy, then Kathy are standing in the middle with Douglas to Kathy's left. Miss Gracie is in front of them, seated. Douglas is snappily dressed in a dark suit, standing firm and serious, the footman once more. His diminutive and dignified Mama

48

is wearing that special dress she kept locked in her room. Look closely. Kathy's hand is tenderly resting on Douglas's shoulder.

Behold the perfection of this moment, ladies and gentlemen, and let us raise our glasses: To the muggy, horsefly-bit days and crisp, clear evenings of summer. To the autumnal beech trees exploding in bronze, yellow, and red among the crumbling corn husks. To Dr. Zhivago's winter palace, the virgin white blanket below, cloudless azure skies above, and in between the squeals of children careening down the hills in sleds. To the lonely dandelion birthed by gentle rains poking through the softening soil, with chocolate Easter eggs hidden under bushes and on tree limbs, awaiting the hunt, announcing the spring, when all starts anew.

Yes, raise your glasses high!

To that perfect gentle knight who was born there, was raised there, and cared for her throughout his entire life, that simple man with the grand heart who was her soul. And to his sweet, gentle mother. To Douglas and Miss Gracie, two of God's finest creations.

Raise them higher still!

To those ten redheaded children running wild, carefree, wondering who among them could climb the highest branch on the tallest tree, hold his breath the longest in the pool, or just eat a plate of spaghetti the fastest while their mother wasn't looking. To the six who would marry, the three who would choose not to, and the one who became the priest. To their twenty-nine children and the forty of the next generation with at least three more on their way.

To that tall, lanky, handsome lad from Omaha, Nebraska, the master orator with the towering intellect, whose idea of an earthly Eden was a cold gazpacho in the shade after an afternoon on his hands and knees working the vegetable gardens in the sweltering heat, sunburn and mosquito bites be damned.

To his bride, the product of high society in Sharon, Connecticut, the delicate lass with the effervescent smile and golden hair who could ride a horse like a champion because she was one and might have become a concert pianist had her future husband not come into her life, he a convert to the faith and she born into it, for them both the cornerstone of their lives and the single highest imperative for their children, not just to believe it, but to live it, and they chose this place to do so.

So yes, let us toast that bucolic place just a stone's throw from the city and also light-years away. Let us toast her moment, when time existed for those who wanted it, and those who lived there did not. Let us toast her name, her history, and her significance, first as that place in the mountains in the Navarre region of Spain where at the point of the gun Catholicism was defended, and then to that place in the foothills of the Blue Ridge Mountains of Virginia where one hundred years later it was so vibrantly lived.

To Montejurra!

SECTION II

SPAIN

1. El Escorial

"Papa wants to know, do you want to go to school in Spain?"

It was February of 1970, and I was in the second semester of my freshman year at The Hill School in Pottstown, Pennsylvania. There was nothing wrong with The Hill School as American prep schools go. My brother Chris, five years my senior and on his way to a successful career in business, had graduated two years before having enjoyed it immensely. My brother Michael, then a junior and two years older than I, did not. I fell somewhere in between. As advertised, the academics of this school had been demanding, even exhausting. Weekdays were regimented with perhaps an hour or two of social time and another couple for sports. Every other moment was devoted to class, study, eating, or sleep. Weekends allowed for more social time but not much more. The Hill School's first priority was always academics.

I'd made friends during my freshman year when everything was at its newest and most exciting. On the other hand—and for a young teen this was huge—The Hill School was an institution for rich kids, and that's something we were not. We were allotted twenty-dollar monthly allowances to cover pretty much everything from the necessary to the frivolous. Where others might order mouth-watering pepperoni pizza nightly, we might need to save for a couple of months to pay for one. Where others had their parents personally outfit their dorm rooms, we scrimped. A two-by-two-foot remnant rug next to the bed—five dollars. A second-hand reading lamp—ten dollars. A little used record player—twenty-five dollars. Records—borrowed. Academically, we fit in. Socially, we did not.

We were sitting on the bed in Michael's bedroom. He'd spoken by phone to Papa and was relaying the offer: Did we want to transfer to Spain for the following academic year? The offer came with a catch, which was not surprising since Papa had a knack for throwing curves. We would be in Spain by ourselves, living in the town of El Escorial by ourselves, and attending the Real Colegio Alfonso XII, an all-Spanish boarding school. This surely would have intimidated the Bradys or the Partridges, but not the Bozells.

Our family had lived in Spain before, from 1961 to 1963, in that very town. In fact, we'd even attended that same school, Michael in the third grade, I in the first. Nor were we the first to undertake this high school sojourn. Sister Kathy had traveled there two years previously to complete her junior and senior years in the town of Ávila living with old family friends. But this time, we'd be entirely on our own. Michael and I looked at each other, contemplating the options for only a moment before we both jumped in glee. There was never a doubt. I would spend three years there, the first with Michael, the second joined by Johnny, and in my final year with Johnny alone.

The very name *El Escorial* sings, as it should. Located in the Guadarrama mountains about forty-five miles northeast of Madrid, today the town is a weekend escape for affluent Madrileños, a residential mecca for artists, and a mandatory stop in Spain for tourists all over the globe. The hillside is dotted with modern weekend chalets that look down on the ancient town with its narrow, one-way cobblestone streets filled with tourist shops, art outlets, swank clothing stores, local cafes, and international restaurants, and clogged with drivers looking everywhere for an open parking space (there aren't any). The town is brimming with metrosexualized men and colorless women, their eyes dutifully glued to their smartphones, oblivious to the magic that surrounds them. So let's not consider this town by its obnoxious modern footprint.

Rather, let's look at El Escorial when we first lived there in 1961, back when life was ordered. Papa had hitchhiked around Europe in 1948 after the war, and in so doing discovered El Escorial. It left its mark with the twenty-two-year-old. Always the romantic, thirteen years later he would return, this time with a wife and eight children in tow.

El Escorial was an insignificant village in Spain during the Middle Ages. Then the most powerful man in the world came knocking. Philip II wanted something built, and when your official title was *The Most Illustrious Philip, by the Grace of God, King of Spain, King of Aragon, Valencia, Mallorca, and Sardinia, Count of Barcelona, King of Granada, Lord of Álava, Guipúzcoa, and Vizcaya, King of Navarra, King of England, King of Ireland, King of France, Duke of Milan, King of Sicily, and King of Jerusalem, Duke of Brabant, Count of Flanders, Duke of Limbourg, Duke of Luxembourg, Count and Marquess of Namur, Count of Holland, and Lord of West Friesland, Count of Zeeland, Duke of Gelre, Lord of the Ommelanden, Hereditary Lord of Utrecht, Count of Drenthe, Lord of Groningen, King of the Spains and the Indies, King of Portugal and the Algarves, and King of Ceylon*—things got built.

In 1563, construction began on El Real Monasterio de San Lorenzo de El Escorial, a magnificent feat of architecture to project the might of an empire "where the sun never rests." In 1584, the project was completed. (Great trivia question: Who introduced the world's first known Workmen's Comp program?) In the Golden Age of Spain, if Madrid was the capital, El Escorial was Spain's Catholic heart.

El Escorial actually comprises two towns: the original town of El Escorial down the hill from the monastery that would come to be known as "El Escorial de Abajo," and the new town above, built to service the needs of this massive new complex. This town would take the name of its patron, Saint Lawrence, and come to be known as San Lorenzo de El Escorial. Combined they are simply El Escorial, and for the Bozells they were heaven on earth.

The Monastery of El Escorial is a stunning masterpiece, and in my certainly biased opinion the most beautiful edifice in the world. Built in the Spanish classicist Renaissance style, it is solemn and austere, like Philip himself. Designed in the shape of a grill to commemorate the martyrdom of Saint Lawrence, this gigantic structure boasts numbers that jolt the senses: sixteen inner courtyards, four thousand rooms, twelve hundred doors, eighty-six staircases, seventy-three sculptures, eighty-eight fountains, a staggering 2,675 windows, and fifteen miles of passageways including, as my brother Michael would discover, hidden underground tunnels serving as emergency royal escape routes.

The complex was designed to project the might of imperial Spain and built to hold everything a Holy Roman Emperor could possibly want. That included a massive Gothic basilica; the royal library; a monastery originally hosting the Hieronymite Order and now the Augustinians; a royal (and garish) eighteenth-century palace, constructed during remodeling; the Pantheon of the Kings and the Pantheon of the Princes, each with its own decaying chamber accessible only to the monks, appropriately called *el Pudridero* ("the Rotting Room"); and finally, El Real Colegio Alfonso XII, the school we would be attending.

2. Life with Franco

Spain's halcyon days of empire were but the stuff of history books by 1961. One might even argue that Spain had become a third world country. The savage Civil War in the late 1930s, pitting anti-Catholic liberals, anarchists, and communists against Catholic monarchists, conservatives, and fascists under the command of Francisco Franco had left the country in tatters. Because of Franco's support of Germany during World War II, the international community declared Spain a pariah and abandoned her. This ignores the full picture. During the Spanish Civil War, Franco also crushed the communists, saved the lives of thousands of priests and nuns, and restored the monarchy. In short, he saved Spain.

What today is the most popular tourist nation in Europe, back in 1961 was isolated, ignored, and underdeveloped. Modernity was in scarce supply in El Escorial back then. There were a handful of cars rumbling about, mostly battered SEAT 600s (the Spanish cousin of the Fiat), Renaults, and cheap, rattling, clumsy, misshapen Citroëns. Most villagers availed themselves of simple putt-putting motorcycles, led by the iconic and virtually indestructible Vespas.

There was the occasional bus crawling along while belching suffocating clouds of black smoke with every acceleration. These vehicles had company on the worn cobblestone streets: animals. It was common to see the grizzled farmer in his omnipresent black jacket and black cap, an unfiltered cigarette dangling from his lips, switch in hand, alongside his mule laden down with product for the market, or leading oxen hitched to ancient wagons carrying mountains of hay. The food—all the food—was fresh and delicious.

There were no grocery stores, let alone supermarkets. Fresh fish could be found packed in ice at the *pescadería*, meat hanging on hooks at the *carnicería*, aromatic bread at the *panadería*, cakes and sweets at the *pastelería*, and so forth. Women were seen all day walking around town with shopping bags picking out food for the day's meals.

We lived a couple of kilometers outside El Escorial de Abajo in "La Madalena," a sprawling country estate we'd leased for two years. The air was always fresh, no matter what season, and crystal clear. We had a breathtaking view looking west to the monastery resting on the hill. We'd hear the glorious bells pealing every quarter hour, the larger ones booming on the hour. More memorable still was the soft, lazy clanging of ancient, handmade bells of the sheep grazing nearby.

The cost of living was a fraction of what it had been in the States, allowing us to live like royalty with maids, cooks, gardeners, drivers, and a governess. It was then that my parents discovered Mercedes Bravo, a young woman they invited to move to the United States upon our return in 1963 and who spent forty-four years in their employ until her full retirement in 2006. Now age eighty-two and living in Madrid, this woman quickly became a member of our family sixty years ago and remains one today.

I have vague recollections of others, like our young driver Jose Maria, but in his case not for who he was, as much as what happened to him—and me. It involves bullfighting. Every old town in Spain has its bullring, usually a relic of better years when the art was more popular and entertainment options more limited. The *Plaza de Toros* in El Escorial de Abajo was built in 1957, making it rather new when we were there. El Escorial is a secondary stop on the bullfighting circuit, but nevertheless a good one even for full-fledged matadors. My bride attended her first bull fight here in 1983 and, as she'll attest, the ring was sufficiently run down that an angry bull could—and, when we were there, did—blast through the wooden retainer wall and charge into the stands, scattering panicked onlookers. It was curious that Norma kept her face covered during the first engagement, yet by the sixth and final fight she had become a full-fledged aficionado of the art.

That's the *corrida*. The *novillada* is another story. By definition a novillada is a bullfight using immature, overage, or defective bulls, the perfect match for a young man, an old man, or in the case of Jose Maria, a drunken fool. It was a hot August afternoon, and the stands were filled with citizens gaily celebrating the feast day of Saint Lawrence. The wine was flowing freely. The fans would bellow an exaggerated "*Ole!*" when a pass was executed correctly and hurl resounding but jovial obscenities when not. Throughout it all, old untuned trumpets accompanied by battered, out of sync drums with dented cymbals accompanied the crowd noise with far more enthusiasm than skill. It was perfect. I cannot recall how many of us attended the novillada that day, but it's fair to say one of them wasn't Papa. There's no telling how he would have reacted when one inebriated patron picked me up and dropped me into the ring in the middle of the action as the crowd laughed uproariously watching this six-year-old redheaded American run for his life (or so he thought) to reach the nearest protective barrier, safely out of reach of his attacker (that probably never saw him). The bulls that day were small with immature horns. Still, they could cause real damage.

Various townsfolk came out with makeshift capes to show off, the drunker the braver. One, of course, was Jose Maria. Too sloshed to move quickly, Jose Maria failed to evade the charge of a little bull whose horn clipped him at his groin. Jose Maria doubled over grabbing his crotch while the crowd gasped. He paused, and then slowly straightened back up. Right out of a Laurel and Hardy movie, his pants fell down. The bull had ripped his belt and nothing more. With one hand Jose Maria held his pants up and stumbled out of the ring, but not before extending an exaggerated bow while the crowd applauded with brio.

And yet El Escorial was sophisticated compared to the smaller villages dotting the countryside. If at times El Escorial felt like a medieval town, in these smaller villages it really was the Middle Ages.

A visit to Gallegos de Sobrinos (population *mas o menos* nothing) outside of Ávila showed me just how primitive rural Spain was just a half century ago. I was seven when Mercedes brought me to her village on holiday. In once Catholic Spain, every town spent a week celebrating its patron saint. Gallegos de Sobrinos was no different. The village was little more than a row of little stone houses on a dusty path off a winding, potholed mountain road. There was no commerce to speak of, no cars, not even running water, at least not in the houses. On the other hand, there were horses, oxen, pigs, donkeys, and chickens everywhere. A wire brought electricity to one light bulb inside the house. The bathroom was the barn next door. But this was the feast day of La Virgen de Chilla, and none of this mattered. The town was celebrating.

I can still remember the gaiety that Saturday when we arrived, the villagers assembled outside, laughing, playing guitars and mandolins, singing flamenco, some seated at the rickety tables playing the Spanish card game *Bastos*, freely drinking wine from their *botas* while eating the most delicious bread, cheeses and—especially!—the most succulent *chorizo* imaginable. Fifty-nine years later I can still taste it. The festivities went late into the candlelit night.

First thing Sunday morning Mass was held. All the villagers filed down the dusty path that led to the main road. There we were joined by the young horsemen from the surrounding villages, dashing and impeccably dressed in their riding outfits, astride horses as beautifully groomed as their riders, their coats shiny black with multicolored plumes affixed to their halters at the forehead.

Near the juncture of the dirt path and the main road, *obreros* worked on two oxen wagons, one on either side of the road facing each other. Each wagon was pulled back and anchored so that the wagon poles were now facing skyward at forty-five-degree angles. A rope was tied to the end of one wagon pole and attached across the road to the other pole, perhaps a dozen or so feet above the ground. Then a very live rooster, its legs tied, its wings flapping helplessly, was hung upside down from the middle of the road.

The riders lined up, and the first one took off, charging down the dirt road with the crowd yelling encouragement. In short order you learned the purpose of this exercise. It was a competition to see who could be the first to jump the highest, and at the most propitious moment pull the rooster's head off.

Easier said than done. It took several tries before one of the lads finally succeeded. The head was yanked off and the rider triumphantly tossed it into the field as the crowd cheered. The rooster, now headless, continued cockle-a-doodle-dooing upside down with blood pouring out where its head once rested, apparently quite annoyed. The winner's prize was the bird.

We rented our *finca* for two years and leased our home for two years, and in 1963 it was time to head back to the States. It wasn't until shortly before her death that my mother told me the full story. As it happened, during those two years my parents had become so immersed in the Catholic life in Spain, both cultural and spiritual, that they came within a whisker of settling in El Escorial for good. Mom recounted to me that, as the deadline loomed, Papa and she escaped to a beautiful old resort in the hills outside El Escorial to discuss their future. Ultimately, they concluded that while their hearts were in Spain, their loyalty was to the United States. There was a political war underway, and both felt the obligation to report for duty. They would do so, but for them this war was no longer political. Catholic Spain had defined them, and they remained so defined for the rest of their lives.

3. Back to the Past

In June 1970, seven years after we left Spain, we returned. By "we" I mean a small army: Papa and Mom, Kathy now eighteen, Michael sixteen, me fourteen, Willie eight, Jamie three, and our beloved ageless Mercedes. But we were not alone.

Papa had selected El Escorial to be the site of his first Institute for the Christian Commonwealth, an intense summer studies program he'd founded to school some three dozen students in the righteousness of the Catholic Reformation, the wisdom of Saint John of the Cross, the justice of Carlism, the virtues of *vino tinto*, and the art of bullfighting. Within days sleepy El Escorial had been transformed into the very lively Bozell world. The institute was ensconced in the *Real Colegio Maria Cristina*, an annex of the Escorial complex, founded in 1892 by Regent Maria Cristina of Austria. It offered everything necessary for the institute—classrooms, dormitories, dining rooms, outdoor recreational facilities, and indoor plumbing. Our family meanwhile took up residence in a four-bedroom apartment on Joaquín Costa, a side street in the center of town. This would be our Spanish home for the next three years.

The relocation hit at once with a delightful wallop. The cloudless skies were bright blue, and although the summer temperatures soared in the afternoon, they were eased by the height of the Sierra de Guadarrama mountains and cooled in the evenings. Noise, noise, noise—it was unending. All day we heard Vespa, Enduro, Montesa, and Bultaco motorcycles brrraping all over town. Large buses rumbled through town bearing tourists, primarily French and Germans who had recently discovered this magnificence, and barely squeezed through the narrow streets. Locals and visitors were everywhere, chatting as they walked. Basilica bells tolled. Town Hall tower bells clapped.

The lack of air conditioning dictated the lifestyle. Always the first one to rise, Mom would go around the block to the panadería for fresh-baked loaves of bread and pastries, perhaps stopping on the street corner where the kindly old lady stacked her mountain of fresh melons and selected the best for us. After a quick breakfast, the Bozells were off to explore anew with stops at the bars for yet another delicacy—*café con leche*—or, if closer to lunch, to enjoy a cold *caña*, the local Spanish beer on tap, which was always accompanied by complimentary *tapas*. Sometimes the day included one or more visits to the Maria Cristina to see Papa, perhaps attending one of his lectures or one delivered by the eccentrically brilliant Dr. Fritz

Wilhelmsen or perhaps by other lecturers whose presentations were equally riveting, at least the small parts we could decipher.

Each day was crowned by a delicious three-course lunch at the school or any one of the innumerable restaurants, after which it was time for the town's collective *siesta*. Stores were shuttered, motorcycles stopped roaring, and the streets were emptied as the hot afternoon sun blazed. Silence. By 5:00 p.m. the town had woken from its nap, shops were reopened, and activity resumed, but now of a different sort. There's a curious tradition in Spain known as *la vuelta*, or "the stroll." At sunset with temperatures falling, villagers seemingly materialize out of nowhere to enjoy the evening air, women walking with arms locked, men with arms clasped behind their backs, and children with arms around each other's necks.

Each group will muster to exchange stories of the day just concluded. Every town has its set location, and to this day they still do it. In Valencia, the locals walk around the cathedral. In Ávila, they walk around the Mercado Grande, and in El Escorial they stroll slowly from one end of the monastery's wide front portal to the other, a couple football fields long, then back again.

After an hour or so of this exercise, the strollers disperse to enjoy other things, the children playing kickball in the streets, or buying homemade ice cream sandwiches from street vendors while their parents mill in the bars for the evening *chato* of wine or *cerveza* with the accompanying free *pincho* of *tortilla* or *chorizo* or *queso manchego* or other nibbles on offer that day. All of these tapas were mouthwatering; pickled pig's ear, not so much. (What does pickled pig's ear taste like, you ask? Imagine a pig's ear, pickled.) Dinner was served as late as 10:00 p.m., after which some citizens returned to the streets for more of the same. Now adults could be found seated on the tables outside the bars enjoying the night. Occasionally we'd come across the mandolin and guitar players, sometimes a lonely flamenco singer booming his lament. Those were local folks playing for themselves. This was an everyday magic lost forever to history.

There was one small problem with Papa's plan to have Michael and me and later Johnny enroll in an all-Spanish school. We still understood the language pretty well, but our speaking abilities were unacceptably limited.

We'd all become fluent during our first stay, so much so that upon our return to the States in 1963 some of us had to relearn English.

But even with a Spanish maid and cook, the memory banks cashed out. By 1970 our Spanish inflicted actual pain on the locals who endured it. So Papa sent me to a bar for the summer, literally. His solution was ingenious, the kind of thinking that defined him and which today would land him in prison and me in a foster home. An hour away from El Escorial, over the mountains, stood the walled beauty of Saint Teresa's Ávila. In 1970, this jewel of a medieval village knew little of the outside world, and the world knew less of it. Any foreigner stood out, most especially a tall redheaded American, sometimes with an elegant redheaded wife and countless redheaded children in tow. Papa was legendary, *"El Gran Jefe,"* as his Abulense (what locals in Ávila are called) friend Sigirano Diaz dubbed him. "Sigi" in turn was Papa's Sancho Panza, short and paunchy, serving proudly as *El Gran Jefe's* aide-de-camp when he came to town. One reason Kathy had studied in Ávila for two years was because she'd been able to live with Sigi and his lovely wife, Tomasita.

Papa knew that the only way for me to become fluent quickly was to be separated from all the Americans in El Escorial and placed in a location where no English was spoken. It was *hundirse o nadar*, sink or swim. Sigi had been tasked with finding a solution to the problem and arranged for me to spend the summer working at El Pepillo, then the best restaurant/ bar in Ávila. It was owned by Don Orencio, a tall, elderly, and kindly man with the elegant features we expect of a Spanish patrician, including the trademark, straight-lined, pencil thin moustache. I was also to live in Don Orencio's apartment. In true Spanish fashion, in recognition of the faith Papa had placed in Ávila to care for me, the entire town adopted me.

I wonder how many fourteen-year-old boys (other than, the next year, my brother Johnny who went through the same drill) have ever spent a summer like mine in 1970. Don Orencio's second-floor apartment was in the same square as El Pepillo, so I commuted about thirty yards to work each day. After breakfast in the kitchen (nothing, but nothing will ever top fresh *churros* dunked in a cup of thick, dark chocolate), the work began. For the first few hours I helped prepare for the busy lunch hour, and then I assisted with lunch, bringing up food from the kitchen to the second floor dining room. There was a break around 4:00, leaving about three hours for a swim, or a walk around town with my new friends, or maybe just a nap. I'd be back by 7:00 for the dinner shift. By 10:30 we were finished. These were twelve-hour work days, six days a week. My day off was Wednesday. Just after dawn I'd walk excitedly to the train station for the hour-long ride to El Escorial to spend the day with family and friends, then back to Ávila that night.

As far as both tourists and locals were concerned, El Pepillo was a first class restaurant in terms of both ambiance and cuisine. What went on behind the revolving kitchen doors was quite another matter.

Spaniards might not be surprised, but if this were in the States, agents from OSHA, the FDA, FBI, and good deed doers from PETA would be storming down our doors. There were rats—not mice, rats—everywhere. In this country we'd call them free-range rats. Cats were allowed to roam to keep the rat population under control, but they were no match for the rodents.

There were smaller creatures with which we contended as well. Our kitchen produced a mouthwatering flan. The cooks would prepare the caramel in the morning using custom-fit pans that were then placed on the counter for the hot flan sauce to cool and harden. Before lunch it was my task to finish the job. I would apply a scoop of vanilla ice cream topped with a cherry over each serving before inserting the tray into the ice box. But first I'd have to wave the back of my hand over the top of the tray to remove the cockroaches feasting on the desert. And that daily insect feast pales when compared to what I witnessed one busy Sunday afternoon.

We had been invaded early by a sizable wedding party that had occupied the dining area and had managed to eviscerate our entire supply of chicken. When they left and the regular patrons took their place, a number of them immediately ordered more poultry. There being no such thing as a Safeway with a ready supply of chickens, we might expect the waiters to calmly alert our guests to the shortage. But this was Spain, and it was 1970, and there was always a solution, in this case alerting the diners that their chicken would be slightly delayed. The head cook's son worked with us upstairs in the staging area. His father came racing up with instructions for him to fetch some chickens. As I watched the boy bounding down the stairs I was puzzled. Where might this mysterious supply of poultry be hidden? After waiting about a half hour, during which time the first courses were prepared downstairs and transported to us via the dumb waiter, I was overwhelmed by an indecipherable cacophony of human yelling and animal screeching.

I happened to be tugging up a dish at that moment. When the succulent dish appeared in front of me, it was accompanied by a couple of floating feathers. Ignoring my food order, I charged down the stairs. When I reached the bottom and looked over the open kitchen, it was sheer pandemonium. There were chickens flying all over the place while the cook and his assistants, including his son, hacked at them with cleavers and knives, dispatching their prey one by one in mid-air. There was blood and feathers everywhere. But there was also the promised missing ingredient for lunch, slightly delayed to be sure, but oh, so fresh.

As compensation for all my work at El Pepillo I received free room, three squares, and every month one thousand *pesetas*, or fourteen dollars American. This was plenty when an entire town has adopted you. The fun began after work. The waiters and bartenders would assemble, and off we'd go. Spaniards, especially those from small towns, are creatures of habit. All of his adult life Sigi enjoyed his sacred Saturday night ritual driving his trusty little SEAT (purchased for him by Papa) around the town walls, stopping in the same half dozen bars, to enjoy the very same *copas de anis*, with the very same friends, standing at the very same spot by the bar. The bartenders at El Pepillo were no different. We'd leave the restaurant, and we'd hit the cobblestone streets, popping into one predetermined bar after another for nightcaps. By 1:00 or 2:00 in the morning we'd stumble back to our respective apartments.

And I mean stumble. There were no cars on the narrow, silent streets, and with crime non-existent, there was no known danger. Arrive at your apartment without your key or the ability to insert it effectively into the lock? Not a problem. You simply clapped your hands loudly. The sound would bounce off the ancient stone walls and echo down the silent streets. Eventually, it would reach the ears of the trusty *serrano*, the old man whose job it was to hold copies of everyone's keys for just such an occasion. He'd shuffle to the door, extract a copy of your key from a massive ring on his person, and after unlocking your door, you'd slip him five pesetas, and you were home safe.

Wait a minute. You're saying you were fourteen and drinking? Would it help if I told you that during the summer I'd turned fifteen? Imagine being fifteen and smoking and imbibing with total cultural acceptance. Believe it or not, I could, and everyone my age did. At least I thought I was drinking. Little did I know that Papa had spies everywhere, and bartenders all over town had been instructed to pour the absolute minimal amount of rum into my *cuba libre*. Here I thought I was getting plastered, but with a couple of notable exceptions I was getting ripped on Coca Cola. How those bartenders must have enjoyed the summer-long charade!

There was the occasional evening or afternoon when Don Orencio would have other plans for us. We visited the bullring several times. One Sunday I was honored to watch two of the nation's greatest matadors on the same bill. The stern-faced Santiago Martín Sánchez, popularly known as *El Viti*, was further nicknamed "The Ace of Spades" for his workmanlike accuracy with the sword and his ability to dispatch his target with deadly efficiency. Paco Camino, young and dashingly handsome, was nicknamed *el Niño Sabio de Camas*, "the clever boy from Camas." He was just the opposite, sometimes wild and actually afraid of the bull, but at other times dazzling with his gods-tempting, gasp-inducing style. You never knew which Paco Camino would show up for work.

At each bullfight three matadors were assigned two bulls apiece. At the conclusion of each twenty-minute engagement, the crowd loudly, and if necessary, ruthlessly worked the judge. If the fight was lousy, then nothing was awarded. If the effort was just passable, the matador might be allowed one trip around the ring, with men tossing him botas, the leather canteens filled with wine. If the matador had acquitted himself well, the judge would order a bull's ear cut off, which the bullfighter would hold aloft proudly while completing the circle. If excellent, two ears.

The highest award—I have never seen it bestowed—was the bullfight version of the Medal of Honor: the tail. On this day El Viti was surgically brilliant with his first bull and was awarded one or two ears, I can't recall. Paco Camino was another story. Inexplicably, he was thoroughly intimidated and appeared actually frightened by his first draw. The crowd's boos cascaded into the arena when he finally killed the bull, sloppily. It was painful to watch the master so humiliated. With his second bull, El Viti was again precise and businesslike, the sword entering true between the shoulder blades and angling to the heart for the instant kill.

Now it was time for Paco Camino. The crowd greeted him with another verbal broadside—bullfighting aficionados do not suffer cowards gladly. This time, it was as if he responded, "Message received and understood." Again, inexplicably, the other bullfighter appeared. Paco Camino first silenced the boo birds, then had the crowd clapping, then cheering, and finally thundering its approval as he danced about and mesmerized the beast with all manner of life-threatening moves. In twenty minutes the transformation was complete, and the kill was perfect. When finished, Paco Camino shot the crowd a look that proclaimed, "How did you like *that?*" He then made a ceremonial *vuelta* around the ring, holding both ears aloft triumphantly as the fans roared and tossed their botas in the hopes he'd choose theirs with which to quench his thirst. It was a spectacular afternoon.

Don Orencio also brought me to an amateur novillada. Ávila had its own annual affair, celebratory and boisterous as the townsfolk turned out to cheer or to heckle, but this time good-naturedly. What three men— boys—would volunteer? All week long the bartenders at El Pepillo urged me to enlist. I almost did. One more cuba libre, properly spiked, and I might have. Thank God I didn't.

The novillada was an evening event, with just one bull per teenager. The first lad took one look at his draw and ran for his life. The second boy was serious and wanted the recognition. He actually acquitted himself quite well, and after killing his bull, he was applauded vigorously for his gallantry.

The third engagement, that was one for the ages. As with the first match, our would-be matador was scared witless. This time, the crowd, good-natured as it was, refused to let him leave. Each time the little bull passed, we cringed expecting this kid to get clobbered. Somehow he dodged the bullet each time, and the laughter only grew. When he was handed his sword for the kill, this boy—he couldn't have been much older than I—looked as if he were going to faint. Even the staid Don Orencio was whooping it up and mercilessly needling the poor guy. As the boy lined up to face his foe, I could see the sword wobbling, he was shaking so hard. The little bull charged, and our would-be matador panicked. He turned and ran from his prey, literally throwing his sword at the bull. Now Don Orencio and I were in tears, our heads buried in our hands, knowing this poor kid was about to get ignominiously butted.

When we looked up, the boy was still running, but the bull was lying on the ground. Dead. I will never be able to explain how, but the sword had reached its target, penetrated into the stomach, and killed the little bull instantly. At the sight of the deceased bull, the crowd simply lost it. Rarely have I seen so many people laugh so heartily. A number of young men charged into the ring, hoisted Ávila's new hero onto their shoulders, and carried him out in mock triumph to the nearest bar. There they celebrated his first and surely his last bullfight.

And so it went for eight glorious weeks in the summer of 1970 when life was strange and sweet and somehow ordered. But all things must end. During my final week in Ávila, the Institute in El Escorial wrapped up its summer session, and the diaspora followed: my parents, siblings, and Mercedes headed home to Virginia. With school in El Escorial beckoning, I bid my friends in Ávila farewell.

When I arrived at El Escorial, it hit. The vacation was now over. The town was silent. Tourists were no longer shopping and sightseeing. The omnipresent vendors had vanished, as had their wagons filled with candies and ice cream. Motorcycles had ceased to roar, and, sadder still, everyone I knew was gone, friends and family both. Even the weather had changed. The skies had turned damp, overcast, chilly, and gloomy—the perfect complement to my mood.

I walked the empty streets to our apartment. Michael had returned ahead of me—he'd spent the summer with our Uncle Reid in Comillas—and was equally depressed. We sat in the apartment saying little, brooding.

It had hit us both: the fun was over, and in one week we'd be walking down the hill to the great unknown of a Spanish high school.

Michael snapped out of his funk first and suggested we play a game of Monopoly. We made our *cafe Monkys*, the most delicious instant coffee ever to be visited on man, especially with milk warmed on the stove and accompanied by buttered crackers for dunking. Then the record player was turned on so we could play the same twenty or so albums endlessly. It was cold outside, but inside it was beyond cozy. We played our first game, then another, and another, and another. We played Monopoly for the entire week, day and night, not because there was nothing else to do (and there wasn't), but because we were having a ball, just the two of us, bonded by our loneliness, our fear of the future, and the fun of that timeless board game.

One week later we were in.

4. El Real Colegio Alfonso XII

I can't say for certain why Michael and I weren't terrified. I suppose part of it was genetic. I don't remember either of our parents ever being intimidated by anything, and we were raised similarly. We relished challenges. We had always been different, a large unruly family, Catholic to the core, Irish in our temperament, and with parents eschewing the pedestrian in favor of the eclectic. Two teenaged American boys sent by themselves to another country on another continent to enroll in a new school taught in a different language was just a part of the continuum. But it was also the sheer scale of the proposed new experience that shielded us from what promised to be total culture shock. Everything all summer had been fascinating, so different, and so exciting that we hadn't stopped to consider that perhaps we *should* be intimidated. On the first day of class we walked down the hill to the monastery and stepped over the threshold of the massive green doors—or rather, the human scale door cut out of the massive green doors. Michael was Peter, and I was Edmund, and together we were entering Cair Paravel.

We were now under the control of the Augustinian monks at El Real Colegio Alfonso XII. For the record, I have no clue why this school was named after such an utterly undistinguished monarch. This fellow accomplished nothing that qualifies him for this honor. But who needs public acclamation when you're king? Alfonso XII named the school after himself.

I was immediately struck by the magnitude of it all, the wide stone staircases worn in the middle from centuries of use, the cold stone walls, the musky hallways, but mostly the cacophony of a few hundred boys running about and excitedly becoming reacquainted with old friends. Of course, they shot looks in our direction wondering who these two redheaded strangers might be, but happily the looks didn't kill. They just raised questions.

Michael and I were instant attractions. The Spanish students looked us over with quizzical wonder, much as the simians did Charlton Heston in *Planet of the Apes*. They did everything but smell us. *Americanos!* Most had never met an American. They were not just intrigued but genuinely pleased that we were there and immediately wanted to share their profound knowledge of the American scene. We went through this exchange, several times, in labored English no less:

"Where you from?"

"Virginia."

(Eyes wide open in joyful recognition). *"Veergeenia Ceety! Los Cartwrights!"* (Mock pistols drawn.) *"Bang! Bang!"*

Apparently, we were not from Virginia. We were from Bonanza. At times their knowledge of the American pop music scene was equally tortured, as with our discussions about those two folk rock sensations from New York, *"Seemon y Gar de Foonk."*

Upon our arrival in Spain we'd known little about dress—shorts for teens were taboo; culinary habits—too many eggs make moles grow out of your ears; and stretching—by God, *never* stretch at the dinner table. We also learned no one is more expressive than a Spaniard. *Coño!* meant many things including "No kidding!" *La Madre que le parió!* —"The mother that gave him birth!"—was also their way of saying, "No kidding!" And they loved to cuss, publicly and enthusiastically, again with expressions that bewilder. *Me cago en la mar!*—"I shit in the sea!"—was still another way of also saying, "No kidding!"

We were no longer brushing up against Spanish culture. We were living it. We were becoming Spaniards. I would go days without seeing Michael (later Johnny too) except for meals, and even then we were separated. I'd be with my new friends, and they with theirs. We quickly felt thoroughly at home in our new surroundings.

You think your high school alma mater has history? Try attending a school in a building whose doors opened in 1587. It had been a busy time in El Escorial. In 1554 Philip II had married Mary I of England, making him King of England, but she died in 1558, and his monarchy there was kaput. The throne was transferred to Elizabeth I, much to the chagrin of England's Catholics, who in turn supported Mary Queen of Scots as the legitimate ruler. The Protestants had other ideas.

In 1556, they put Mary on trial and found her guilty of plotting to knock off Elizabeth. In 1587, while Philip was ceremoniously cutting ribbons at El Escorial, Elizabeth's henchmen were unceremoniously cutting off Mary's head. One year later Philip decided to even the score, but 1588 was not a good year for revenge. His mother of all armadas had the living crap knocked out of it.

Philip was at El Escorial when the messenger arrived on horseback with the devastating news that all was lost. Try to imagine yourself in his royal slippers, learning your navy, the one you'd bankrupted your country to build, had just been annihilated. Philip's reaction was a testament to his amazing faith. He ordered a *Te Deum* Mass, giving glory to God. Once upon a time, when Spain was Catholic…

But let's get back on track.

I suppose ours was your typical sixteenth-century royal education center. In 2008 it was still listed by one ratings organization as the best "luxury high end" school in Spain because "though not as expensive as other schools the prestige of going to school in a palace with an opportunity to board can be called nothing but luxury."

Although we lived in town, we boarded Monday to Friday at the school. This was altogether necessary if we were to become fully integrated into Spanish culture. We awoke around 8:00 a.m. and in a most obnoxious way. A monk walked throughout the dormitory slowly, methodically clapping his hands, a sound more insulting to the ears than the most annoying alarm clock ever devised. At 8:30 we entered the dining room, one of the few rooms with even a hint of the twentieth century about it. Seated at our assigned tables, we waited until the monks, usually three or four of them, had assembled on the dais.

After grace was pronounced and students had taken their seats, the waiters marched out from the kitchen with trays. Yes, we had *waiters* and they *served* us. For the next three years the breakfast routine did not vary—on one day a fresh loaf of bread with butter and marmalade and a large bowl of coffee in which to dunk the bread, and on the next day a fresh loaf of bread with a large bowl of hot chocolate in which to dunk it. I never tired of the routine.

After breakfast it was off to the first two classes with a break at 11:00 to go outside and play kickball or simply gossip with friends on *La Lonja*, the massive stone paved courtyard across two sides of the building. Two more classes, and lunch was served at 2:00, after which students were sent down the hill to the *bosquecillo*, the area behind the school with its dusty, makeshift soccer fields, allegedly for exercise. By 5:00 we were back inside for the final two classes, followed by a study hall and another short break.

Dinner was served at 8:30. Some final free time was allowed, and then it was off to the barracks to bunk with some fifty classmates as well as the mice that scavenged nightly for food scraps. Speaking of food scraps, a word about dinner: it was as awful as the simple breakfast was delicious. Each night, they served up the same tasteless slop: an old, overcooked slice of cow with watery gravy, a clump of boring potatoes, and lettuce soaked carelessly in oil and vinegar. The rolls, now stale, tasted like wallboard. After a few weeks of this, Michael and I decided it was time to introduce this school to a time-honored American tradition unthinkable in Franco's Spain: the strike. We recruited co-conspirators, and, as a group, we convinced the entire assembled student body to refuse the meal the following night with the demand that the menu be changed.

The excitement in the dining room was electric that evening in anticipation of what would happen when the waiters entered with their trays. As one, we would reject the food! Demand better! Attica! Attica! It was straight out of a prison movie. Unfortunately, word had made its way to the monks about the planned resistance, and they had prepared a clever counter assault.

After grace, the kitchen doors swung open and the waiters entered. Our jaws dropped. For the first time ever, the plates were laden with succulent fried chicken whose delicious aroma quickly flooded the room. Damn those men, cloth or no cloth. I watched in horror as one student after another eagerly abandoned our righteous cause in favor of this extraordinary meal. Resistance everywhere was collapsing. I frantically looked to Michael, seated at the far corner, to rally his side of the hall. When I caught his eye, he was ripping off a mouthful of chicken, and his smile said, "The hell with you and your stupid strike." Out of pride I held out by myself, which was a useless gesture. We never struck again.

About half the students lived in Madrid so, like us, they boarded only on weekdays. On Saturday, we opened with a 9:00 study hall, with the option to attend Mass. Most of us enterprising lads headed off to one of the remote and beautiful side chapels given the Mass lasted only fifteen minutes, after which we learned to hide from the monks for the remainder of the hour. After breakfast the school was dismissed, and boys poured out the doors to freedom, those who could to go home, and those who could not to spend the day in town.

There were no TV rooms because there was no television worth watching. Spain had two government-owned stations, each broadcasting a few hours a day, first with government propaganda and later with the occasional American western or cop drama, terribly dubbed, all in black and white. Every few weeks the monks transformed one of the classrooms into a makeshift theater and showed some old American movie in black and white. We were grateful for any nugget of entertainment, no matter its vintage. Who would have thought a high school boy in the early 1970s could pine for a movie starring Doris Day?

Many an American today contemplating what life was like for a teenaged boy in Spain in that era would be horrified by some of its cultural mores. I make that observation with a wide smile on my face. Imagine a society where boys (not girls) smoked at will, whenever and wherever we wanted. American tobacco being an expensive delicacy, we smoked local, harsh, pungent, black tobacco. We smoked it in hallways, in restaurants, on the street, on the trains, in movie theaters, in bedrooms—everywhere.

I am told I first smoked at age—ahem—five, stealing cigarettes from the learned conservative polemicist and old family friend Willmoore Kendall, then extinguished them on the bed sheets and wondered how I got caught. It took a heart attack almost five decades later for me to end this awful habit, and even then quitting was met with stiff resistance.

But as a teen I was in Spain, alone, in a society that loved not just the sinner but the sin itself. *Free at last, free at last....* Away from home, now I could smoke with wild abandon. So of course I did. Knowing Papa would eventually be visiting, I screwed up the courage to write him first, to make my case. "I just turned fifteen, I know, but everyone here smokes, and can we agree I am NEVER going to quit?" When his response arrived granting me permission, I felt like a convict whose reprieve from the governor came as the guy in the black hood was plugging in the chair. I was relieved, to say the least. But what choice did Papa have? He knew he was licked.

Which is not to say that Papa didn't get the last laugh on this one.

A couple of months later, he came to visit us. We went to dinner by ourselves at *Casa Larios*, one of our favorite little family-owned restaurants, which is to say they turned the living room into a dining room. As was customary at the time, Papa smoked before, during, and after the meal. I hid my cigarettes in my pants, not in the shirt pocket. I was far too embarrassed for a public display. The more I watched him smoke, the more desperate to have one I became, but still I could not bring myself to smoke in front of him. Papa knew this too. As we were having our desert, Papa lit yet another cigarette, took a huge, satisfying drag, and as he blew out the smoke mischievously teased, "I know you're dying for a cigarette, aren't you?"

With that I took out my pack and—so embarrassing!—smoked in front of him for the very first time. Maybe we were raised not to be intimidated by anyone, but that "anyone" did not include the man who taught us to be this way.

Social interaction was conducted in bars. That was another little culture shocker. In 1970 there was no drinking age. Fifteen years old and in the mood for a bottle of wine? If I had the ten pesetas, fourteen cents, it was mine. That and my ten peseta pack of *Ducados* cigarettes, along with perhaps twenty-five or so pesetas for the ever-present pinball machines, and I was set for the afternoon. Spoilsports ended this joy ride three years later, shortly before I left. An official edict from on high was posted in every bar: *Absolutely NO ONE under the age of fourteen allowed to drink in bars.* Crackdown!

Where afternoons were concerned, we had about three hours of recreational sports activity, but the Bozells had better plans for their free time. Rather than follow our classmates down the hill to the bosquecillo soccer fields for the afternoon, at the propitious moment we'd peel away and sneak into the town, Michael to engage in various forms of misbehavior or just to relax at the apartment, Johnny to chase girls, and I to head for an old, decrepit, literally nameless bar we'd grandiosely dubbed, "El Casino." There was nothing inside the joint except some old tables and chairs and a simple bar with an occasional bored bartender serving only a handful of drinks. On the counter you could grab an old chess set, but we'd choose a deck of very used playing cards and a box of little metal disks that served as chips.

We'd buy our perfunctory beers and then settle into our designated table, and the poker game would begin. We'd play for real money. The stakes were low, but sometimes the winnings and losses exceeded two hundred pesetas ($2.80), a small fortune for high school students. We'd play every minute of our free time, then slip into the line of students reentering the school. If friends were in town for the weekend, we might play Saturday, then head back Sunday for more. I was pretty good, and so was Johnny, and we augmented our monthly allowance by another 10 to 20 percent.

Misbehavior did have its consequences. We were living in a system where corporal punishment was quite the rage, which is to say that if monks were enraged, corporal punishment followed. It came in stages. DEFCON 4: *Kneeling on the floor*. It doesn't sound that bad, but try kneeling on an old wooden plank floor for, say, an hour. Or two. Or three. It hurts like hell. If the transgression had been severe enough, or if there was continued misbehavior during the execution of DEFCON 4, you'd be taken to DEFCON 3: *Kneeling on the floor with arms extended.* Again, try this, even for a half an hour. If circumstances warranted, you'd be hit with DEFCON 2: *Kneeling on the floor with arms extended holding books.* This punishment was unsustainable past a few minutes, so the sentence extended beyond a few minutes.

Then there was DEFCON 1: *Oh, shit.* This was the end-of-life stage when the monk was enraged enough to dispense with the niceties of DEFCON 4–2 and resorted to the nuclear option: the beating. A favorite weapon of these Augustinian monks was the long leather belt that hung down the sides of their robes. It became an instant whip.

Still that was nothing compared to the real beating I watched one monk inflict against a student who taunted him in front of the entire class while at DEFCON 2. Apparently, the student believed this man of the cloth could go no further in the punishment department. Wrong. The monk opened up with both fists and pummeled his hapless victim. The student never challenged this monk again. No one did. The word "deterrent" comes to mind.

Teenagers know everything, and I knew this was so very wrong. At home during our Christmas vacation, I took the opportunity during dinner to bring this injustice to Papa's attention. I chose dinner so the whole family would know just how awful were the conditions under which we suffered overseas while everyone stateside enjoyed the protections of a civilized society. Papa listened quietly, attentively, and yet with obvious bemusement as I gave a thorough report. When I'd finished, quite proud of my dramatic soliloquy, he asked one question, the one question I hadn't expected. "Did the boy deserve it?"

I had to tell the truth, "I...*guess.*" In a flash, just like that, I knew my cause was lost. Papa smiled, and we were off to the next family topic.

About those monks. What thought comes to mind when picturing some two hundred young boys living in the same complex as some two hundred men of the cloth? It's not a pretty picture, is it? Given how a viciously anti-Catholic media have savaged the Church, and how some in the Church have deserved it, the Catholic community in our country is in full retreat. The same holds true today in Spain, but even more so. Catholicism has disappeared. To see this transformation is among the saddest developments of my life.

It was not always so.

A wag once stated, "In Spain there is a church on every corner and two bars in between." Both were central to the Catholic experience. In one God was venerated, and in the other His teachings were lived imperfectly, after which there was the visit to the confessional, after which the process repeated itself.

There were no Protestant churches and no synagogues. You were Catholic or nothing. In that era most everyone was Catholic, and more to the point, they practiced their religion faithfully. There were churches all over every town. On Sundays each church celebrated multiple Masses, and most were heavily attended.

It wasn't just Sundays. During the weekdays most churches celebrated the early morning Mass attended by the elderly men and women, with most widows and widowers wearing their obligatory black suits or frocks. Most Catholics did not miss Holy Days of Obligation. There were priests and nuns, and at El Escorial, monks everywhere. All were in garb, and all were treated with fervent reverence.

The town celebrated the Church. During Holy Week, students were dismissed for the equivalent of spring break. During my first year both Michael and I had the opportunity to enjoy different mini vacations with friends, but there being so many chores to complete around the apartment, only one could go. We flipped a coin. He won; I stayed behind.

I spent the week busily doing this and that, but when Holy Thursday arrived, the tone changed. A solemnity descended on the town. The bars were empty. No one played pinball or cards or music. Silence. That night, while at the apartment, I heard a distant *Thump! Thump! Thump!* Someone was slowly beating a drum. I looked out of the apartment terrace. People were silently leaving their homes, walking in the direction of the drummer, holding unlit candles.

I walked outside and followed, curious. The people stopped at the street running parallel to us, a block away. We stood in the narrow, worn stone sidewalks. At once it came, a slow procession of several hundred men and women, all holding lit candles, carrying on pedestals several of the larger statues from the basilica, quietly reciting the Rosary. As they passed by, the bystanders on the sidewalks would step into the street to join the march, lighting their candles. The procession grew. I joined as well. A candle was provided. We rose up the hill somberly, to the cemetery. Priests awaited. Special prayers were said for the dead, and then everyone returned to their homes, silently.

Catholicism was lived.

And that's where the bars come in. Everyone had his favorite watering hole, the place you went for a quick coffee and breakfast roll early in the morning on the way to work (and when cold outside, perhaps a shot of cognac), the place where you convened with your friends around noon for a caña of beer or a chato of wine or two before lunch and then again before dinner.

To do what? To chat. To catch up on the day's work, monotonous as it might be. To laugh at jokes retold countless times. To talk about bullfights, soccer games, your neighbors—praising the good, raining scorn on the unacceptable, and mimicking the ridiculous. But mostly you went to join with your friends in simple communion.

That communion extended outside the doors. Friends were greeted warmly, strangers with respect. Men whistled innocently at pretty girls, who (normally) smiled back with an innocent flirt. Doors were opened for the fairer sex. A helping hand was always extended for one in need. No money to pay the bill? Catch you next time. Honor prevailed in a society where honor was paramount in an ordered life. A Catholic life.

An American living in today's secular society would never understand what it meant to live in a culture defined by its Catholicism. But let me give it a shot. Some boys in this school, as with any school, were incorrigible. My friend Paco fell in this category. The only thing that saved him from expulsion was his charm. He was well liked by the monks, but they were reaching the end of their tether. One afternoon as students were preparing to descend to the bosquecillo, a monk took Paco aside and invited him for a beer at a bar in town. Paco accepted the invitation and left, but not before telling us of this very strange overture. We had no idea what to make of it. Remember, he was no more than sixteen.

They were back about two hours later, Paco somewhat worse for wear. It was obvious he'd consumed more than one beer with this priest. "What happened?!" we asked in shock.

He told us. They'd gone to a little, nearly empty bar around the corner from the Hotel Miranda. The priest bought him a beer and then began pummeling him with questions about his behavior, delving ever deeper into his soul as they drank. The priest admitted he, too, had been a miscreant in school, and they began openly to trade stories after the priest promised immunity. Eventually the priest brought Paco around to accepting the error of his ways, and Paco apologized. "Are you truly sorry for your sins?" the priest asked. Paco answered in the affirmative, at which point the priest raised his hand, right at the bar, and blessed him declaring, "Then by the power of God, I absolve you of your sins."

The monk had wanted to hear Paco's confession, and if it took buying him beer in a bar, by God that's what he was going to do.

One hundred and sixty dollars. That was our monthly allowance. It had to cover rent, food, clothing, and toiletries. It had to cover all social activities, including the rare meal at a restaurant, the occasional movie, pinball games, and, yes, cigarettes. It had to cover all transportation, be it to Madrid or to Ávila or to any other port of call and all expenses once there. It also had to cover the services of Lola, a sweet old lady Mom had hired to come once a week to clean up the place but who quickly became so physically depleted we assumed her tasks in return for her occasional delicious meals. Thank God for Michael who took charge and taught Johnny and me how to assume managerial responsibility after he left. Spain was inexpensive, but not free, and somehow we made it work with this pittance.

People rode the trains everywhere, and so did we—usually. Sometimes we took the local buses, but a few times we drove. We learned that the local car rental agency could not discern between an official US driver's license and a learner's permit. We convinced the rental lady that, yes indeedy, in the United States boys were licensed to drive at a very, very early age. On the strength of our learner permits, the rented SEAT 600 would be ours for the weekend. It was the most rudimentary of automobiles. There was a horn, headlights, and windshield wipers, and maybe even brakes. The tiny side windows were optional. Still, it cost money. Capitalists that we were, eventually we figured out we could drive it one day, then sublease it to friends the next, collecting enough money to pay for the whole weekend.

For three years it was like this, the first with just Michael. In the second year we were joined by our younger brother Johnny. We watched with joy as he, too, turned charlatan. The final year it was just Johnny and me, Michael having gone back home to college. Johnny assimilated so thoroughly that he would return a handful of years after his graduation and marry a local girl from Soria. They have lived happily ever after in that city with their two grown sons. To keep the Bozell carbon footprint alive in El Escorial, they now maintain a weekend apartment in our special little town, a half century after we first came, saw, and conquered.

Everything for us was a game, and Spain was our playground. Johnny and I misbehaved, to be sure, but Michael was in a league of his own. Amazingly, he somehow convinced the monks that he was the single most angelic student ever to grace that school. As I write this he's celebrating his fifth decade as a cloistered Benedictine monk in France, a lifelong pursuit of penance for his transgressions in Spain circa 1970–1971.

At the start of this chapter I alluded to Cair Paravel and for good reason. We explored constantly and on one of those adventures with his best friend Pedro, Michael discovered an actual passage inside the basilica of El Escorial. I'll let him explain this one:

> In the basilica there is the main organ in the choir [flanked by] two slightly smaller ones. You will remember that to get up to the *cúpula* "dome," you had to have a door unlocked by a guide which led up from the first story balustrade to the organ on the right. You came out at the organ, crossed, and found a door with steps winding up to the *cúpula*.

But on the left, things were different. The door on the balustrade level was not locked. You could open it and go up to the organ on the left. But now you could proceed no further. If you crossed the organ space and went for the door on the other side, you found that it opened instead into a broom closet of sorts. Your wicked brother thought about this at one point and said, "There's something wrong here. Everything is symmetrical in the Escorial. If there is a staircase on the right, there must be one on the left."

With Pedro, we examined the back of the broom closet by banging on the wall with our feet. The sound we made told us this was a flimsy partition. We came back later that night armed with something heavy (I forget), and banged (the noise echoing through the basilica!) on that brick partition until a hole appeared and cool air flowed in. We had just found our own way up to the *cúpula*. No one ever found our secret entrance because the closet was full of junk deposited at the back over the years.

But someone *had* seen them sneaking about those forbidden passage-ways and reported it to the school authorities. That evening the entire school was assembled for questioning. Only one student was excused from the grilling because it was understood that he simply would never, ever do such a thing. Unfortunately, the report stated that one perp was a redhead, which left the investigators with only one suspect, and I didn't have an alibi. I'd been in town that afternoon playing poker. I guess there wasn't enough evidence to convict, but there was no doubt in their minds as to the guilty party.

How did Michael get way up there behind the massive organ pipes, anyway? Truth is, we could go most anywhere in the complex we wished. We had keys. Better put, we had The Key.

This was Spain, which was not exactly NORAD where security systems were concerned. Before the age of security chips, cryptographic assertions, and Wi-Fi enabled Bluetooth electronic and biometric smart locks, people used…keys. El Escorial had a master key known as *la llave cíen* to signify it could open all one hundred doors in the complex, except there were actually twelve hundred doors, but who would want to have a key known as *la llave mil dos cientos?*

In no time flat each of us had acquired his own llave cíen.

I found that my key to our apartment at Joaquin Costa had been misfiled and required patient jiggling before it would engage. But it opened every single door in El Escorial—without jiggling.

Did I share my key with Michael? That would be too easy.

"The vice principal and other authorities had it," Michael recalls. "One day Pedro asked to borrow it for some legitimate reason. He'd managed to buy or find another like it, and simply filed the second one holding la llave cíen in front of it. That key got us into LOTS of places."

So when Johnny arrived the following year, we gave him copies of our master key, did we not? How insulting to presume that Johnny couldn't do this on his own! He was every bit as accomplished as his brothers.

"Padre Demetrio was our class supervisor, but he wasn't quite cut out for the job," Johnny reminisces. "He would merrily lend us his llave cíen after we got on his good side, thinking we could do no wrong. The trick was to ask for the key right before, even during the outdoor recess when there was fog. That way he wouldn't see you hightailing it into town to make a copy…or three, and racing back to hand it back to him before recess was over. That's how I got mine."

Where did we go with those keys? Anywhere we damned well pleased, that's where. For three years whenever we could, we'd unlock a door and explore. This place with its four thousand rooms was our oyster. Chapels, private passageways, royal library, and pantheon, the royal palaces, hell, even Philip's personal bedroom next to the altar, separated by glass so he could pray in private—we could and did go everywhere. We became so knowledgeable about the layout, we gave nighttime private guided tours to friends and family. Michael went into the palaces one night, wrapped himself in a curtain, and, candelabra in hand, slowly walked from window to window in an attempt to create The Ghost of El Escorial. It didn't take, but it was fun.

Michael was the most adventurous, always. He'd befriended the care-taker of the royal library, Father Gregorio, who told him of the existence of hidden royal escape routes under the monastery. Michael set out to find one—and did. Again he explains:

> I went to the *bosquecillo* in my first year and was horribly bored, which is not a good place for Michael to be. I forget how and such, but to make time pass pleasurably, I convinced a fellow classmate to accompany me in my latest scheme.
>
> "Qué quieres hacer?" he asked. "Why, what do you think, estúpido? Let's find the underground passage that leads up to the monastery." Anyway, one afternoon we opened a manhole behind the monastery. Gaping beneath us was a brick cylinder dropping down into darkness. We'd found the entrance!
>
> A week later we returned with candles. We pulled aside the cover and slithered down. At bottom there was a slim corridor descending from the monastery. Water trickled down. We lit our candles and walked up for about two hundred yards. We found ourselves in the foundations of the monastery. The palace, to be exact. We were in a taut hallway that circled around a wall. I knew what it was. I'd been told that the pantheon of the kings and queens of Spain, under the main altar of the church, had leaked for one or two centuries until some character came up with a plan to dig a sort of moat around it so that the water could flow downhill. We were in it.
>
> After exploring what we could, we hurried back as our candles were practically gone. As we neared our manhole, we could hear calls. "Bozell! Alemani! Estáis alli?" Needless to say, we spent hours on our knees with our arms stretched out on either side [DEFCON 3] in front of the dean's office in the days to come.

I wasn't there to witness that. I was you-know-where.

Twice annually Francisco Franco, *el Caudillo*, would come to visit, chauffeured in the absolutely gorgeous Mercedes-Benz gifted to him by Hitler with a second gem of a Mercedes behind to serve as decoy. Prince Philip and Princess Sofia arrived by helicopter with their own decoy behind them.

Every February 2nd they came to celebrate the Fiesta de San Lorenzo, accompanied by government officials, dignitaries from foreign embassies, military brass, and all manner of cardinals, bishops, and priests. While they were inside the basilica attending Mass, the students were hustled into the *Plaza de Reyes*, the large inner courtyard, outside the basilica, and lined up dutifully with instructions to cheer wildly when he walked by to enter the church and later when he emerged from the church. This perfect moment was captured on state television for that night's news.

The Mass concluded, the VIPs came out and lined up across the wide expanse of stone stairs, Franco front and center. As the dignitaries filed down the steps that emptied into the Patio of the Kings, the students lined closest to the church were moved so as to file behind the entourage. I watched and to my surprise saw Michael coming down the steps about four rows directly behind Franco. Surprise turned to horror when I saw him stumble forward, pushed from behind by a fellow who lost his balance. Had Michael not managed to right himself, he might have flattened the little dictator. Not a good move with so many soldiers holding so many machine guns with the safeties off.

Monkeys that we were, we loved exploring the roofs. After opening a locked door and ascending up the staircase to the bell tower on the school side of the monastery, we discovered a large window with metal bars blocking passage, but one bar was inexplicably bent just enough to allow a boy to squeeze through. From there it was a three-foot drop to the top of a roof, and off Michael, Johnny, and I went countless times to explore, under the stars.

Just try to imagine what might be discovered in an edifice as large and complex as El Escorial. Now factor in the element of danger. The roofs were steeply sloped, the slate was always slippery, especially after a rainfall, and the wind gusts were powerful enough to knock us off our feet. We were several stories off the ground. One bad slip, and it was curtains.

Happily, our guardian angels were on high alert. We traveled all over the endless rooftops, but the ultimate goal was the cúpula—not the base but the top of the cúpula. The rooftops led to the tower with the stairs that rose to the pathway circling the base of the massive dome. From there we could see for miles or open the little door and peer down, straight down, to the bottom of the basilica. (Imagine this from the opposite direction: a tourist looks up to study the unfinished portrait of King Charles I on the dome only to see a tiny door open and a little red head appear looking down at him.) From the base we could go up to the next level, climbing the stone steps cut into the curvature of the dome with a metal rail for balance.

This climb would take us to the top of the cúpula, but we faced one final challenge: to reach the steeple some ten feet higher, we had to pull ourselves up an ancient rusted metal rod hanging from the top. We did this in the knowledge that if this old pole wasn't firmly attached, we were heading for a Wile E. Coyote *splat* below.

At the tippy-top there were four plaques, each perhaps one foot by one foot, with royal pronouncements inscribed in Latin, giving glory to God or something equally lofty. Legend had it that these plaques were made out of gold. So, of course, I wanted one. One night I made the impossible climb to the summit and, with tools in hand, detached one of the four. At my first opportunity I snuck it out of the monastery and up to the apartment for safekeeping. It was brass, not gold. But no matter. I ran into Michael a few times that week and teased him about the wonderful find I couldn't wait to show him, but he'd have to wait for the weekend. When the magic day arrived and we were together, I triumphantly brought my plaque out, the master trophy to end all master trophies. Michael smiled in appreciation, then jumped up. "Let's compare!" Into his room he went, and out he came with his very own plaque. He had ascended that same week with the same idea in mind.

The one area I dared not fool with was the sacred monastery itself, magic key or not. It was entirely uncharted and teeming with meandering monks who forbade any outsiders to enter, most especially pesky redheaded students. I'd stepped into their lair only once, and only for a minute before hightailing it out with the heebie-jeebies. Michael, on the other hand, had no such trepidations. One afternoon Pedro and he not only entered the forbidden territory but also actually ascended the highest tower on that end of the complex. There they entered a dusty room with artifacts strewn about, including some royal paintings at various stages of composition. Pedro chose one he liked, and Michael another, and after rolling them up carefully they tossed them out the window to the boxwoods several stories below. From there they were transported to the apartment.

Michael's was special, an unfinished portrait of a Spanish king. The artist was Juan Carreño, a disciple of Diego Velázquez himself. Our very own royal portrait was hung in the apartment, but not for long before our future monk felt it necessary to return it to its rightful owner, and not before it almost got us into a heap of trouble. Michael takes the baton here. "When the man who ran the shop where Mom used to buy her antiques came by and saw it, he gasped, 'Where on *earth* did *that* come from?' We opened our eyes with that practiced Bozell innocence and said we'd found it at the Madrid flea market."

The adventures in Spain were endless. In Ávila one dark night we climbed to the top of its cathedral to ascertain if the rumor was true that grass actually grew up there. (It does.) It was my stupidest brush with death. I was standing on one roof, needing to get across to another roof a few feet away. The drop between them was several stories. The problem was that it was too far to jump. The roofs were attached to the tower, and I spotted a large nail protruding from the tower wall, halfway across. I reached out and grabbed it, thinking I could use it to swing across. Wrong. I swung but I didn't reach the other end and instead was left dangling by one hand. I could not go forward to reach one roof or back to return to the other. With my free hand I desperately felt in the darkness until finally I felt a slight indentation in the wall. Pressing the fingers in my free hand into it with all my strength, I managed to pull myself to the other side, barely making it across.

We did love teasing the Spaniards, especially strangers who were never sure quite what to make of us. Often in a public setting the Spaniards listened to us speak English and assumed we were unschooled in their language, so they'd chat away about us, poking fun at our accents, or dress, or our red hair, believing we couldn't understand their zinging commentary. Usually we didn't care. We'd wait until the propitious moment and then switch to Spanish, damn near perfect Spanish, and watch the mortified expressions on their faces.

But one time we did care. Michael and I were on the train returning to El Escorial after an outing in Ávila. There was no one in our car except two older women facing each other at the far end of it on the other side of the aisle. We were close enough to hear each other. They could tell we were Americanos, and they were making some disparaging comments about us, giggling. We knew what they were saying, of course, but ignored them. They were obnoxious but innocent. Still.

After a few minutes, Michael got up and walked to their end of the car. I assumed he was going to the bathroom, and my thoughts drifted off as I looked out the window. A couple of minutes later I heard screeches and turned to see the cause. Michael had not gone to the bathroom after all. There he was, on the other side of the train. *Outside* the train. He'd walked to the platform connecting our car with the next, opened the door, and holding on to the step rail, swung himself into the open so the wind pushed him up against the window where the old shrews were sitting, and offered them a big smile. Needless to say, they ran from that car. A minute later Michael was back in his seat, and now we did the giggling, well satisfied.

Perhaps the best adventure took place in Segovia, in *El Alcázar*, the magical castle of Ferdinand and Isabella, *los reyes Católicos*, who in marriage united Castile and Aragon and forged the military muscle to expel the Moors altogether from Spain in 1492. While living in this castle they did some interesting things, such as, oh, dispatching Christopher Columbus to discover the New World. Like so many other castles, only a fraction of it was open to the public, with the rest a mystery, except, in this case it was known that the Alcázar also served as the national headquarters of the notorious *Guardia Civil*, Franco's omnipresent military police.

Johnny, Michael, and I arrived one snowy Sunday afternoon in the dead of winter when there were no other tourists around. After visiting all that was permissible, Michael, as was his wont, announced a game: Who could be the first to find a way into the forbidden 75 percent of the castle? We were certain that if we could find one entrance, everything inside would open up. We set off in different directions to find it. I found a way to open a padlocked gate, but it led up to some obscure tower, nothing more. Michael discovered a floorboard that secretly opened to stone steps leading down to creepy subterranean passageways. It was an incredible find and is still there today, except at some point the authorities nailed the floorboard shut. Still: nothing. Finally, Johnny hit the jackpot. Not far from that very floorboard there was a large wooden door, which, of course, was locked. But above it he'd noted a wood-shuttered window that served no discernible purpose since it was an interior door. Michael and I hoisted Johnny on our shoulders. Bingo! The window was unlocked. Up and over Johnny went, dropping down the other side to open the door.

We were in. Given it was the weekend, there were no *guardia*, and now the entire castle was ours to explore. Gleefully we took off in different directions, again, periodically bumping into one another with "Oh, my!" smiles, too excited to stop and report our discoveries. At one point I came across and entered the executive offices of the Guardia Civil. I found the office of *el comandante*, pausing with trepidation, not keen on getting bamboo chutes jammed under my fingernails should I get caught. (Habeas corpus was a nonstarter in Franco's Spain.) I stepped inside, nervously, only to find Michael sitting behind the desk of one of the most feared men in Spain, his feet comfortably resting on the table, chomping on a pilfered cigar for comedic effect as he quietly leafed through some very private police files.

Eventually I found the jackpot inside the jackpot: the only door with a lock, specifically a chain and padlock. Something special had to be inside. Calling my brothers to the door, we inspected the security challenge. Michael left and a minute later returned with a crowbar. (How he instantly got his hands on a crowbar in the middle of the castle I'll never know.) We popped the chain and entered the room. There were amazing things in there, everything from a breathtaking stuffed peacock to...well, let's just leave that story there.

While we entertained many visitors from the States, none was more welcome than our parents. Mom came several times, but sadly, on a few occasions it was to recover from physical exhaustion. The strain of a full-time job seventy miles from home along with the care of the remaining half-dozen children was taking its toll. Several times Papa dispatched her to us with instructions that she be totally pampered, a task we eagerly undertook. Mom normally spent two weeks, the first doing nothing but resting, which in her case meant joyfully relaxing on the couch reading her Agatha Christie novels. Engines refreshed, during her second week she ventured out more, visiting, walking to the basilica for her daily 6:00 a.m. Mass, shopping, and the like. Papa usually joined us at that point, and the love birds would now be in their heaven.

When Papa came by himself, it was another story. It was his belief that the appreciation of Catholic Spanish culture was every bit as important as the pursuit of academics and perhaps even more so. It meant the inevitable road trip. We never knew what to expect, which did nothing but add to the excitement.

One day at school I was notified that we had a visitor in the lobby. Who could that be? What joy when we saw him: Papa had arrived without alerting us! Even better, he was there to spring us out of school! Michael, Johnny, and I rejoiced at our freedom while the Augustinian monks shook their heads in bewilderment, surely wondering, as they did so often, if this was how children were raised in *los Estados Unidos*. No other students in that school would ever be allowed to do this. No parents of any students at that school would ever think to do it either. We relished the difference.

Papa invited us to pick a destination, and we chose the historical coastal town of Cartagena on the southeastern tip of the country, home to the Phoenicians, the Greeks, the Romans, the Visigoths, and for a couple of days, the Bozells. While only five hundred kilometers away, driving the primitive road systems in Spain made this a two-day journey, especially with Papa's meandering directional, which was just fine by us. That just meant more days out of school spent with him. We left the first evening with the plan to have dinner in Aranjuez, site of Philip's summer palace. I remember this part of the trip not because of Aranjuez, which is rather boring, but because of the drive there. "Tell us a story!" one of us pleaded. At age sixteen, Papa had bested sixteen thousand contestants in an American Legion national oratory contest, earning him a scholarship to Yale, and no one, but no one could tell a story like this man.

The topic was selected: the Korean War. For an hour, maybe more, we relived the war with him, his tale interrupted only by the long drags of his cigarette, making it flicker orange in the darkness. Our attention was focused completely on the driver who spoke crisply, his noise rising with drama, lost in his narrative. *And then the Communist army crashed over the border, a million strong! Our soldiers were suddenly in a fight for their very survival, fighting not just a million Reds, but fighting in weather so cold that ice gathered on their grizzled beards, unkempt from days of unrelenting war*—I made that up, but it was that sort of thing. He was mesmerizing.

On another trip we traveled to Yuste, final home of Philip II's father, Charles I, the warrior monarch who conquered everything in his path and then suddenly abdicated the throne in 1556 at the apogee of his power. He was giving it all up to live out his final years in quiet contemplation with Our Lord in the monastery of Saint Jerome Yuste.

Again it was the trip, not the destination, that was most memorable. At one point the route called for a steep ascent up the Sierra de Tormantos mountain. When we reached the summit, Papa stopped the car, turned to me, and to my shock and horror (shared, I'm sure, by Michael, who was there), he declared it was my turn to take the wheel. I was still brand new to this driving thing—I did not even have my learner's permit then!—but Papa didn't care. After a quick tutorial on the peculiar placement of the reverse gear in the rented Simca ("Over to the left, then up, and *dammit use the clutch!*") which resulted in the prerequisite grinding of said gears, we were headed down the treacherous mountain in a country that did not believe in guardrails.

As on most mountain roads in Spain, we could actually see the occasional car obliterated below. I was panicked, but in short order I wasn't alone. Papa realized the mistake he'd made, but it was too dangerous to stop, and there was no room to pull over. We had to get to the bottom, hopefully one way and not the other. Finally we made it, and Papa ordered me to pull into the first available bar. Ashen-faced, he bolted out of the car to settle his frazzled nerves. I don't recall him ever asking me to drive again.

Which is not to say he was much better. Papa was notoriously absent-minded. Throughout his life there were numerous incidents where *his* exhausted guardian angels had to save his bacon. Sometimes even they couldn't pull it off. Example: To drive from El Escorial to Ávila, about an hour away, we had to cross over Mount Abantos. At the summit one can still find La Cruz Verde, a lonely little bar that served as a pit stop for travelers. Back then Spain was unfamiliar with *Madres* Against Drunk Driving, so drivers regularly pulled over for a glass (or bottle) of wine. Papa made this trip by himself one day and later reported to us an incident only he could create.

Papa had parked his Hertz rental car outside the bar and ducked inside for a glass of wine (or probably several glasses of wine if he was enjoying himself enough, which normally was the case if he entered into conversation with the locals). Exiting the bar, he found the car was gone. Vanished. Vamoose. This of course was impossible. There was no one at the top of that mountain except the bartender the entire time. It was also inconceivable that in Catholic Spain the rare driver on that quiet mountain road would pull over and have a companion jump out to hijack a parked car. So what in the world had become of it? It wasn't long before the bartender solved the puzzle. The dirt parking area next to the bar ended at the side of a cliff. There was no guardrail. Standing on the edge, he beckoned Papa over, and pointed down. The hapless Hertz rental car was lying at the bottom of the mountain, smashed to smithereens. Papa had left it in neutral.

In the fall of 1971 several siblings arrived for a celebration. Our sister Kathy, then nineteen, had been dating a man with whom the entire family, especially our parents, had become instantly enamored. Cy and Kathy were visiting us in El Escorial when they announced they were engaged. Hooray! Kathy being the first of the siblings to marry, the reaction was instantaneous. Papa and Mom came rushing across the pond, followed in short order by both Chris and Maureen, neither of whom was going to miss this spontaneous party.

Two more family friends joined us, Brad Evans and his wife, Paula, six months pregnant. Brad had arrived from Austria several months before on his honeymoon, having stopped in Milan to catch a performance of *Tristan and Isolde* at the famous La Scala opera house. Sigi and Tomasita Diaz beckoned, so everyone headed to Ávila. That beautiful town is remembered for its medieval walls, its patroness St. Teresa, and for some of us, one whale of a bar fight.

One of the most iconic sites in Ávila is *Los Cuatro Postes*, The Four Posts. This small monument in the plains outside of town offered a spectacular view of the town walls, especially when lit at night. It was here where Saint Teresa stopped after storming out of Ávila in a religious dispute. Turning to face the town, she shook the sand from her sandals saying, "From Ávila, I take with me not even the dirt!" (She and Ávila subsequently reconciled, which is fortunate for many reasons including the fact that this story would not be possible otherwise.)

As with other landmarks, Spain marked the site with a bar, also named Los Cuatro Postes. Small, old, and quiet, it was a favorite watering hole for Sigi, and that's where the men headed after dinner. It was getting late, and we were the only patrons there. Carefree or not, I was still sixteen, the youngest there as Johnny had not joined us. I was not about to chug-a-lug wine in front of Papa, so I sat at one of the few tables, joined by Chris. He had arrived from the States that morning, was jet-lagged, and in no mood for heavy drinking. Sigi, Cy, Papa, and Brad stood at the bar.

Oh, did I mention that Brad Evans was gigantic? Bearded with a deep baritone voice, Brad stood about six foot five and weighed nearly three hundred pounds. He once played college football against "Mean" Joe Greene, and need I say more? He could be loud and bombastic, but he was also a gentle man who liked pranks, loved playing with children, and could be found air-conducting operas in our living room. But on this night, after consuming copious libations, Brad was boisterous and pompous enough that Papa finally opined, "Brad, you have no humility."

It wasn't a challenge or even an accusation. It was a quiet observation, but Brad was in no mood to be analyzed. "I dare you to say that again!" he challenged Papa, whereupon Papa without hesitation or even emotion simply repeated, "Brad, you have no humility." And that was that. Fists started flying everywhere.

Brad's fists, that is. Before anyone could respond, never mind resist, Brad had flattened everyone except me. Utterly unsuspecting that his words would trigger this fate, Papa was the first one slugged, and a bloody gash opened over his eye. At that Chris and I jumped out of our seats. I didn't get two steps before Chris shoved me away, and thank God for that. A nanosecond later Brad's fist came whistling by my ear.

Chris dove into the fray and right back out, twice, each time punched in the chest. Then it was Sigi's turn. Our little fat Spanish friend was punched hard enough that his face bounced off the bar, opening a cut over the bridge of his nose. Finally, it was poor Cy's turn at bat, and he was summarily dispatched, also a bloody mess. With that, Brad stormed out of the bar and into the night. The entire fight had lasted some thirty seconds.

Before anyone could stop him, Cy angrily charged out of the bar in pursuit. Cy was nearly a foot shorter than Brad and almost exactly half Brad's weight. But he was also a seasoned merchant marine captain, and God only knew what kind of fury our future in-law could muster. Our response was a collective OMG. *Mayday, mayday*. There was going to be no wedding. Cy was going to die. Everyone followed him out. The moment we stepped into the parking lot the owner slammed the door shut behind us, locked it, and turned off the lights. We watched Cy disappear into the brush in the darkness of night. He summarily ignored our pleas for him to stop.

Silence. We looked at each other. There was no telling where he'd gone so we listened intently hoping to hear something, anything. After a few minutes it came, softly. A sound. Little by little it increased. Wait…is it…could it be…what? A song? Singing. Yes, indeed. The voices became louder, and it was clear they were coming toward us. They came out of the shadows, and we saw them, Cy and Brad with their arms around each other's shoulders, stumbling and belting out some grand Irish folk song. It was over, meaning it was time to celebrate this too. We piled into our cars and took off in search for another bar, finally finding one still open. There was lots of commotion in this busy bar when we entered it for another copa, but as everyone stood at the bar with his drink, the crowd fell silent staring at these Americanos in stunned disbelief. Everyone had forgotten a little detail, the need to wipe the blood off his face.

The next morning it was comeuppance time with the women. They gathered in the courtyard outside the cathedral. Brad had thoughtfully purchased apology flowers for all the men to give to each of their respective ladies. Tomasita looked at the flowers in horror. It turns out these were designed specifically for funerals, which, come to think of it, may have been fitting. Chris was physically unscathed, but sore, and gave his girlfriend and soon-to-be fiancée Mary (Baker) her bouquet. Next was Papa, who had to explain away his black eye to Mom. "I ran into a door," he said meekly. Sigi followed suit to explain his shiner. "I ran into a door," he repeated to his wife. Cy came last. Cy had two black eyes. "Two doors."

Three or four days after his arrival, Chris, Johnny, and I set out to hike up the forested hills above El Escorial, looking, as always, for adventure. We came across the reservoir that supplied the drinking water for the town below. An unimposing fence with a perfectly scalable locked gate was what protected this site from meddlesome interlopers. It was defended by a guard in a little shack. But not really. He was a very old man and, to make things even funnier, when we came upon him, he was sound asleep. If we'd chosen to flood the town below, he'd never have known. Even if he did see us, there was no way he could stop us from mischief. But what might happen if he did? It was then that one of us (I put my money on Chris) suggested we find out. "Let's get arrested!"

It's important, dear reader, that you understand this point. In Franco's Spain, lawlessness was virtually unknown, partly because Spaniards were then naturally good and honorable but also, and let's be honest here, because there was no telling what might happen should the Guardia Civil arrest you. But we were intrigued by the unknown. We decided to find out.

We climbed over the gate, the *No Entre* signs deliberately ignored, and loudly began depth charging rocks into the water until we finally awoke our slumbering guard. Stepping out of the shack, shaking out the cobwebs, he furiously and clumsily attacked the countless buttons on his colorful ceremonial guard's uniform. We could have just walked away, literally, but that wasn't the plan. We waited patiently for him to finish dressing, and on his command, surrendered. We were under arrest, he proclaimed authoritatively, it probably being the first time he'd ever arrested anyone. We were to follow him down the mountain to be delivered to the Guardia Civil station below.

There was something about our family, something that continues to this very day. As I noted earlier, we love to role-play. I cannot tell you how many different manifestations this has taken over the years, but when the opportunity presents itself, we pounce. As we descended toward town we discussed openly in English the need to assume new identities for the confrontation that awaited us. We couldn't deny we were the American Bozells because we were known to everyone as such. But we could assume new personalities, couldn't we? And so we did. Chris would play a deaf-mute, our own Harpo Marx. Johnny, who had the ability to stay in character no matter the circumstance, was to be just plain…dumb. I'd play the straight guy.

But first we had to do something about this grouchy old man who was starting to grate on us. As we descended the mountain we were met by hikers coming in the opposite direction. As our paths crossed, the guard would bellow, in that exaggerated macho, chest-thrust-out, arms- gesturing-wildly, voice-raised-dramatically manner common among Spaniards, that these Americanos were attempting to sabotage the water supply of El Escorial and he—*yo!*—had effected the arrest, thus presumably saving thousands of lives; and he—*yo!*—was going to see that we were delivered to the Guardia Civil for *la justicia*! The first couple of times he did this we were amused, but we soon tired of the routine so we turned the tables on him. Now when we passed a hiker, we—*nosotros!*—declared with our chests extended and voices raised that we had found this ceremonial guard undressed and asleep on the job and we—*nosotros!*—were effecting the arrest. This only angered our poor captor the more.

It was late afternoon when we were arrested, and it was twilight when we finally made it to the police station, a nondescript little building in the middle of town. We entered a small, dark room with a policeman seated at a desk to the right of the entrance. In front of us there was another policeman behind a protective grate, protecting himself from what I have no idea since no one in his right mind would dare enter that station to create trouble. As the *militares* looked in bewilderment, the old man proclaimed (here we go again) with dramatic gestures and a voice torqued up yet another notch that he had apprehended us would-be terrorists and brought us to la justícia!

Time for our show. The policeman behind the grate looked at Chris as the eldest and asked him (I cannot remember why) how much money we had. Chris in turn pointed to the pen on the desk, silently requesting permission to use it. As the military cops watched, Chris nonchalantly began to draw a one hundred peseta bill on the wall. They did not like that, ordering him to cut it out, and who the *demonios* did he think he was? I spoke up to explain, a thousand apologies *señores*, that my poor brother was a deaf-mute (they never thought to ask why, if that was true, he'd understood their request) and couldn't speak for himself. Chris looked at the man without expression, as if he now didn't understand a word of this. Next they turned their attention to Johnny, our unfortunate little brother who was, well, slow. The cop asked him a question, and Johnny in one motion delivered a performance worthy of an Oscar. Staring at the floor with a look of utter stupidity—he never did break character—he gave a hell-if-I-know-because-I'm-stupid shrug that left them visibly befuddled.

I asked to speak to the comandante. This was a most important matter, I said. The old guard and I were led downstairs to the commander's office. It was right out of *Midnight Express*. Another cramped, dark room with a light bulb hanging over a small, battered wooden table with four chairs and nothing on the dirty old walls except an aging photograph of *el Caudillo*, which was hung behind the desk ridiculously high on the wall, with the nail far too long, making Franco tilt forward, looking disapprovingly at everyone below. The feared comandante, rank unknown yet most certainly exaggerated, was prosecutor, judge, jury, and executioner here, and now he demanded answers.

The guard repeated his version of events, his oratory now reaching Shakespearean proportions. Then I gave mine: Why, we as Americanos were on a leisurely stroll and, unfortunately, we just didn't understand the warning signs, but then we found this man asleep! And barely dressed! For all to see! Disgraceful! We felt it was our duty to bring this to the attention of the authorities, and so yes, we'd gone along with this arrest so we could report the transgression, and here we were.

My explanation was preposterous enough to be believable. Besides, we were the American guests living in their midst. The commander turned on our hapless victim and gave him a thorough tongue lashing, promising to mete certain punishment should that disgraceful behavior ever repeat itself. While the God-and-Guardia-Civil-forsaken guard listened in astonishment, I received an apology for having been so terribly inconvenienced. Up the stairs I went, and, reunited with my brothers, we were allowed to leave. Once outside the station we laughed merrily as we returned to the apartment. Mission accomplished.

There were so many such adventures over those years, enough for their own book. I hope these stories will give you a flavor of what three teenagers could do when living alone across the ocean in another country at another time in another culture among some of the loveliest and most forgiving people God ever placed on this earth.

But now it was time to come home. Over the winter of my third year I applied for admission to the University of Dallas. The form asked me how many years I'd have completed at the end of the semester. I told the truth but not the whole truth. I answered four (remember, I'd undergone my freshman year at Donald Trump Jr.'s alma mater, The Hill School), but what I chose not to disclose was that the high school system in Spain demands not four but five years. In late April I was notified I'd been accepted, which begged the next question: Why finish a school year that lasted through June when I yearned to be back with my family in the States? So I booked a flight departing two days later. In record time, I wrapped up all my affairs. This included selling my beloved Swedish Hagstrom electric guitar for $110, the cost of the plane ticket.

True to form, the day before I was to leave I couldn't find my passport. The only place it could be was at the apartment, which I tore apart for hours. We tended to leave important documents on a tray on top of the little entryway table. I checked, then rechecked every possible spot. I don't know how many times I looked inside that tray, which is what you do when you're sure it was there and it's nowhere else. Hours later, having exhausted all possibilities, and fearing the worst—I couldn't leave—I turned to Saint Anthony, offering a silent prayer promising something rather dramatic, whatever it was, if only he'd help me. Ten minutes later I found my passport. It was in the tray on the little entryway table.

SECTION III

ROAD TRIP

Okay, so one final adventure in Spain.

This story first was made public in a most unusual way on the most unexpected platform.

Americans have enjoyed efficient phone service for over a century.

Not so in Spain. In the 1970s phones were still a luxury. Your phone might or might not work, which often was irrelevant since the odds were pretty strong that the party with which you wanted to communicate didn't have a phone. A call overseas was even more precarious. You had to request an international line and be by the phone when the opportunity presented itself. The quality was awful, and the rates were astronomical, so the calls had to be kept short. This was rarely an issue since the call was usually dropped before you were finished.

If ever there was an urgency, the only recourse was the good old-fashioned telegram. Looking back, I can't believe we actually had to send them. Stop. Keeping words to minimum. Stop. Costing fortune. End. If there was no urgency, we wrote letters. We had my father's portable Royal typewriter, and on weekends one of us could be found at the living room desk, coffee in hand, hammering away with a letter to our parents, and less frequently, to siblings and friends. Letters were typed on the ubiquitous thin, rough, yellow typing paper, of which we had a seemingly endless supply.

The correspondence was usually several pages long because there was so much material to cover. It would take at least a week for a letter to wing its way across the ocean, and at least that long for its reply to find its way back. Taking into account the time it would take to produce the letter, it boiled down to about one exchange per month with our parents. That was it. The other lifelines to news about the mother country were our subscriptions to our parents' *Triumph*, our uncle's *National Review*, and *Time*, a magazine that once mattered. Given the limited access to information, we gleefully devoured every article in every issue when each arrived.

Tim Baker and I had met in Detroit in December of 1972 when his sister Mary was wed to my brother Chris. Tim was in his second year at the University of Dallas, and I was in my final year of high school with the intention of enrolling at UD thereafter. At some point during the wedding festivities I'd met Tim's classmates, Mike Cochran and Joe Stahler. They would all be spending the following semester in Rome participating in UD's overseas studies program. We agreed to rendezvous there. The plan called for me to find a way to Rome during our spring break, after which the four of us would travel together back to Spain for Holy Week.

Four months later it was time to pull the trigger on the proposed expedition. I had exactly five dollars to my name, but Tim had assured me that if I made my way to Rome, he'd take care of expenses for the trip back, so what the hell. On the appointed day I walked to the edge of town, stuck out my thumb, and off I went. I was back within a week and shortly thereafter sat down to write my report to my parents.

That letter speaks volumes about an era exactly a half century ago. It also speaks volumes about the world today.

It is simply inconceivable that someone my age would do what I did fifty years ago. I was on another continent, traveling through three countries over three days, on a course I'd chartered privately that required hitchhiking and riding rails, sleeping wherever possible, and eating frugally because I was virtually penniless. And I was sixteen. And I was alone. But perhaps most poignantly as I reflect back on it, I was incommunicado. From the time I left El Escorial and arrived in Rome almost three days later, no one knew where I was, nor, for all intents and purposes, could I communicate with them. And yet…and yet…it was nothing at all. There was no concern, none whatsoever, on my part. This was an ordered world, and in an ordered world things went right. It did not matter that I was a foreigner; it was expected that I would be treated as a guest. It did not matter that I was no more than a child; it was expected that should any trouble befall me, I would be aided. It did not matter that I might be riding with strangers in their cars, or alone on trains; it was expected that I'd be given safe passage. It did not matter that I had only a handful of dollars for this trip; it was expected that there would be charity if needed. There was no need for communication because all would be well. Of course not all went as planned, and there was one part that almost went very, very wrong. (Think J. Paul Getty's grandson. He was my exact age. He was in the same city. And it was only a few months later.) And yet when I recounted that part of the story to my parents, I did so cavalierly, as you will see. False bravado? Not at all. I expressed the fear I felt—but it was only at the moment because once it was over, it was over. We were back to an ordered world.

Now put yourself in my parents' shoes when they received the letter. To the best of my knowledge they had no idea I was embarking on this trip; or if they did, they certainly didn't object. It just wasn't out of the ordinary that one of their children might do something like this, because they'd been raised to be independent, encouraged to be adventurous, and taught to be self-sufficient. They were also living in a part of the world where the culture was still Christian. My parents never expressed anything in return that might betray shock or even surprise. Their response was quite different.

Several weeks later a new issue of *National Review* arrived. There on the cover was the headline, "A Sixteen Year Old's European Vacation." I'd not known that Mom had shared my letter with her brother Bill, who liked it enough to reprint it in his magazine, untouched for purposes of authenticity. My guess is that each had believed the other informed me of the letter's impending publication. Neither had. Here is the letter, still untouched. Note just how politically incorrect it is by today's standards, which only serves to underscore how once upon a time man could be

irreverent and still not offend. If I upset the perpetually offended now—
no apologies.

Dear Mom and Papa:

Today is Sunday and school is out until Tuesday due to some feast
so I'll get around to writing about my trip to Rome. It's about time,
isn't it?

I'll try to keep it short because if I were to tell everything that
happened of interest, it would take a week to write this. I caught the
ten o'clock train going to Barcelona, and got there at eleven P.M.
[Edited out for brevity: I hitchhiked to Madrid first.] After finding a
pensíon (a literal hole) and going to a bar to have a bocadillo, I went
to another bar to have a coffee, but ended up in a house of ill fame.

Oops. Next morning, Thursday, I started hitch-hiking toward the
border; Tim Baker was so right: The French don't take anybody! By
four, I was in Figueras, a town about 120 kilometers from Barcelona
and about twenty from the border, and from there nobody would give
me a lift, so I decided to take a train to the first French town, called
Cerbère. but I didn't know it was up in the mountains (i.e., in the
middle of nowhere). After trying unsuccessfully for a couple of hours,
I got a ticket on a train to Aries. [Note for the record: I rode the rails
to preserve cash.]

The train left a little late, and I woke up at Nice, on the Riviera, at
about ten A.M. (Friday). The road to Italy was on the beachside, so it
was packed with people and cars, but once again, by mid-afternoon I
still hadn't gotten a ride. At that point I made revised calculations and
figured out that I had drastically underestimated time and distance for
the trip, in such a way that at the rate I was going, I would never have
time to get to Rome. At that I decided to take a train straight to Rome.
[Note for the record: Again I declined to pay, preferring to hide from
the porter.]

I got to Rome at twelve P.M., whereupon I took a cab to Tim's
place, but when I asked the driver how much it cost, he told me $8,
so I got out. As I was looking for a bar to call him up, two things

100

happened: First of all, I saw a fight in the middle of the road between five sluts and five other women – I don't know what it was all about, but it sure was funny; they were so wop-ish, stopping all traffic and pulling at each other's hair!

Secondly, I realized that not only had I left Tim's phone number in the cab but also your friends' address in Viterbo.

Sorry. I decided to sleep in the train station (there was no way I could get to Tim's place at that hour). As I went in, I realized that the waiting room was locked, so I decided to look for some hole some-where. When I found the perfect hole, it was being presently occupied by five drunks and a Moor (I think more Moors live in train stations than in Africa!). At around two A.M. the entire train station closed down and we were thrown out. This was awfully strange, but then again, a lot of strange things went on there while I was there!

Outside of the station I was met by two men who looked like perfect hoods. They asked me if I was looking for a hotel. I said yes, if it was cheap. One went off one way while the other one led me further and further down a semi deserted street. I kept asking for the "hotel" to which he would answer "later, later." From the start I had been suspicious but I had decided to try my luck out anyway. We ended up in a bar where hood #2 came in. With him entered a "she" (the fact that he/she wore lipstick I guess was proof enough). Off they went into one corner speaking in low voices and looking at me. At that I started getting really scared. So when the three left and told me to wait, I took off and ended up in the BEA-BOAC waiting room. I told the man at the desk that I was waiting for a flight going to the States and went to sleep on a bench. The fact that there was a cop in the building worked like a sleeping pill! At about 6:30 I was courteously asked to leave: There was no such flight.

At about seven I caught a bus to Tim's place. When I got there I asked if Tim was there. No, he was in Yugoslavia. Did he leave a message saying I could use his room? No, he hadn't. Could I use his room? No, I couldn't. At that I tracked down the dean, Mr. Scully, and told him that I was Chris Bozell's brother and that maybe I was going to go to Dallas University next year, and that Chris had spoken very highly of him, and COULD I USE TIM'S ROOM!? He let me.

I slept all Saturday. On Sunday, I went to Pope Paul's eleven o'clock Mass, where, when he was marched down the aisle I was no more than a yard away from him! After that I stayed in the plaza until he gave his blessing. I walked around Rome for a couple of hours.

On Monday morning, Tim came back. After lunch a bunch of us went back to the city. We walked around Rome for about five hours, going all over the place. We went up two of the seven hills. On the top of the second hill we got to this house with two busts of Nero, so we guessed it was his place. There was about one square mile of gardens, which I think are the most beautiful in the world, with underground gardens. We saw a palm tree surrounded by a bunch of bushes. The only way to get to the tree was to follow the pattern of the bushes, a type of labyrinth which took about five minutes to follow to get to the tree.

On Tuesday I went to Assisi. It took me three trains and four hours to get there and as it turned out I only had an hour and a half to see everything. I saw the main church (where he is buried) and then spent the rest of the time walking around the town. I can see why you liked it so much! If someone were to take all of the tourists and buses out, I think it would be the most beautiful town in the world! I really loved it.

I still hadn't seen the Sistine Chapel or St. Peter's entirely, for that matter, so on Wednesday I tried to see them. The Sistine Museum was closed, but I did see all of St. Peter's (I still like El Escorial more, though). I think that the thing that most surprised me (and that I thought was the funniest thing in Rome) were the posters on the walls. On one block I saw a big Communist poster, alongside of which was a big poster put up by the Neo-Fascist people, followed by a poster about the Social Democrats, followed by a poster announcing the Communist victory in Vietnam, followed by another poster about the South Vietnamese victory. No wonder there's chaos in Italy!! That night Tim, two other friends, and I left for Spain.

The trip back, I think, was the most original and the strangest in history. The three of them had Eurail passes which let them travel freely through Europe. We decided to try our luck at passing them around (using the three passes for the four of us). Our first train left at 8:30 and got to Nice the next morning at ten. Half of the Italian army was with us and every compartment was absolutely packed, so we had to get seats (pullout) in the aisles. We knew that we weren't going to get any sleep so we started telling Italian jokes: since the people there realized we were laughing at them, they gave us quite a few sweet smiles. One of us got on the baggage rack on top of us at which point this old grouch started going on, and on, and on about him until he ran out of breath. The rest of us had put our bags on our laps and tried to sleep that way. It worked out ok until I realized that the old man was resting his bag on top of my head! At that I guess I kind of blew up, because I knocked over a bunch of bags and also got on the baggage rack, and when he started yacking about me, I dropped my bag "accidently" on his head. That shut him up for the rest of the trip.

At Nice we decided to get off and spend the day on the beach, where we all slept. That night we took a train to Barcelona (ten hours). Once again I had to sleep on the luggage rack.

Friday morning we got into Barcelona and found out that we had to wait until nightfall for the train to Madrid. We spent about two hours looking for a place with showers, but everything was closed, so we remained filthy. At three o'clock we went to an outside service at the cathedral where they were to bring out a statue of Christ and there would be a short service. We got some seats and went to sleep until it started, but as it did this man came around asking for payment for the seats, which got us so disgusted, we left. Can you imagine a charge for going to a church service?

For the next train we decided to reserve some seats. The three of them got some, and then Tim passed me his Eurail pass, and when I went, the man told me that there were no more reserved seats but he gave me a ticket anyway! That night we got on the train, and got kicked out of first class I don't know how many times. Even though we had seats, they were very uncomfortable, so Tim and I decided to move into first class. A while later another friend came in too. I went back after a while to speak with the guy that had stayed behind, and in came the other two saying that they had been kicked out. To make things more comfortable, I got on the racks again and another person got on the floor, while the two remaining people were able to stretch out. At around two, thinking that the ticket man would not come around anymore, I went back to first class and got into a compartment with two girls, and when I had just gotten comfortable on two opposite pull-out seats that formed a bed, in came the ticket man, and out went I. At around 10:30 A.M. Saturday morning, we finally made it back to El Escorial.

All in all, the trip may not sound as interesting as it really was, but I can assure you that I really had a great time, and only wish that I had had more time to spend in Rome, because I saw very, very little over-all. Moneywise, I kept it down to only going over $20, which I owe to Tim, and will pay out of my allowance. I wasn't able to meet Johnny, because I also left his address in Rome (I'm not too good at keeping addresses am I?). Will stop now, because I'm going to go broke on postage for this!

All love, Brent

SECTION IV

PLANES, TRAINS,
AND AUTOMOBILES
(BUT REALLY JUST PLANES)

Fly as much as I have—several million miles, I suspect—and something noteworthy is bound to happen. I give you several moments, in no particular order. Here are the first three.

1. Stupid Move at a New York Airport #1

It's 1961 and we're all headed for Spain. We are at Idlewild Airport waiting to board our overnight flight. A number of us have been given matching light overcoats for the voyage. How can I possibly remember that detail given I was only six at the time? Because I was playing on the escalator, seated as it moved up, and somehow I managed to get the back of that new coat sucked into the slit at the top. Screams for help. Frantic effort to shut the escalators down. Back of the overcoat looks like it's gone through a paper shredder. Very unhappy parents.

2. Stupid Move at a New York Airport #2

It's ten years later, and I'm returning home from Spain. I've managed to acquire a thirteenth-century warrior's sword that I'm bringing with me on an Iberia airline flight. *On board. Unsheathed.* Such were the travel possibilities in that time not so long ago. Landing at JFK, formerly Idlewild, I transfer to LaGuardia for the shuttle to Washington, DC, carrying my unsheathed thirteenth-century warrior's sword in my hand. If the bus passengers are staring, I don't notice. I'm in a teenaged jet-lagged haze. I walk into the terminal and right through the metal detector holding that unsheathed thirteenth-century warrior's sword in my hand. Picture that. Next thing I know, I'm in mid-flight, headed for the nearest wall. A very large cop apparently was not impressed. I am momentarily detained, then released with an admonition not to do everything I just did ever again. I arrive at the gate. The Eastern Airlines Shuttle is less accommodating than Iberia. They make me hand the unsheathed thirteenth-century warrior's sword over to the captain who takes it into the cockpit and returns it to me as we disembark in Washington, DC.

3. Smart Move at Barajas Airport, Madrid

It's the same general time period, and you can credit my brother Michael with this one. After a few trips into that airport, we've figured out their intricate baggage scanning procedures. As luggage enters the terminal on the conveyor belt, a member of Franco's Guardia Civil awaits, brandishing an ominous weapon: a piece of white chalk. He systematically scratches check marks on the suitcases as they go by—except for the random bag he selects for inspection for whatever reason. The suspicious item continues on its voyage until a second member of the Guardia Civil grabs it off the belt and away it goes for inspection.

Well, we have no use for this. We are hiding nothing (going into Spain, anyway), but we are impatient Americans and this is a nuisance. Michael arrives at the solution. We bring our own chalk and position ourselves between Guardia Civil *Uno* and Guardia Civil *Dos*. So long as that system is in place, no piece of Bozell luggage is ever threatened again.

NCPAC

1. "Everybody failed."

It was late October, 1979, and I was in the US Senate cafeteria having coffee with Morton Blackwell, then a legislative aide to New Hampshire senator Gordon Humphrey and later founder of the Leadership Institute. I'd been sent to him by Representative Robert Bauman, with whom I'd met a week earlier. Bauman was a family friend and a rising star in the party until his shocking arrest in a late night drunken stupor trolling in a seedy part of town attempting to seduce a sixteen-year-old gay prostitute. (But otherwise...)

My wild Spanish youth and my mischievous college days behind me, I'd returned to the Virginia area as a near facsimile of a grown-up. Now twenty-four, I arrived with my bride, Norma, our two-year-old, David, and Brent IV ("Zeeker"), not yet one. Having family in the area was one reason for being there, but there was something else. The Reagan Revolution was underway, and I wanted to be part of it.

How, I had no idea, and so I was looking. It said something about Morton Blackwell—I've repeated this countless times in many lectures at the Leadership Institute over the years—that he spent almost three hours with a complete stranger that afternoon, painstakingly giving me an intel dump on one contact after the next. "If you're willing to wear out two pairs of shoes, you'll definitely find a job in Washington." It turned out I didn't even need to break in the first one.

At the top of Morton's list was John T. ("Terry") Dolan, founder and Chairman of the National Conservative Political Action Committee (NCPAC). I'd never heard of him, nor his organization. I wasn't even sure what a political action committee was. Morton told me NCPAC ("Nick-pac") was the largest conservative organization dedicated to electing conservatives to every level of public office while conducting all manner of mayhem on other fronts.

One of NCPAC's many programs was a four-day Campaign Management Training School, and Morton recommended I attend one if possible. The following day I called the NCPAC offices and was surprised when I was put right through to Mr. Dolan. I was in luck. He was holding a training seminar the very next week in Arlington. Better still, there was an opening for me. Best of all—it was free.

About forty of us convened in one of those lifeless meeting rooms at the Key Bridge Marriott the following Monday morning. When Terry strode into the room, he was not at all what I'd expected. He was so young, just twenty-nine years old, short, and slender. He sported one of those serious Mark Spitz '70s moustaches. His wide necktie was loose, and his top button unfastened. He seemed always to be distracted, almost to the point of disinterest.

As the first order of business he passed out a piece of paper for all of us to fill out. On the front there were ten questions of a political nature. Who are the two senators from Virginia? Who is the prime minister of England? What's the Ninth Amendment of the Constitution? That sort of thing. On the back there were another ten questions, but these were of a pop culture nature. Which movie won the Oscar last year? Who won the 1975 World Series? Who sang "Hotel California?" And so on.

When the surveys were completed, he provided the answers.

He asked for a show of hands of those who answered at least eight of the political questions correctly. Most hands shot into the air, triumphantly. He then asked for a show of hands of those who answered at least eight of the pop culture questions correctly. There were audible dismissals as virtually no one rose to the occasion. A few actually chuckled at the thought that people would care about such tripe.

Then Terry passed judgment: "Everybody failed."

Andrew Breitbart is credited with the quote, "Politics is downstream from culture," but Terry introduced the concept while Andrew was still watching the *Brady Bunch* back in LA. This was lesson number one in Terry's playbook, perhaps also the secret to his success. The role of the campaign manager is to elect his client, he explained. In order to do so, the campaign message must connect with the audience. Like it or not, the average Joe out there knows little about civics and couldn't care less about the identity of the prime minister of England. But he does like movies, watches television, enjoys sports, and knows who sang "Hotel California." Selling a candidate is no different than selling a washing machine. Connect with the consumer on his terms, not yours, and you win elections.

It's the culture, stupid. With that, the school was underway. For almost four full days we were put through a grueling ordeal, learning the essence of every element of campaign management, be it polling, scheduling, advance work, candidate management, advertising, public relations, small dollar and major donor fundraising—everything. One by one Terry would bring in the very brightest in the conservative movement to teach his specialty, and then Terry would leave the room to work on a funding appeal, pour through a mountain of polling data, or as I'd learn later, to sneak into the game room to play Ms. Pac-Man.

Just as he did with the initial exercise, it was Terry who oversaw the final exam. He broke the group into teams of five and laid out a real-life scenario from a congressional campaign in South Dakota in 1976. The conservative Republican incumbent was crisscrossing the state in a media blitz. There was one female reporter representing a small paper from some insignificant town, and she was being a special pest, stalking him every-where, constantly jabbing a microphone in his face, and peppering him with "gotcha" questions.

After a hard day's campaign the candidate was in his car when the obnoxious journalist stuck her mic in his window to nag him yet again. He'd finally had enough of her and pushed the door open. It sent her to the curb on her butt. The next morning a front-page story appeared in her newspaper: The candidate had assaulted a female reporter.

What was a campaign manager to do? That was the exercise.

The teams huddled. For several hours we discussed every single aspect of the campaign and how it should react. Given the firestorm coming, where should we schedule the candidate? Face the music or hide him from sight? If hiding, should we also make the campaign disappear and pull our ads for a while, or should we do the opposite, cutting new ads letting them respond for us instead? Should we invest in polling to provide us strategic advice on public reaction? Use this or not use this in our fundraising? And on and on. No strategy was left unexplored.

When we were done, the teams took turns presenting their plans, in as specific detail as possible. Each presentation lasted a good fifteen minutes. Terry listened patiently. When they were all complete, he pronounced judgment.

Flashing his trademark Cheshire Cat grin, he declared that, yes, we had all failed once again.

We had all missed the clue. He reminded us that the reporter worked for a nothing paper in Nowheresville, South Dakota. No one would have read what she wrote. It was a nothingburger issue that would probably never see the light of day. (This was pre-internet.) Except now, thanks to us, it had been elevated to a major crisis known by every single reporter in the state, and through them, every voter. Fact is, we may have just cost our candidate the race. The correct answer was: do nothing. Then Terry started laughing. A part of you wanted to kill this man. The other was in awe.

The final assignment was to fill out a questionnaire outlining our areas of interest, our availability, our willingness to relocate, and a bunch of other wishes and fears. Terry hoped to place each of us in the campaign where we could be most effective. I declined to fill out my form. I had no interest in working on a campaign, I told Terry. I wanted to work for him.

Funding always being an issue—Terry could spend money at the speed of light—he had no full-time work for me, but over the next few months did contract with me on a couple of projects, one to produce a very sophisticated analysis of all the conservative funding organizations in America, as an aid to candidates, the other an opposition research paper on Missouri senator Tom Eagleton, which turned out to be entirely unnecessary when the news broke of his fragile mental condition, forcing him to withdraw from his reelection campaign.

In June, Terry called again. Would I be interested in a job as a full-time fundraiser? This field was of no interest to me. In fact, it was off-putting. Worse yet was the pay. Terry might throw money around recklessly but not toward salaries. He was notoriously frugal in that area, paying himself $24,000 annually, and for everyone else it was less. He offered me $15,000 and 3 percent commission on net monies raised. It was a pittance, but with a bride, two toddlers, and no other prospects, I had no choice and took the offer. So began a six-year adventure working for a strategic and marketing genius who founded and ran arguably the most powerful political operation in America. He also did more to elect Ronald Reagan than most anyone in the country. It is shameful that only a handful of conservatives today even recognize his name, and of the few who do, most know little more than the manner in which he died.

2. Terry Dolan

Terry was twenty-seven when he launched NCPAC in 1976. He had two partners, Charlie Black and Roger Stone. They left shortly thereafter to cash in as political consultants for the swamp. He later told me with disgust that he suspected Stone was double-dipping into NCPAC's meager war chest to cover personal expenses. Alongside Richard Viguerie, Howard Phillips, Jerry Falwell, Paul Weyrich, and several others, Terry was one of the fathers of the New Right movement. It was birthed out of an opposition to the moderate wing of the Republican Party that was unwilling to challenge the liberals in the Democratic Party as well as frustration with the Old Right mainline conservatives who had lost their spunk. These young Turks wanted action. NCPAC began with nothing except the fundraising signatures of two men. One was North Carolina senator Jesse Helms, oftentimes the lone and so much maligned conservative in the

Senate, the 1970s version of Jim DeMint. The other was a Californian by the name of Ronald Reagan.

NCPAC would last only a decade but would launch the careers of some of the most successful conservative activists today. Craig Shirley came from the Republican National Committee and took a job as NCPAC's press secretary. He'd leave NCPAC to start his own successful public relations company and from there to become the foremost biographer of Ronald Reagan with four bestsellers to his credit. Brent Baker arrived as an intern and would leave to help me launch the Media Research Center. Today he's recognized as the single most knowledgeable analyst of the news media in America. A long-haired Leif Noren would take a job as an assistant bookkeeper and would rise to be NCPAC's executive director. He also helped launch the MRC, serving as its first executive director and shortly thereafter helping me start Creative Response Concepts (now CRC Advisors), where he served as chairman until his retirement in 2020.

Greg Mueller joined NCPAC's sister, the National Conservative Foundation (NCF) as an intern, left to work for Shirley's new company, and then assumed the presidency of CRC. Today he is the CEO of CRC Advisors. Richard Kimble joined us straight out of the University of Maryland, working under me in the fundraising operation. Today he sits at the head of the fundraising table, having raised hundreds of millions of dollars for a wide swath of conservative causes. Vic Gresham took the job of NCPAC's political director; today he directs many campaign efforts throughout Virginia. John McLaughlin didn't work directly for NCPAC but learned his polling craft designing surveys for NCPAC, was constantly in our offices, and today heads one of the most prestigious polling firms in America. There were others. Collectively we were dubbed by one conservative leader as "Terry's Kids."

Ever the opportunist, Terry had discovered a loophole in the campaign finance laws at the time—and pounced. "Loophole" is the wrong word if, like Terry, you believe there should be no campaign limitations. For him it was simply a way around stupid federal laws created to limit personal involvement in campaigns because Bebe Rebozo chose to secretly bankroll Richard Nixon a decade earlier.

Campaign finance laws stipulated that individuals could give no more than $5,000 for the primary and a similar amount for the general election campaign, with a maximum of $25,000 allowed annually for all federal efforts. But in the famous *Buckley v. Valeo* case of 1972, former Senator James Buckley of New York successfully persuaded the Supreme Court that the Constitution allows for unlimited personal participation in the political process. If an individual had no contact with either the candidate or his campaign, he ought not be bound by campaign finance regulations. With that the independent expenditure effort (IE) was born. While others practiced it, Terry mastered it. NCPAC would become one massive independent expenditure effort.

Terry kicked the IE tires in 1976 with Orrin Hatch (once upon a time, a long, long time ago, a conservative) in Utah, and again with Gordon Humphrey in New Hampshire in 1978. Each was challenging a powerful liberal incumbent in the Senate. The conventional wisdom had it—and still has it, thanks to incompetent campaign managers—that the public focus on campaigns starts after Labor Day, therefore the campaign should do the same. But Terry found the flaw in this thinking, or better put, saw the opportunity.

In politics it is always harder to diminish a negative than increase a positive. If you put your opponent on defense early, you control the narrative. As Richard Viguerie famously said, "In politics it's define or be defined." Terry never waited until Labor Day. He went in a year early to do just that. His targets were almost always incumbents, partly because they had voting records, making them politically vulnerable, but also because Terry relished overturning the Capitol Hill applecart.

The first order of business in a campaign was to conduct a statewide survey to determine the incumbent's weakness. Where did he stand on some important issues that were in opposition to those held by his constituents? And how might his support be affected if his constituents learned of that position? Terry would pore through hundreds of pages of polling data until he found the "Aha!" revelation, the one issue that would cause the incumbent the greatest political heartburn. In today's bifurcated climate, a candidate like, say, Trump, or even Obama, could successfully campaign despite massive negatives. Back then the formula was different. If the candidate's favorable rating dropped under 50 percent and his unfavorable rose to over 25 percent, he was in political quicksand.

The issue identified, Terry would bring in his advertising posse to produce ads hitting the incumbent on this issue. For two weeks he would saturate a media market with television, radio, and print ads, and then conduct a follow-up survey. If he'd moved the needle sufficiently and could extrapolate that a full-fledged campaign might defeat the incumbent, off he'd go to raise the money. Campaigns back then cost a fraction of what they cost today, especially in states with smaller populations. A test could be conducted for as little as $50,000, and the rollout of a Senate race might carry a million-dollar price tag, sometimes even less.

Terry bristled at the term "negative campaign." There was nothing negative about a discussion of an incumbent's votes. If anything, the accusation only emboldened him. From his perspective, it underscored the arrogance of Washington elites who believed someone like Terry Dolan had no right to question their records.

Terry never indulged in character assassination and would have nothing to do with anyone who did. Nor would he allow a label tougher than "liberal," no matter how dishonestly his opponents might label him or his preferred candidates. But he did attack, and he scored every time. He picked a fight with the incumbent knowing that both the incumbent and NCPAC would be bloodied. That was fine with him given that one was running for reelection, and the other wasn't. Meanwhile, the challenger—Terry's candidate—could rise above the fray and connect with the voters with a positive message. We never consulted with campaigns we were trying to help once they were official and underway. Most, but not all, were smart enough to stay out of the way.

Orrin Hatch was one of the smart ones. In 1976, with Terry's help, he beat three-term incumbent Democratic senator Frank Moss. Gordon Humphrey played it smart too. In 1978, with Terry's help, the little known Gordon Humphrey beat three-term incumbent Democratic senator Thomas McIntyre. They took the high road while Terry did the brawling.

3. "Target '80"

It was 1980, and Terry was going big. The summer before, he had announced "Target '80," publicly declaring war on five of the most powerful and liberal Democrats in Washington. George McGovern of South Dakota, who had been his party's presidential candidate just eight years previously, was the best known. But conservatives in the movement knew the rest: Frank Church of Idaho and John Culver of Iowa, Birch Bayh of Indiana, and Alan Cranston of California. "Target '80" was audacious to say the least. Terry was proposing to take down the liberal hierarchy of the United States Senate.

It was an issue-rich environment that year. The Carter agenda was in tatters, both domestically and internationally. The economy was in a free fall with gas lines, rampant inflation, skyrocketing interest rates, and surging unemployment. Overseas the Soviet Union was on the march everywhere. History has its moments, and Ronald Reagan arrived in the nick of time. He promised to destroy the Evil Empire while making America once more the shining city on a hill.

Reagan and Dolan were political revolutionaries. They had similar DNA that showed itself in their optimism, their confidence, and their sense of purpose. The major difference between the two was that Reagan wore gloves, and Dolan preferred bare knuckles.

When Terry announced his $8-million "Target '80" campaign at a packed national press conference, he left out one minor detail. NCPAC had no money. But what he lacked in paid media resources he more than covered with his earned media shenanigans. If he couldn't pay for his commercials to sell his message, he'd get the press, or even better, get the incumbent himself to do it for him. No one had Terry's chutzpah, and he'd chuckle with glee every time his daring worked, which was often.

Here's one example. When George McGovern announced his Senate reelection campaign, NCPAC had just $14,000 in cash in the bank. Terry read McGovern perfectly, harkening back to the 1972 Democratic convention when McGovern had so foolishly tried to publicly negotiate with yuppie radicals who were rioting in Chicago, only to have his futile effort backfire. Terry emptied the bank in order to run one full-page ad in the Sioux Falls *Argus Leader* titled, "Ten Questions We Wish the Media Would Ask George McGovern." It ran through a litany of issues on which McGovern's votes or positions ran contrary to the beliefs of South Dakota's generally conservative voters. One referenced an incident several months before that had caused a minor uproar within the national conservative community but minimal press coverage in South Dakota. "Why do you feel it's okay to publicly share an ice cream cone with Fidel Castro?"

Poor McGovern bit—hard. Rather than ignore us, as Terry's campaign school had taught us to do, McGovern enlarged the ad, put it on an easel, and, at his own presser, proclaimed to the assembled journalists that he was going to respond to "every single one of these scurrilous charges!" And there it was, on every local television set that night and in every newspaper the next day: our ad with McGovern in a defensive crouch trying to explain himself point by point. Define or be defined. Local news now became national news: McGovern was under assault from a national conservative organization. Conservative donors learned of this effort, and money began to pour into NCPAC's coffers to fund it.

A few months later Terry got him again. Polling data that year showed that voters were enraged that so many elected officials were so out of touch with their constituents. Many citizens would be willing to vote these officials out of office for that reason alone.

Our goal was to prove just how out of touch with the people of South Dakota McGovern really was. With the help of terrific oppo research, Terry learned that McGovern owned no property in South Dakota and did not even live there. Terry addressed that issue in a television ad and created a simple tagline for it: "George McGovern. Out of touch with South Dakota." McGovern rushed to the press to denounce NCPAC for this, playing the populist card. It was absolutely true, he said. He could not afford two residences and had opted to sacrifice on behalf of the good people of South Dakota by living in Washington, DC. Blah, blah.

Did I mention that Terry had a terrific researcher? Terry was ready for that disingenuous answer, and McGovern wasn't ready for Terry's response to it. He ran a new TV commercial citing McGovern's own words followed by a picture of McGovern's private farm in…Nova Scotia. "George McGovern. Out of touch with South Dakota."

Checkmate.

Terry wanted national press for "Target '80" because that attention would raise not only the credibility of the effort but also the cash needed to fund it. The head of a large labor union, I forget which, had publicly denounced Terry during the 1978 campaigns. So Terry set his sights on him for another audacious move. He had his creative people draft up a "confidential" game plan for "Target '80," describing all the targets and the attendant efforts planned for each. Making the plan even more credible was that all its information was true! Once it was prepared, Terry took a big red magic marker and in bold letters scratched, "YOU MUST STOP THESE PEOPLE!" He then mailed the plan anonymously to the labor union leader. The poor sap took the bait. He publicly released this "confirmed" secret strategy and announced a massive national effort to terminate this threat to Western civilization. And there you had it: NCPAC v. Big Labor. National press. National funding. Terry laughing with his Cheshire Cat grin.

What stuns in retrospect is the size of his internal political staff in 1980 when he declared war. He had his political assistant, Lisa Stoltenberg, and an occasional intern. That was it. But Terry also had the New Right behind him. Never before or since has the conservative movement been so united with so many top-shelf leaders. Paul Weyrich (Free Congress Foundation) was a master strategist. Richard Viguerie (The Richard A. Viguerie Company) had developed the entire direct mail fundraising business. Arthur Finkelstein (Arthur J. Finkelstein & Associates Inc.) was one of America's foremost pollsters. Howard Phillips (Conservative Caucus) was the right's resident anti-communist leader. Ed Feulner (The Heritage Foundation) led the intellectual firepower on Capitol Hill. The Reverend Jerry Falwell brought the religious right to the table. There were others as well. Each was an expert in one or more aspects of a successful national movement. Terry? Terry excelled in all areas.

But it was also deadly serious stuff. "Target '80" was *mano a mano* warfare between NCPAC and an alphabet soup of leftist organizations.

Terry won one skirmish after the next not just because of his political expertise but because of his connection to popular culture. He attracted conservative Hollywood celebrities like Susan Howard (*Dallas*) and Scott Baio (*Charles in Charge*) to serve as spokesmen. He sponsored chili cook-offs in Texas, a Barbara Mandrell concert in Kentucky, a Roy Orbison concert in Virginia, and even tried to sponsor a NASCAR vehicle (he couldn't afford it).

No prize seemed to be out of this wunderkind's reach. Time and again he raised a possibility that left the rest of us shaking our heads in disbelief at his audacity. These moves were the political equivalent of my brother Michael swinging outside the railroad car to scare the old shrews.

One day the manager of an unknown young rock musician approached Terry. He needed money to launch his client's inaugural album. Would NCPAC be interested in putting up fifty grand for a piece of the action? Terry asked my advice. I thought it was a ridiculous idea and said so. But Terry was curious and sent me to a bar in Georgetown where this fellow was performing to check him out. I went and reported back to Terry that the guy was perfectly awful. It was only then that Terry abandoned the idea. So Stevie Ray Vaughan had to find someone else to help produce his first album.

On Election Day 1980 Terry pulled off perhaps the most successful feat in modern political history. It was 10:00 p.m., and one network reported that with 3 percent of the total counted, Senator Church was down just a tad in Idaho. I told Terry this as he walked by my TV screen. Even with that miniscule percentage reporting, Terry knew he'd won. "We got him!" he exclaimed with a triumphant smile, punching his hand. Church went down. McGovern went down. Bayh went down. Culver went down. Only Cranston had survived, and only because California was a bridge too far financially. The Democratic majority, along with much of its liberal leadership, had been decapitated. One can argue that had those four leftists remained in the Senate, the Democratic majority in that chamber would have blocked Reagan's entire agenda, both economic and foreign. Think that through, and you'll understand the magnitude of Terry Dolan's contribution to his country.

4. Animal House

Nowhere can perception and reality be more different than in the world of politics. Now more than ever. Terry was seen by leftists in the media and the political world (I know, I know: the same thing) as an ogre, a threat, a dark, perpetually angry fanatic heading an existentially threatening dangerous enterprise manned by Middle-earth trolls.

The reality was just the opposite. NCPAC was *Animal House*, and Terry Dolan was Otter. John Belushi would have felt perfectly at home working at NCPAC. Not including our phone bank there were about twenty of us. Our average age fell short of twenty-five. Some staffers were just out of college. One or two were still in college.

Our offices were located in Rosslyn but looked like they belonged in Sarajevo. Typewriters were constantly clicking away, but if one broke, it stayed broken. Posters on the walls dangled because no one bothered to tape them back up. Stacks of paper cluttered on old army surplus desks peppered the place. Broken chairs, like their defunct typewriter cousins, sat idly in corners. Blinds worked, or didn't work. Coffee stains were everywhere. My first office was in a hallway. I was given an old foldout metal patio table as my desk. My phone was on the wall. I learned to be extremely careful when I stood up to take a call. If I accidentally bumped my "desk" on the way up, it would collapse and spew all my junk on the floor. It had only three legs.

We helped elect many other candidates in 1980 with cash or in-kind contributions. One Senate candidate from Florida we successfully supported was Paula Hawkins. Shortly after her victory she graced us with an appearance. She explained that when she came to Washington looking for financial sustenance, "I tripped on the plush carpets" of most groups, but when she got to NCPAC, "I slipped on the paper all over the floor. That's when I knew who would be helping me."

We were the most successful independent political action committee in the conservative movement, but in some ways that was in spite of ourselves. Terry was a political genius but a management disaster. The organizational chart was self-explanatory. It was Terry at the top. The second layer of command was everyone else. There was no discipline. Any time staffers needed anything we just waltzed into Terry's office and asked for it. We weren't tasked with offering solutions to problems. Too much trouble. We waited for Terry to resolve our issues for us. If we needed, say, a pen, we went to the "supply" closet only to find that no one had stocked it—with anything. There were no regular senior staff meetings. From time to time Terry would convene one, but it could last hours, not because of the intensity of the agenda, but because there was no agenda. Any discussion could easily be derailed into an argument over the best sitcom on television, the juiciest gossip on the Hill, or why the Yankees sucked.

After the extraordinary successes of 1980, the organization grew financially. By 1982 our annual budget reached $14 million, and our staff had doubled. Yet it seemed that as our staff grew, in equal proportion our effectiveness diminished. Much to Terry's horror we were becoming a bureaucracy. We were the Monitor morphing into the Merrimack. Terry finally hired a consultant to come down from New York to make sense of it all. We knew we sorely needed some adult supervision, and if this New York consultant fellow had something, anything, constructive to offer, we'd take it.

Ahead of his first visit he requested a copy of everyone's job description. If anyone didn't have one—which is to say almost everyone—we were to give him as best we could a description of the job we'd been hired to perform. When he arrived a few days later, he collected the job descriptions. In return he handed everyone several outlined sheets of paper. For two weeks we were to report on one line what work we'd undertaken every hour of the day. After two weeks the pages were collected and sent back to New York.

A few weeks later the consultant returned with his analysis. Every employee had been graded on his level of efficiency. We were assembled in Terry's office, and each of us was given his report card. I looked at my grade and was stunned. Out of a possible 100 percent I had scored a twenty-seven. I erupted. Looking at Terry, I asked who this garbanzo was that he could score me like that. I pointed out that I was presently running campaigns in five states, raising money for the foundation Terry had launched, lecturing at his campaign schools, helping produce a documentary as well as a proposed public affairs television series, and, oh by the way, I had met and surpassed all my fundraising goals. And for that my grade was an "F?"

Terry listened and then burst out laughing. "How do you think I feel? I got a seventeen!"

The consultant's explanation was painfully obvious, and it spoke volumes that we didn't see it. He'd reviewed our job descriptions, then measured what percentage of time we had spent on it during that two-week period. All my other spectacular achievements were irrelevant. I was spending only 27 percent of my time on that for which I'd been hired.

With that, everything changed. We were instructed either to apply ourselves to our initial job descriptions, or our job descriptions were changed to reflect present realities. Next, Terry hired an executive director to manage the daily operations that would allow Terry to focus on the 83 percent of his own job he was ignoring. He tried a retired army officer first. That fellow arrived first thing Monday morning, took his lunch break, and never returned. Next Terry tried a retired marine captain (note the trend?), and this time succeeded.

It took this fellow only a couple of weeks to separate the wheat from the chaff. One third of the staff was fired, another third put on work performance notice, and the rest of us awarded long overdue but unanticipated raises. Eighteen months after my hiring I was promoted to national finance director, and ultimately president of the corporation.

Besides organizational incompetence there was another reason for the cavalier attitude toward professional discipline, and this is where *Animal House* enters the picture. We were more like the Delta Tau Chi fraternity than a professional enterprise. To say we were raucous is an understatement. There were stunts, games, and pranks seemingly every day. No one misbehaved more than that supposed perpetually angry ogre Terry. Parties could become wild drinking affairs that spilled into nearby bars. Engagement celebrations were even more outrageous. More than once a stripper was brought in to scandalize the bride-to-be (no, it never went that far). There were interdepartmental clashes but also forced alliances for the common defense when under assault by other companies, such as the time Viguerie's office blasted our office with a barrage of water balloons before fleeing.

The press just didn't know what to make of, or do with, Terry Dolan.

5. Target Terry

After the 1980 victories we were contacted by *60 Minutes*. Would it be okay if Ed Bradley tailed us for a few weeks for a profile piece on NCPAC? I firmly objected. Clearly, these people's only purpose was to embarrass us. Terry overruled me, confidently declaring we had nothing to hide. Camera crews followed Terry around the country for several weeks, taping speaking events, a campaign management school in Houston, and other political gatherings. Finally they informed us they had all they needed and left. We never heard from them again. They'd found nothing with which to hurt us.

Then there was the day *Doonesbury* comic strip creator Garry Trudeau and Robert Redford arrived at our offices to meet privately with Terry. They tried sneaking in, but Redford was recognized, and every woman in Northern Virginia came to gawk. The two were whisked into Terry's office to discuss a possible movie project about NCPAC, with Redford taking Terry's role. (How's that for an ego boost?) After doing research, they, too, concluded that the reality of NCPAC didn't match the perception of an evil organization, and as with the *60 Minutes* idea, it was abandoned.

Those two episodes had an element of fun, even if the intention of our would-be chroniclers had not been so noble. Other signs pointed to a darker reality. There were some powerful people who wanted Terry destroyed.

We had at least one mole, a fellow placed there by then Connecticut senator Lowell Weicker. Dolan and Weicker shared the same state but came from opposite ends of the GOP and despised each other. Weicker's plant took a job in our phone bank. Apparently, he never got the memo that calls were screened by supervisors, and he was nailed on his first day.

You can chuckle at that *Keystone Cops* escapade too, but what happened shortly after the 1980 victory was not at all amusing. In early January I was notified that a gentleman wanted to visit to discuss a major gift. When he arrived he was not as I'd expected. He was perhaps forty-five years of age, six feet tall, and extremely well-dressed—custom-made suit, polished shoes, expensive watch, the works. His diction was as elegant as his appearance. Even more interesting, he was black. We wished it were otherwise, but there weren't many black conservative donors in 1982. I didn't know of any besides Count Basie.

He introduced himself: Gideon Clements.

Clements had an interesting proposal to say the least. He told me he'd heard Terry speak at the prior year's Conservative Political Action Conference (CPAC) and concluded he wanted to help us. He represented a consortium of wealthy businessmen who wished to remain anonymous but would divulge their identities once an understanding was reached.

He came with an offer. He and his colleagues were willing to provide the National Conservative Foundation (NCF), Terry's tax- deductible educational arm, with all the funding it would require over a two-year period. The goal was to firmly establish the conservative movement within the American popular culture.

There was a catch, of course. Nothing in this town was ever free.

His partners and he had a plan for the private sector to recover debts owed the federal government, and they wished to present the plan to President Reagan's chief of staff, James Baker. No, I replied, this was something Terry would never do. It simply was not in his DNA to push for any political favors.

No, no, Clements protested. I'd misunderstood. They were not looking for any government funding. What they wanted to propose was something they'd finance themselves. Their compensation would come from monies recovered. All they wanted was an introduction to Baker. They would do the rest. What they required in return was a written funding proposal from me, and again, they'd do the rest.

It was an odd request, but I saw no problem in presenting it to Terry. He, too, found it strange, but no harm, no foul. If that was all he was being asked to do, I had the green light to propose a plan for Clements and see where it took us. I had the proposal ready two weeks later. It would require $500,000 for each of the next two years.

We met at our offices at the end of January. Clements reviewed it and rejected it. It seemed I was not taking him seriously enough. He wanted a grand plan, not something like this, and make no mistake: Clements and his colleagues would fund it in its entirety.

In early March we met for the third time. On this occasion I presented a far more complex proposal. It would cost Clements $3 million for each of the next two years. This time he nodded in satisfaction. After some more discussion he left. He called the following day to say his partners had accepted the proposal. The first million would arrive by the end of March, the second by the end of April, and the third by the end of May. The second year's installment would be sent in January 1982.

I was well pleased, to say the least. I wanted to flesh things out more thoroughly so I suggested another meeting, this time at his office in Washington. When I arrived two days later the office was not what I'd expected. Its location was off the beaten K Street path. It was on 6th St. SE, what was then a still underdeveloped and, in some places sketchy, neighborhood.

His office wasn't exactly an office. It looked a whole lot like a townhouse with a few metal file cabinets lining the walls. The cabinets had various labels. One major header read: "The Manhattan Project." This, he said mysteriously, was "the plan."

Intrigued, I started to ask him about this "Manhattan Project," but he looked at his watch and cut me off. He'd made reservations for lunch, and we needed to leave. He jumped in his car and I in mine and headed for the Capitol Hilton on 16th and K. We parked in separate areas.

Clements had entered the hotel ahead of me and hadn't realized I'd caught up to him by the time he approached the restaurant front desk. The maître d' looked up and recognized him immediately. "Good afternoon, Dr. Johnson. We have your table prepared."

There was no protest. "Good afternoon," "Dr. Johnson" replied, smiling as well.

Clements, or whatever his real name was, turned around looking for me. I acted as if I'd not heard anything, and Clements bought it. We sat down to eat. Alarm bells were ringing inside. We made small talk as we ate. It became apparent he was not interested in talking business. He was interested in my personal life, in Terry's personal life, in life at NCPAC—that sort of thing. He probed deeper. When had we last taken vacations? We were working too hard, he said. And deeper still. What did we like to do on vacation?

I was about to say that with a young family my options were limited, but he interrupted before I could finish my sentence. The point he was trying to make, he said, was that Terry and I needed real vacations. We needed to relax. And he wanted to help. He owned a private villa in the Caribbean—he didn't pinpoint the location—and it was where he went to escape all of life's tribulations. He looked at me conspiratorially and winked. "You want women? Terry and you can come and have them. You want drugs? Whatever you want, we get you."

The trap was being set. I went along with it, intrigued, wondering where we were going with this conversation, now trying to get as much as I could out of him. But he was being coy and unresponsive. Finally, I told him I couldn't speak for Terry, and I was married, but still, well, let's see what Terry wanted to do, okay?

After lunch I returned to the office and beelined it to our ED's office. He was not just NCPAC's executive director, he was retired military, and I figured he'd know what to do. He immediately rang an old friend who had retired as the DC police commissioner and now ran his own detective agency. He came over. After hearing me out, he had a forceful response. Whatever I did, I was not to accept any money from this man until he approved it. If any check arrived, I was to turn it over, uncashed, to our attorneys for safekeeping. He wanted to interview this man personally.

The following morning, I called Clements/Johnson to tell him how much I'd enjoyed our lunch. I reported that Terry was quite pleased to learn of the funding timetable because it now allowed him to begin his work. But there was one item we needed to address. I explained as judiciously as possible that Terry had many enemies and as a result we needed to be as diligent as possible, especially since he was being asked to convince the president's chief of staff to take a meeting. Given our security concerns, would Clements/Johnson be opposed to an interview by an agency we used to handle these things (as if we'd ever done this before)? Of course not, he replied. He understood fully. The interview was arranged for the following day.

We spoke a bit more about the program. Clements/Johnson assured me the first installment would arrive as scheduled in a few weeks.

A week later the detective came to our office to give his report. We sat in silence as he pronounced that everything about Clements/Johnson was a lie. During the interview process Clements/Johnson stated he'd graduated from Brown University. In fact, he never attended. He professed to have served in Vietnam. He was never in the military. His business was not registered anywhere. His national office address was a post office box.

The day after the interview with Clements/Johnson, the detective had visited the townhouse. The owners would not divulge the name of the renter, but no matter: he was gone, and the apartment was empty. The phone number had also been disconnected.

We never heard from Gideon Clements/Dr. Johnson again.

Who was he? What was his design? Was it an attempt at bribery? Probably not. We'd already agreed to do as he'd wished. Blackmail? Probably so. I wasn't the target. I was the means to the end. Clements was the agent, not the instigator.

So who was behind it? We'll never know.

6. "Target '82"

After 1980 Terry continued logging victories, but of a different sort. Early in 1981 he was summoned to the Oval Office for a briefing from the president. Reagan outlined his economic recovery program and requested support in convincing enough Democrats to cross the aisle and give him his congressional victory. Terry suggested that Reagan travel the high road and let him take on those waffling Democrats. Reagan nodded and thanked him for coming. Longtime confidant Ed Meese was in the room, and when he escorted Terry out, he put his arm around him. "That's just what the president wanted to hear." Off to the races Terry went, launching ads targeting some of the "Blue Dog" Democrats from the South who could be brought into the Reagan camp. Most came kicking and screaming— and cursing Terry Dolan to the high heavens. But they came.

Terry threw himself into other projects as well: helping the Nicaraguan Contras and the mujahideen in Afghanistan, fighting nuclear disarmament, organizing demonstrations at Lafayette Park opposite the White House to protest what he saw as a weak response to the downing of Korean Airlines Flight 007 by Soviet aircraft, supporting the administration's decision to liberate Grenada by force, advancing the pro-life movement, and helping out with numerous other efforts.

But nothing motivated Terry Dolan more than his contempt for an ever-increasing federal government. Anything that grew the state he opposed; any proposed reduction he embraced. Reluctantly, because he wanted most of Washington abolished, not reduced. Terry made it clear that aside from the necessities of national defense, weather forecasting, and mail delivery, the federal government needed to do no more. Were he alive today, Terry would argue that the private sector could now manage everything but national defense.

As the 1980s progressed, the relationship between conservatives and the news media grew more strained. To ease the tension, some well-meaning fellow on NBC's *Today Show* arrived at a clever idea, one that, if successful, might please both camps. Recognizing Terry's media skills, *Today Show* execs offered him a unique proposition. He could pick any recent NBC news story he felt was biased and produce his own segment addressing that subject from a conservative's perspective. NBC would run its story and Terry's response side by side and invite the audience to comment. If the feedback was strong enough, NBC brass would consider making this a regular feature. NBC would grow its audience, and we'd be given a forum for our message. Win-win.

Terry jumped at the opportunity. He selected an NBC story suggesting the Soviet Union could be trusted to abide by the Intermediate-Range Nuclear Forces Treaty (INF). The segment projected the Soviet Union as a reliable prospective partner in nuclear disarmament. The leftists interviewed for the segment all but said it was the Gipper who needed to be schooled in the politics of peace. The video featured stock footage of a Soviet May Day parade. Nothing says "peace" quite like Soviet trucks carrying nukes.

Terry took that very same footage, but this time used other voices, including that of British prime minister Margaret Thatcher, to highlight the dangerous expansion of the Evil Empire. He made one strategic edit of the video by zeroing in on a faint image on one of the missiles, the Statue of Liberty, the missile's intended target. Terry's sources reported that the segment was one of the most popular in the history of the *Today Show*. Too popular, apparently. We never heard from them again.

NCPAC's signature continued to be the negative independent expenditure campaign, but this time we could not repeat the spectacular results of 1980. The first midterm election for an incumbent president's party almost always results in a loss of seats, but Terry chose to ignore history. He'd gotten a bit too cocky and now felt invincible. Rather than carefully retrench and consolidate, he went in the opposite direction, announcing "Target '82." This time he put twenty Democrat incumbent senators on notice that he might come after them. He had neither the organization nor the finances for anything this bold, especially given that under normal circumstances most incumbents would have sailed home safely.

But things were shaping up more ominously than we expected.

For starters, the professional political class was on the rise. The class of 1980 was filled with Reaganites, but by 1982 for many the energy and altruism were gone, replaced by personal ambition. The movement had lost its purity and its innocence. Some of the subversives were candidates; others were consultants who had once punched the conservative time clock but now were selling the political equivalent of snake oil. Both were making their fortunes and careers at the expense of the movement's success.

More than one campaign turned on Terry.

Representative Larry Hogan, father of the present governor of Maryland, was considering challenging incumbent Senator Paul Sarbanes, one of the most left-wing senators in the country. Hogan came to our offices to solicit our help. Given he was not an official candidate, we could still talk. Terry urged him to run and promised that NCPAC would enter the state to help if he did. Shortly thereafter, Hogan announced his candidacy and then shocked us by holding another press conference to join Sarbanes in denouncing outside interlopers—us. I urged Terry to go public with Hogan's duplicity, but Terry refused to do so. He was monitoring polling data coming out of the state. Every time Hogan attacked us, seeking political opportunity, his numbers actually dropped. And for good reason. Liberals were never going to vote for him, but conservatives would—except those who watched him attack fellow conservatives and were increasingly questioning Hogan's conservative bona fides—as they should now question his son's. Terry quietly pulled out. Sarbanes squashed Hogan like the worm he was.

Montana was a similar story. Senator John Melcher was the Democratic incumbent and another target Terry had put on notice. Early in 1981 I received a phone call from Billings businessman Larry Williams, inviting me to his state. We met and discussed an independent expenditure campaign (again, legal since he was not in the race). I projected it would cost $50,000 to conduct a test. Williams pledged to fund half of it and soon mailed a small stack of checks totaling $25,000. The test showed possibilities, and with that we announced a formal campaign for the state.

On the eve of Larry's campaign announcement, a source alerted me that Williams was intending to attack us the next day, again as uninvited outsiders. I informed Terry, and this time he blew, one of the few times I ever saw him truly angry. He told me to convey a message directly to Williams. If a single negative thing about NCPAC were to come out of his mouth the next morning, Terry would be on the first plane to Billings to hold a press conference denouncing the hypocrisy, which presser was guaranteed to sink the Williams campaign on its very first day. Williams backed off.

But Terry's heart clearly wasn't in Montana. He'd not only soured completely on the challenger, he'd never felt comfortable challenging the incumbent to begin with. No matter how liberal he was on other issues, Melcher was a strong pro-lifer. We did little, then pulled out.

Williams, too, went down.

More importantly, the Democrats had figured us out and unleashed a devastating counterattack. We were shown a pilfered strategy memo from a Democratic National Committee meeting outlining their "How to Stop NCPAC" plan, and we were helpless to combat it. There were several components, but only two mattered. First, rather than fall for the trap of having their candidates respond to us, the Democrats would launch their own "independent" organizations in the states we'd targeted with the sole mission of eviscerating us with vicious attacks. If we were to bite, which we never did, we'd be engaging with an irrelevant force while letting the prey escape. But define or be defined. If we ignored them, they'd be able to destroy our reputation, labeling us liars, fringe right-wing extremists, interlopers, and the like. Concurrently they would unleash a battery of attack lawyers in each state to meet with local television managers, promising hellfire defamation lawsuits if they ran our "dishonest" advertisements. Never mind that nothing we said was untrue. Knowing they were under no legal requirement to run our ads, one by one station managers declined to do business with us to avoid legal harassment. Try as we did, we could only get a handful to resist the intimidation.

Combine the two counter strategies, and in some races we were effectively neutered. The '82 results were a mixed bag at best. We won a few races, be it through cash or in-kind services, but lost most of the independent expenditure challenges.

Terry didn't know how to take his foot off the gas. In 1983 he was recruiting candidates, crisscrossing the country in search of funding, and providing all manner of assistance to campaigns. He was also launching new initiatives of his own. In the spring of 1983 Terry announced a new project, this one through his National Conservative Foundation (NCF). It was one I'd proposed to him in the Avis car rental parking lot at the Dallas/Fort Worth Airport in 1982. We called it the Media Research Center.

On to 1984. The name of the game was again Reagan, and Terry threw everything he had into his reelection. Reagan often spoke of the everyday Joe doing his part to advance the American dream as an "American hero." Terry borrowed the phrase as the title of his new multimillion-dollar independent expenditure, "American Heroes for Reagan." This time it wasn't all negative campaigning (against Mondale). Reagan had logged so many victories there was much to celebrate, and NCPAC did its share on his behalf.

Once more Terry was in his element. He produced many ads, but the cleverest was the one that ran only once. He sent a film crew to Grenada to interview one of the American medical students freed by the 82nd Airborne that had been sent there by Reagan to wrest the island from Cuban control. In the ad the student recounted the rescue and thanked the president for saving his life. Then Terry, always with an ear tuned to pop culture messages, borrowed a line that American Express had used thousands of times in its commercials and which by now was ingrained in the American memory bank. Just as that company had flashed its credit card at the camera, so, too, did the student now display his "American Heroes for Reagan" membership card. "Don't leave home without it," he smiled.

A call from American Express attorneys put an end to that commercial.

NCPAC offered a wide array of programs, the most notable being a one-hour documentary, "Ronald Reagan's America," which was produced by Mark Barnes, about whom we'll speak in the following chapter. We were able to negotiate placements in local markets throughout the country, but the film's shining moment came at the Republican National Convention in Dallas that summer. Imagine our surprise when the GOP launched its convention with a sixty-minute documentary called "Ronald Reagan's America," with precisely the same message, up to and including using some of the very same stock footage in our film. We decided to accept this imitation as flattery. Besides, to whom could we complain? "American Heroes for Reagan" was an independent expenditure campaign, meaning there was no one with whom we could even speak.

That included family members. Throughout the campaign Terry not once spoke with his brother Tony, then a speechwriter for the president.

Again Terry set out to recruit celebrities to sell our effort. Terry and I went to Hollywood to meet with three of them, and all agreed immediately. We returned to Virginia to announce the good news. Michael Landon, Robert Conrad, and Robert Stack would serve as cochairmen. Our glee lasted less than forty-eight hours. Within two days, all three backed out. It seemed that the official Reagan campaign's Hollywood coordinator wanted not some but all the Reagan supporters in Tinseltown helping her. Three quick phone calls with three quick explanations: If they helped NCPAC's independent expenditure, by law they could have no access to the president, but if they were with the campaign, all manner of presidential access could be made available. We never stood a chance.

NCPAC's singular moment in 1984 had nothing to do with a political program. It was an independent fundraiser unlike anything the political world had seen before, or perhaps since.

Dallas, Texas, was a terrific choice for the 1984 GOP Convention given its powerful conservative Republican roots. Terry and I traveled there in the spring to meet with Nelson Bunker Hunt, the billionaire oilman who was donating to conservative groups such as ours when he wasn't trying to corner the world silver market. His "Circle T" ranch was as iconic as it was enormous, twenty-five thousand sprawling acres to feed his cattle as well as his prized Thoroughbred horse collection. We proposed a fundraising event at his beautiful ranch house and suggested we'd be able to sell as many as twenty-five tables at ten thousand bucks apiece. That's silly money today, but in 1984 it was serious ka-ching. Bunker agreed.

The 1984 Texas Gala invitations were mailed, and solicitors got on the phones to smile-and-dial. Two or three tables sold quickly, as they normally do, then the team settled in to fill the rest. But then an invitee called *us*. And then a second, and a third. We were no longer making outgoing calls. We were taking orders. Two tickets here. Four tickets there. A table. Then another table. Then another table. Finally the venue was filled—and still the orders came. Something was happening. This had become *the* event during the convention. *Haute* Texas society was on high alert. Anyone who was anyone just had to go.

Change of plans. I'd been introduced to Jack Calmes, an event producer extraordinaire whose accomplishments included managing a nationwide tour for Paul McCartney's "Wings" as well as the unveiling of the Dallas Reunion Tower with its iconic kaleidoscope. We met at Bunker's ranch, where Calmes had assembled his team, *Mission Impossible*-style. He had his talent guy, his stage guy, his lighting guy, his sound guy, his food guy, his design guy, but then he had another group of "guys" responsible for other, more eclectic assignments. He laid out his vision. I played with it. We finalized it and parted ways. We met again two days before the event for final revisions.

What began as a typical indoor major donor event now was an outdoor spectacle.

Convention organizers had assigned us to the ghastly airport Amfac Hotel for our headquarters. Tables were set up for our staff to coordinate logistics, and the phones were ringing off the wall. I decided to help out our haggard staff and at one point found myself holding a phone to each ear. On one side I had some local business leader begging for a ticket. On the other end I had a furious congressman who had just learned we'd rescinded the invitation for his wife.

We were no longer inside the house. We were inside the largest tent available in the United States of America. We were not just sold out. We were oversubscribed. I'd attempted to shoehorn as many tables as I could and had exceeded the sixteen-hundred limit. The fire marshal had nailed us and demanded the extra tables be removed. We obeyed, somewhat. But people were just not understanding the world "no." Later that afternoon someone located my room and thrust a $3,000 check in my face when I opened the door. He was offering that for just one seat. Up until the very final moment they tried. As our buses pulled out of the Amfac to convoy some of our guests, a man literally chased one of them, waving wads of cash, pleading for a seat.

The event was scheduled for August 22, when the Texas heat can easily hit a blistering 102 as it did that day. How to keep a tent cool when it's a blasted furnace outside? No problem. Jack's AC guy (see?) had requisitioned two air-conditioning systems used to cool oil rigs off the Gulf Coast. They managed to keep the tent at 68 degrees at the cool cost of twenty-five grand. There was the custom-built stage with state-of-the-art sound and lighting. There was linen, crystal, silver, and china on the tables. There was…there was…there was….

How about this. How about I let the *New York Times* tell the story, from its August 23 edition:

> Nelson Bunker Hunt, the Texas billionaire, was strolling down a hill on his Circle T Ranch near here Tuesday night when he noticed a clear plastic fork on the lawn. He picked it up, brushed it off and put it in his pocket.

"That's the way you save money," he said with a small grin.

Mr. Hunt and his wife, Caroline, were on their way to an awesome party called the Texas Gala, held on the grounds of their 2,000-acre ranch 29 miles north of Dallas. It included cowboys, Indians, tepees, stagecoaches, hot-air balloons, 24 bars and a huge air-conditioned tent, with Pat Boone as the master of ceremonies and Bob Hope as the entertainer.

The five-hour-long party was a fundraiser for the National Conservative Political Action Committee, whose chairman, John T. Dolan, said he expected to raise more than $1.3 million from the event.

"Only in Texas," said the Rev. Jerry Falwell, who gave the invocation at the dinner. "This is true Bunker Hunt style. We Baptists don't quite do it this way. But Bunker asked me to bless this mess and I will." A total of 1,650 people paid $1,000 a head to attend what was certainly the most elaborate of many social extravaganzas related to the Republican National Convention. "It's at least 50 times as large as any party I've ever been to," said Senator Jesse Helms of North Carolina.

"I'm awed and overwhelmed," said Richard A. Viguerie, publisher of the Conservative Digest, who wore a cowboy hat, a suede vest and blue jeans. "I've long since ceased to be amazed by anything Bunker owns or does, but this is more than I expected even from him."

Senator Orrin G. Hatch of Utah looked out of place in his gray pin-striped suit. Most of the other guests were wearing 10-gallon hats or boots or other Texas touches. "I left my cowboy boots in my hotel," he said. "I was so busy making rounds that I didn't have time to change."

Other guests included Senators Paul S. Trible Jr. of Virginia and Chic Hecht of Nevada; Howard Phillips, chairman of the Conservative Caucus; Mr. Hunt's brother, Lamar; John D. Murchison, of Murchison Oil; Charlton Heston and Chad Everett, the actors; Wayne Newton, the singer; the Osmond Brothers, the singers; Ed Jones and Danny White of the Dallas Cowboys, and Steve Lundquist and Rowdy Gaines, swimmers who won Olympic gold medals.

During the cocktail hour, the guests strolled the grounds, watched a cutting horse competition and listened to a mariachi band. They ate appetizers that included barbecue from two sides of beef roasted over mesquite; tortillas, and sautéed oysters.

One of the most popular attractions was Tex, whose owner, Rorie Cowden, described him as "the world's largest saddle- broke Texas longhorn steer." Dozens of guests climbed into the saddle on Tex's back to have their pictures taken. Anne Stallworth of Dallas, whose husband, Robert, is in the oil business, even climbed on Tex wearing a pleated lime- green dress by Mary McFadden and strappy gold shoes.

The four Osmond brothers said they had canceled several concerts so they could attend the Texas Gala. "We wanted to come down and be a part of this whole howdy-do and be counted among those who support Ronald Reagan," Alan Osmond said.

After holding a private cocktail reception in their ranch house, the Hunts and their house guest, Elizabeth Fondaras of New York, strolled down the hill to the huge, air-conditioned 120-by-250-foot tent, where the dinner was served.

"I was pleased to come," said the 58-year-old Mr. Hunt, who was wearing a light blue western shirt, matching pants, a tooled brown leather belt with the name "Bunker'" on the back and a leather bolo tie fastened with a silver dollar.

Mr. Hunt laughed when a reporter asked if it was true he was worth $2 billion. "You must be quoting my debt," he said.

Asked about his new slimmed-down figure, the once portly oilman said he had recently shed 65 pounds on the Pritikin Diet. "And that's hard work when you're a hard-core eater," he said. Mrs. Hunt, who was wearing a peach-colored silk blouse and matching suede skirt and cowboy boots and a diamond horseshoe pin at her neck, was asked if she usually entertained on such a grand scale.

"You've got to be kidding!" she said. "We have 12 grandchildren and it's usually with them." Then the Hunts entered the mammoth tent, which was cooled with 500 tons of portable air-conditioning. "We didn't want people to have heat prostration," Mrs. Hunt said.

The guests dined on beef tenderloin, pasta with red peppers and black olives, marinated asparagus and carrots and hot peach cobbler with homemade ice cream. The red and white wines were from California.

Bob Hope had a field day with jokes about Mr. Hunt's wealth and his unsuccessful attempt to corner the silver market in 1980. "He owns so much silver, he won't die, he'll just tarnish," Mr. Hope said.

That night former President Gerald Ford was the featured speaker at the GOP convention. CBS panned the arena. Party convention halls are always filled to capacity. It was a third empty. A perplexed Bob Schieffer asked Ed Bradley where everyone was. "I heard there's a big party at Bunker Hunt's ranch tonight," Bradley replied. It wasn't just convention-eers who had bailed. It was the press itself. "I had to babysit one hundred seventy-five reporters and twenty-six cameras," recalls Shirley. It was so jammed, "I was wedged between Bob Schieffer and Maria Shriver, and she was yelling, 'Gangbang! Gangbang!'"

It was a smashing success.

Attendees didn't have a good time—they had a very good time. Too good a time, it turns out. This was *the* party. The next morning we had a serious conference planned for those who wanted to hear serious things from the likes of Gramm and Heston. We'd invited all of the attendees and had taken RSVPs totaling some 360 guests. The morning of the Texas Gala we'd reconfirmed them all. But that was before the party. The morning after the Texas Gala only fifty-six showed up.

One fellow recounted his wife's reaction to the event and summed it all up, albeit a tad irreverently: "The Bob Hope event was the most fun she had ever had with her pants on." The gala netted well over a million dollars for our coffers, more than five times what we'd projected. Thank God for that. Two weeks later the bottom would fall out from under NCPAC.

For the uninitiated, let me explain the process of direct mail prospecting because it's important to the narrative. To test the strength of a fundraising appeal, an organization typically rents and mails five thousand names from each of five other organizations' donor files. The purpose is not to make money. It's to gain names that will provide funding from subsequent appeals.

Back then (industry rules have changed over time) a test was considered a success if the list mailed broke even. What followed was the 5/25 rule: go deeper into the file, but do so carefully. Now you mailed 25,000 names from that specific donor file, but no more. If *that* mailing was successful, then you knew you had a homer and could consider mailing that organization's entire file. Concurrently you would be testing the same letter with new lists from other groups. By the same token, if a letter failed to break even with one list, that list was avoided in the future. In short, it could go from one extreme to the other. The goal was to raise as much, or lose as little as possible.

Terry had tested a direct mail piece a few weeks before the GOP convention, and the results were phenomenal. Every list fared well.

Indeed every list tested had made an eye-opening profit. It spoke to the possibility of record-smashing income with an ambitious rollout. The experts running our direct mail operation proposed the ultimate: Forget the 5/25 rule. Mail virtually every known conservative donor in America. The costs alone would be in the millions of dollars, but based on test projections we'd get our money back and then a lot more. Even better, we'd have potentially hundreds of thousands of new supporters to bankroll us for years to come. Visions of sugar plums.

Leif Noren, now NCPAC's treasurer, and I argued passionately against this. We had only a few hundred thousand dollars in the bank—Terry was always spending—and if something went wrong, it could spell disaster. But the vendors carried the day. Terry gave the green light.

Millions of fundraising appeals hit the mailboxes a week after the convention. Two weeks later Terry walked into my office, closed the door, and slumped into a chair. He was pale. The millions of dollars anticipated never arrived. The mailing lost $4.5 million. Our worst fears were realized. NCPAC was broke.

Polling numbers explained the catastrophe. When the test solicitations had hit mailboxes, Reagan was actually losing to Walter Mondale. Donors were worried and eager to open their checkbooks to save the Gipper. But the GOP convention had given the Reagan campaign rocket fuel, and he surged to a twenty-six-point lead. When our multimillion-dollar mailing landed in donors' mailboxes, they were now quite content and feeling no need to dig deeper. Reagan streaked to a historic forty-nine-state landslide. We limped over the finish line drowning in red ink.

Something else was happening. Terry was becoming increasingly ill.

We began noticing the decline two years earlier. From time to time Terry would find himself dragging, as if with an unrelenting flu. He'd go to the doctors and return with the news that there was no news. They couldn't pinpoint the problem. He was on a strict exercise and diet regimen, but that wasn't helping either. His condition worsened. I knew it was serious when we traveled to Kansas City for a fundraising event. Always fluent and ebullient in his presentations, Terry inexplicably stumbled. When it was over Terry looked visibly shaken. I asked him if he was okay.

He was not. "I went blind."

In the middle of his speech he'd temporarily lost his eyesight. We chalked it up to physical exhaustion and finally convinced him to take a vacation. A couple of weeks later he returned, but his situation was unchanged.

On a separate track there was another issue that threatened the well-being of the organization. Rumors were floating about, some credible enough that the press was reporting them, that Terry was gay. If true, this could prove calamitous for NCPAC. Any homosexual conservative leader would have a media bull's-eye on his back, not because he was gay, but because of the presumption that he was a hypocrite.

Except he wasn't. Terry openly fought the gay rights movement because he genuinely opposed it. Terry was a radical libertarian. He despised the intrusive nature of the federal government, and with the exception of the unborn, he felt that no element in society had any "rights" deserving of federal action. This included gay rights. He'd told me he'd attended a meeting of the gay organization Log Cabin Republicans and shocked them by denouncing their gay rights agenda. In fact, he made me attend a meeting in Dallas with a gay father-son tandem—try to fathom that one—at their gaudily decorated apartment. They represented a large group of well-heeled potential funders and promised substantial bling—if only

Terry would embrace their gay rights agenda. He'd made me join him so I could witness his denunciation and refusal to accept their offer.

That said, being one of the best-known leaders of the traditional values movement left Terry particularly vulnerable. At this time, too, less than forty years ago, most movement leaders and even more donors would desert Terry if the rumors proved true.

We never put two and two together. AIDS would not hit the public consciousness hard until the death of Rock Hudson in 1986. AIDS was the scarlet letter signifying deviancy. It was impossible to picture Terry this way. There was no evidence, only gossip about Terry's alleged homo-sexuality. Besides, so little was known about AIDS that few could readily discern its warning signs.

In late 1985 Terry called Leif and me into his office. He swore us to secrecy. Not even his own family knew what he was going to tell us, and it needed to remain that way: he was dying. The cause was still unknown, he explained, but the symptoms were such that his body was no longer producing white blood cells to combat his mystery illness. He was defenseless.

He had two requests to make of us. The first was that I personally break the news to my uncle, Bill Buckley. Terry considered Bill the godfather of the movement and as such Terry felt he deserved to know. But no one else.

I called Bill, and he invited me to lunch at his home in Stamford, Connecticut. I broke the news during the meal. Well-grounded in the New York arts scene and not one to pull punches, Aunt Pat homed in immediately. "Is it AIDS?" Of course not, I answered honestly. The illness was inexplicable. Bill asked me to convey his grief and his willingness to do whatever Terry asked of him. I left, but not before reminding them that our discussion was had in utter confidence.

Back in my home that night, I got a call. Terry's brother Tony Dolan was on the line. He was beyond furious. He was cooking at his grill, he explained, when Bill called—Bill and Tony were very close—expressing his sorrow at the news of Terry's impending death and his willingness to help. Tony wanted to know what in the multiple-expletives-deleted I was doing telling Bill his brother was dying. I forget how I answered, but I remember him slamming down the phone before I finished. Can you blame him? It was a helluva way for a brother to get the news. Years later I shared this story with my mother, the sibling closest to Bill. She laughed in horror. "Honey, you didn't know? Tio [our nickname for Uncle Bill] could never hold a secret!"

For his second request, Terry wanted us, Leif, really, to oversee a search committee whose mission was to find his successor. Leif cast his net widely, but there was only one serious bite. Former Delaware governor Pete du Pont was interested, but ultimately our debt was too off-putting. In the spring of 1986 we advised Terry it was time for him to office out of his home and that jointly we'd run the ship of state in his absence. I'd assume the title of president and manage the programs, and Leif would become the executive director and control the finances. Terry would remain the chairman of NCPAC. We'd come to his home to brief him weekly on our activities. We felt it important for him to keep an emotional bond to the organization. He agreed to our unorthodox proposition.

During the first few weeks apart, we communicated regularly about most every facet of the operation. All the while he spoke openly of his impending death, even joking about it from time to time. I asked him where he wanted to be buried. "On the Washington Mall," he laughed, "facing the Capitol, with my hand coming out of the dirt giving Congress the middle finger."

What I'll never forget was his fundraising instruction. He wished for our direct mail agency to draft a letter for his signature telling our donors he was dying, and please send money. I could not believe my ears. Had I just heard correctly? He read my face and started chuckling with his Cheshire Cat look. "Well, I *am* dying and we do need money." To the end, Terry was always confident, always bold.

I agreed to do as he asked, and a week later I delivered the draft, penned by a writer who told me he never had, and never again would, write in the persona of a dying man. Terry read it over and tossed it back to me. "What a pussy. He's being way too nice! I'm going to be dead! Just say so!" He was smiling again. I took it back but in return handed him a voice recorder. I wanted him to tape a similar message, now in his own words. It was my intention to make copies of it and circulate it to our major donors after his death.

A week later we returned, now with the "Dammit-I'm-dying-send-some-damn-money!" draft. He approved. I asked for the tape. Terry's disposition changed. He hesitated, then shook his head slowly and sadly. "I just couldn't do it." His verve was gone. That's the moment it hit. Terry really was dying.

For as long as we could, Leif and I visited him weekly. Other than immediate family members, we were the only ones given the privilege. Having done so, I became a witness to a powerful spiritual transformation. Terry had always been a paradox: a practicing Catholic who attended daily Mass but a fierce libertarian who engaged in gay sex. Like all of mankind to one degree or another, Terry had his private demons. In a transitional age, his were just more obvious.

A kindly Dominican monk ministered to Terry regularly and toward the end, daily. Terry was now bedridden. Every week we'd arrive at the house, and his mother would let us in. We'd inquire as to his condition, and every time she answered, "Terry is much better." But he wasn't. He'd always been slender but now was increasingly gaunt and ghostly and ultimately emaciated. The disease was destroying him. He no longer was interested in politics. Instead he asked about the well-being of others. He spoke of God. He was increasingly quiet, listening to us speak softly with his father, who lay at his side on the bed running his hand softly through Terry's hair. We spoke in hushed tones, except on the quarter hour when a little alarm on his watch would beep. He'd raise his hand weakly asking for silence and slowly mouth a Hail Mary.

John T. ("Terry") Dolan died on the final day of 1986. He was thirty-six years old.

HOW TO SHOOT COMMERCIALS (AND NOT PEOPLE) DURING A WAR

1. Preparation

It was the spring of 1987, and Ronald Reagan needed money, specifically $20 million from Congress. By today's standards such a request would constitute an asterisk on a footnote in an appropriations bill. Nancy Pelosi could find that much while still getting her hair done.

The Marxist Sandinista regime in Nicaragua was becoming increasingly bellicose toward the United States to the point of inviting Cuban and Soviet military advisors, a direct challenge to the Monroe Doctrine. Opposing the Sandinistas were the Contras, an underfunded counterrevolutionary force. The debate raging in Washington was nearly as intense as the war in Central America. Supporting the Sandinistas, actively or passively, were the likes of Speaker Tip O'Neill and Majority Leader Jim Wright in the House, and in the Senate, Ted Kennedy, Alan Cranston, and the perpetually obnoxious Lowell Weicker. The Sandinistas could also count on the beautiful people in Manhattan, ignorant nuns in the Catholic Church, idiots in Hollywood, fellow travelers in the news media, and aging leftovers from the hippie generation—in short, anti-anti-communist America. The far left was glorifying the noble struggle of the proletariat in Nicaragua while fawning over their leader, Daniel Ortega. Their adoration recalled the welcome afforded Fidel Castro a generation before. And why not? Both were communist thugs running banana republics, blaming America for all the disastrous consequences of their actions, much to the delight of the "Blame America" crowd here at home.

Ronald Reagan and his conservative supporters were backing the "freedom fighters," as he dubbed the good guys. The Contras' political leader was Adolfo Calero. The military was commanded by General Enrique Bermúdez. "Military" was a bit of a stretch. There were some seventeen thousand peasants under arms living in the swampy jungles of southern Honduras. The goal was to increase the number to thirty thousand. "Under arms" was also questionable. The Contras had miscellaneous small arms and a handful of new Stinger missiles, the latter to defend against the devastatingly powerful Soviet Hind helicopters roaming the skies. That was pretty much it.

They had a helicopter too.

The Contra cause was kept alive by the largesse of some wealthy Americans. Calero was traveling around the country recruiting men like Spitz Channell (for whom I worked at NCPAC, and who later worked for me), General Jack Singlaub, and a fellow named Lt. Col. Oliver North, who kept conservative leaders privately apprised of the situation in this country while also doing some stuff quietly with Iran. I knew many of the men and women helping bankroll the effort. All were patriots.

Perhaps the liveliest was Ellen Garwood, a feisty and wealthy philanthropist from a prominent family in Austin, Texas. This diminutive octogenarian hated communists, pure and simple, and made no apologies for it. When the Iran Contra story broke, and she was called to testify before Congress about her participation in this cause, her family was rightfully concerned. Not Ellen. I asked her about her upcoming appearance, offering to help shield her from the Beltway piranhas, but she was all in.

She looked me right in the eyes and said with steely resolve, "I want to testify!" A true Texan. She'd given the Contras a pile of cash with which they bought a dilapidated Vietnam War-era helicopter which was refurbished and then re-named the "Lady Ellen." The Lady Ellen roamed only when capable of flying, which wasn't that often. Her job was to shuttle Contra leaders and their guests from one location to the next.

The Contras needed humanitarian assistance as much as they needed weapons. The freedom fighters were on the brink of collapse when Reagan appealed to Congress for the $20 million. If this aid could be delivered, the anti-communists could live to fight another day. Without the money and a clear commitment from Washington that the US was firmly behind them, the Contras were finished. By themselves the Sandinistas posed no threat to anyone outside their borders, but they had no intention of keeping to themselves. They were openly inviting the Soviet military, along with their Cuban underlings, to build bases and establish their long-sought toehold in Central America. That was a concern of monumental proportions. What better way to solve that problem than by invoking the Monroe Doctrine and fueling a civil war inside that country?

The Reagan people believed that the Monroe Doctrine was now more critically important than ever. The anti-anti-communists were equally committed to the proposition that the Contras were nothing more than a terrorist rabble committed to overthrowing the noble Sandinistas. The Reaganites wanted Ortega gone, but leftist Democrats controlled the purse strings in Congress and were solidly in the "No way José" camp.

Only a wave of public opinion could sway the more moderate "Blue Dog" Democrats to join the Reagan camp. But public opinion was being pushed in the opposite direction. The coverage from the American news media was decidedly and unsurprisingly hostile to the freedom fighters' cause, siding firmly with their leftist allies in Congress and giving the "terrorist" label oxygen whenever possible. That's where we came in. Our job was to offset their dishonesty.

I decided to use the National Conservative Foundation as our vehicle. I was the executive director of NCF. How I came into that position was another Terry Dolan special.

We need to back up four years, to 1983.

I was in my office one day when Terry burst in, furious. Terry was seldom angry, and until this moment he'd never been upset with me, but on this morning he barged in waving a small stack of financial forms.

"What have you done? NCF is broke! I can't believe you let this happen!"

As opposed to NCPAC, which was primarily concerned with federal elections, NCF was a tax-deductible foundation focused more on educational matters, except now NCF couldn't be because apparently it was busted. Terry pointed to the financial reports. The numbers were alarming. There was virtually no cash in the bank. It was in the red in direct mail, and there was no income coming in from the major donor fundraising arena, my specialty at the time. NCF wasn't just taking on water. It was sinking.

I looked at him quizzically. "Why are you looking at me?" "Because you're the executive director! This was your responsibility!"

I knew Terry better than anyone there. I knew this was going to be good.

"I am?"

"Well of *course* you…." and then his voice trailed off. At once his angry tenor softened, first in confusion, then doubt, then embarrassment.

"You mean I didn't tell you?"

I slowly shook my head, smiling. This was spectacularly disorganized Terry at his finest.

I asked when this vaunted title had been bestowed on me, and better yet, why.

So he told me. Terry Dolan was a founding member of the Council for National Policy, a rather secretive gathering of several hundred national conservative leaders of all stripes, except most were traditionalists, and they were at war with the libertarians. Though Terry supported virtually every social issue on the right, the CNP traditionalists distrusted Terry's libertarian leanings, and more than one was suspicious of his purported homosexual lifestyle. Although no one was willing to challenge him—Terry was a force of nature when provoked—they sure as hell didn't want him to have backup, which they assumed I'd be when he nominated me for membership in the organization. The old CNP hands rationalized their opposition to me by claiming that since the bylaws forbade any fund-raising, they also forbade any fundraisers. And so they voted me down.

My rejection predictably got Terry's dander up. What followed was a furious debate. I was told later by one participant that mine was the most hotly debated nomination to date. Terry finally found a way around his critics. He announced to the membership that I was no longer to be considered the national finance director of NCPAC. I was now presented for membership as executive director of the National Conservative Foundation. With that, their argument was neutered. The opposition collapsed, and I was in.

Except he'd forgotten to tell me.

Terry's embarrassment lasted only a moment. Now that it was established that I was the executive director at the NCF, he placed the depressing financial report on my desk, well satisfied he'd successfully passed the buck, and I'd now have to handle the crisis (which eventually I did).

I had one more question to ask him. "Exactly how much were you paying me for this?"

Now it was Terry's turn to smile. "You never asked for anything!" Out the door he went.

Three years later Terry had succumbed to his illness. We were now into the spring of 1987. Leif Noren and I were running NCPAC jointly, and I had sole control of NCF. I had the foundation back in the black financially, even if just a bit, but enough to run an advertising campaign to help the Contras.

Now to put together the campaign. I'm tickled that at times like this everyone calls himself a producer. I qualified, I supposed. I was putting the operation together, finding those to create the commercial while iden-tifying the agency that would place the ads. In principle, as the producer I'd have the power to tweak things on both the creative and placement ends, except that back then I had no expertise with either. I'd need experts to help with both. The first order of business would be the production of the ads.

Who to make them? Over the years at NCPAC we'd worked with several television production firms in the Washington, DC, area and as a result I felt any one of them would give me favorable rates. No such luck. When I called, all of them wanted to charge me double their normal rates because we were going into a war zone. I couldn't afford that. So I threw a Hail Mary pass. I called Mark Barnes, a man I'd come to know over the years, and with whom I'd established a friendship. But he was on the other end of the country, then deeply immersed in California politics. I knew getting him was a long shot at best.

"Are you up for an adventure?" I asked. "I want to do some ads to help Reagan with the Contras and want to shoot them in Nicaragua. To save you the trouble of asking, no, I can't afford to pay war wages."

I expected either the perfunctory, "Sorry, can't," or else a pregnant pause followed by a long list of questions. I'd seen Mark in action before. He was a perfectionist who left no detail to chance, but in this he didn't hesitate for a moment.

"Sure."

"Sure, what?"

"Sure."

I should have seen it coming. Mark hated communists, was an adventurer, liked a challenge, and knew instinctively we were going to have fun. He didn't even ask what I was willing to pay.

Now it was my turn to pause, unsure what to say next. Mark bailed me out. "When are we leaving?"

A few words about Mark because you need to understand this unique character. I met Mark in 1980, at the start of NCPAC's independent expenditure campaign for Ronald Reagan.

This short and portly pipe smoker exuded an air of scorn bordering on contempt, at least to those who didn't know otherwise. In fact, the cynic was just a role he played. How he could stay in character was a mystery. In reality, he was affable and kind to a fault, with a tremendous sense of humor to boot. He had a zinging wit to match his irreverent sense of humor. Political incorrectness was his signature. Instead of asking a pregnant lady when she was due, he'd inquire nonchalantly, "When are you calving?"

He could also be very direct. In 1992, I finally convinced Bay Buchanan to talk to him about producing commercials for her brother Pat's presidential campaign. She instructed me to call him so he could make his pitch to her. I did as asked. His response was unexpected but should not have been. "Tell Bay she can make *her* pitch to *me*." Needless to say that idea went nowhere.

When it came to his craft, Mark was the consummate professional. I'd watch him do thirty takes of a thirty-second commercial I'd requested, admonishing me to "Be quiet!" when, hearing the cash register in my head, I had the nerve to ask why we couldn't settle on take fourteen.

In 1980 Terry needed him to produce a thirty-minute documentary—right now—and invoked his friend's commitment to the cause. Mark was on a plane from the West Coast that night. His documentary was completed in just a handful of days and would win the Pollie Award for the best political documentary that year. He was that good.

I should have known to expect that reaction again. A few days later Mark called. His team was ready. He would serve as director. He'd recruited Larry Cushman to be our cameraman. Larry was then an independent contractor specializing in direct response infomercials. Larry was not just good at his craft, he was enthusiastic and committed, and we became instant friends. Finally, there was John Carvelli, then still in college. John would be our sound man, pack mule, soul mate, and most importantly, entertainment. What I brought to the table was my Spanish. My job was narration and logistics, before, during, and post production. It was my responsibility to map out the campaign, land the interviews, serve as translator, and then deal with the myriad of problems one encounters with this kind of shoot, especially in a third world country at war with itself.

We discussed our options and decided we'd first go to Nicaragua to interview Sandinista leaders and gather footage of the nation's growing squalor. Then we would make our way into the Contra camps in Honduras to talk to the rebels.

2. The Sandinistas

For help with the first leg I made some phone calls to the White House, which in turn led to phone calls with the State Department, which led to phone calls with the American embassy in Managua, which led to phone calls back to me to discuss and arrange interviews.

We were advised to be careful. No surprise there. Apparently, communists don't cotton to folks who come to their country to create ads designed to topple them from power. We would be seen as adversaries if we arrived with cameras but without the sponsorship of some western fellow travelers or, better yet, an invitation from the Sandinistas themselves.

How to thread this needle? How to convince the Sandinistas of our good intentions when our intentions were anything but? After much back and forth we decided to go as fellow travelers—American journalists. We'd have to fake our credentials, hoping they'd never be checked, since no journalists were welcome in Nicaragua without the government's permission.

Larry's wife, Paula, was tasked with creating the false media credentials. Each of us had his black and white picture taken and sent to her. Paula worked her magic and presto! The credentials almost convinced me that we were officially representing that world-renowned news service, "Newswatch."

Larry and Mark assembled all the equipment necessary for the adventure and on the appointed day met John and me at the Miami airport where we had dinner and drinks and became acquainted. Early the following morning we were en route to Managua. Its airport was pretty much as expected: dirty, disheveled, depressing, and dysfunctional. There were no shops, no restaurants, no bars—just a dimly lit, dilapidated walkway taking us to the baggage area. The airport was eerily quiet. Very few people could afford, or were allowed, to fly out of the country. Even fewer wanted to fly in. Even so, there were plenty of *soldados* with standard commie AK-47s.

When our bags were brought out, we saw the damage immediately. The cases were scratched and dented. Somewhere between the airplane and the baggage area someone or some people had obviously slammed the equipment onto the pavement. We weren't in Kansas anymore. We opened the battered cases fearing the worst, but damn if they didn't live up to their reputation for indestructibility. The camera was still intact and functional, and our project was still alive.

The only place less inviting than a communist third world country is a communist third world Central American country. The heat and humidity—especially the humidity—are oppressive in Nicaragua. I've been there several times. I don't care what anyone says. There is no one season preferable to any other. They are all equally miserable. The weather was a perfect complement to the condition of the nation's capital. This was no ordinary struggling third world country. We were looking at a nation falling apart.

I'm sure some neighborhoods were elegant, but they were reserved for the elite. This certainly was not our destination. We stayed in real Managua.

Most buildings were shacks, one-story structures with unfinished or broken wood or brick siding, most without windows, and all of them with dilapidated, bent metal roofs. Some didn't even have that. There were almost no trees, only shrubs. Virtually no grass, only dirt. No sidewalks, only cracked streets. One building after another was damaged or destroyed, by natural disaster, man-made violence, or just neglect, and left to rot.

The Old Cathedral of Managua was badly damaged, first by a volcanic eruption in 1931, but more recently by a Sandinista attack. There were almost no street signs. Ask directions and you'd be instructed to take a right at the green shack with the blue tin roof or a left at the red broken fence. And then there were the cars. Most every car we witnessed on this visit—we made it a point to check them all—was visibly damaged some-where. Most had dents and scrapes. Many had broken windows covered by plastic. More than a few coughed noxious gases from busted lifters. Others roared because of missing mufflers. Most had some sort of rope holding something together, a door, a window, the hood, the trunk, you name it. Other than the party leadership, no one could afford anything approaching new. So what was already damaged became more dilapidated by the day.

We caught a cab—no taxi was undamaged either—and headed to the only vestige of hospitality in the entire city, The Hotel InterContinental.

Few other buildings in the capital city could boast of modern amenities like air conditioning, elevators and, most importantly, cable TV. That said, the phones worked only sporadically, the tap water was undrinkable, and the food was barely edible. On the positive side the hotel had a pretty good bar. Plus, with the Sandinistas controlling the national news organizations, only at the Hotel InterContinental could we *extranjeros* get a peek into the outside world and that through CNN.

After unpacking and not enjoying a meal, we headed out for our first assignment: collecting footage of this mess of a city. We piled into a taxi with our equipment, and off we went. We had specific destinations in mind, but first we just wanted to drive around to see what might be worthy of recording. It took only a minute to figure out the driver was a government informant. If there's one thing you'll learn from these despotic regimes it's that they have clumsy government agents. The conversation went something like this:

"We'd like to have you just drive us around the city, *por favor*."

"*Si, señor*. And can I ask where?"

"Just around the city. We'd like to get to know it."

"Of course, señor. And might I ask…why?"

"We just want to get some footage."

"Very good, señor. And can I inquire…for whom?"

"How about we go back to the hotel?"

The second cab driver was just as obvious. But Government Agent #2 preferred the public relations strategy. After we told him of our desires, he purposely headed to any place that might offer even the slightest opportunity for positive spin. His job was to praise everything as a testimony to the historic triumph of the Sandinista revolution and its dazzling leader, *el Presidente* Daniel Ortega. We stopped at a few recommended spots that must have pleased Government Agent #2 to no end.

At one site, we filmed a monument dedicated to "the true heroes of the revolution." It featured an imposing statue of an Adonis-like Sandinista soldier, holding high his trusty rifle in triumph. The driver next took us to a schoolyard where grade school children, dressed in uniforms featuring the ubiquitous colors of the revolution—red for blood and black for death—marched and yelled Marxist, anti-US slogans they couldn't understand, under the stony gaze of their female minder. We then directed him to the one specific destination on *our* itinerary that day.

The very name "El Chipote" struck fear in families all over the country. It was the national dungeon where the Sandinistas held their political prisoners. Eerily it was belowground in the city. Although somewhere below our feet, we had no idea of its exact size or its population or the sentences being served by its prisoners. Neither did our driver. Neither did anyone who didn't have to know. But the prisoners had a name, a unique and frightening name, one that spoke to the brutality of the Sandinista regime. They were *los desaparecidos*, "the disappeared ones." These were the men and boys snatched off the streets, or pulled out of homes, or caught hiding in the jungles. They were accused of sedition, and if not shot on sight, were hauled away, many never to be seen again. Brutalized, tortured, executed—no one knew, but the stories of horrific treatment flew among the *campesinos*. The Sandinistas had every reason for keeping the prison out of sight, even denying its existence.

When we told our driver we wanted to be taken to El Chipote and at once, his pleasant demeanor disappeared, replaced by a look of pure fear. "No, no," he said in an earnest, low voice, his head shaking for emphasis. "This cannot be done." But he'd just admitted he knew of its existence, and we knew at once that he had no desire to take us anywhere near there. We settled the matter when we convinced him to drop us off far enough away that he wouldn't be seen.

The entrance was unmarked and had some sort of gate, locked of course. We approached it and began filming and immediately were stopped by three soldiers. I don't know where they were hiding. I just knew they were pointing very nasty looking AK-47s at us. "*Párense!*" they barked. They demanded to know what we were doing.

But first they angrily ordered Larry to turn off his camera. Larry knew full well what they wanted because of their hand gestures and immediately took his eyes from the lens to look at them, raising his left hand to convey, *Yes, señor, of course. As you instruct.*

Larry had real *cojones*. John, Mark, and I all noticed what these three commandants were too ignorant to see. The camera was still resting on his shoulder, and the red "record" light was still on. The shot of Sandinista goons pointing weapons at Americans would become a tasty ingredient in the final ad cut.

Now to answer for ourselves. The memory banks are a bit fuzzy, but I have to think our story had been rehearsed beforehand. Pointing to our credentials, I explained in purposely fractured Spanglish, *señores*, that we were a film crew from "EhnewseWatch" working for "el Señor Tohm Brookah" from "Las Noticias NBC, a companía muy, muy importante," so "importante" in fact that "el Señor Brookah" was coming the following week for an interview with "el presidente" himself to mark the anniversary of the Sandinista revolution. "Señor Tohm Brookah" had instructed us to go about town gathering footage. "Forgive us, *señores*, if we have done something wrong."

It worked like a charm. They were not about to interfere with a news crew gathering footage in Managua for a story about el presidente. They lowered their weapons. Still, they said, this was a restricted area, and instructed us to leave.

By this time Carvelli had returned. Here was another man with his own set of cojones. While our soliloquy was taking place, John had slipped away with his photo camera and gone through the bushes to the entrance to El Chipote. We may not have gotten video footage, but we did get some photographs. Good enough.

We returned to the Hotel InterContinental, happy to rid ourselves of our driver. The feeling must have been mutual. We called the American embassy, and a new driver was promised, one we could trust.

The following morning Luis arrived. He charged a small fortune, the going price for trust. The first order of business after breakfast was the gathering of more B-roll footage. We hit pay dirt immediately, figuratively and literally. Our first destination was the local market. It was the pure essence of wretched poverty. It had rained the night before so the dirt street was now black mud. As Larry recalled the scene in a recent conversation: "Hot, humid, filthy dogs that shouldn't be around, flies on the little kids—not a good situation, truly third world." It's too bad Larry's camera couldn't record the smell. What a stench! It smelled as bad as the raw sewage looked. Peasants were kneeling on old sheets draped on the ground to protect themselves from the stinky mud. On those sheets they sold their wares, wares defined as anything they could find to sell. A broken toy. A broken plate. A pair of worn shoes. One man was selling a single worn shoe. The most pathetic item I found was a rusted, bent door hinge sold by a woman equally old and tragically broken. It was all she had to offer.

Sell for what? The national currency was the *córdoba*, and nobody wanted them. The inflation rate was Venezuela-like, daily streaking toward the heavens. Those burdened with córdobas carried wads of paper currency, literally in the tens of thousands, for the simplest of purchases. It was basically worthless currency. They'd have taken Confederate money were it offered.

We didn't interview anyone. The pictures told the story better. We were happy to leave this human tragedy, heartbroken for those condemned to live out their lives in this picture postcard of communism, powerless—then—to do anything about it.

Our second stop was as comedic as the first was depressing. The local supermarket was a state-run enterprise designed to project the prosperity generated by the Sandinista experiment. Fail. It was a warehouse held together by Scotch tape. The paint was peeled, the sign was missing letters, and like everywhere else, there was filth. But it was the inside that told the real story, and again we hit pay dirt.

There was no air conditioning, of course, and even with the door open it was hotter and more humid than outside. One glance at the shelves, and Larry's video light turned red. In a word, the store was selling what was available—that day. And that day little was available other than paper towels—row after row of them. There was a second item, maybe a third, and that was that. Every other shelf was empty except for the one closest to the door. It was packed with what every starving peasant would want: book after book, pamphlet after pamphlet, on Marx, Marxism, communist struggles and, naturally, communist victories. These were not new publications.

They were worn and in varying stages of decomposition. They'd obviously sat on these shelves, and other shelves, for a long, long time.

We were having a grand time with the videotaping, but we felt hostile eyes following us as we filmed, so we tried to behave. But when we arrived at the box Marxist book bazaar, we could no longer hold back and started laughing. That's when the angry government store manager threw us out. But we had what we wanted.

The third stop was an interview with Enrique Sotelo Borgen. He'd gained a level of infamy for providing legal support for CIA agent Eugene Hasenfus, who was shot down over Nicaragua and accused of helping the Contras, which one hopes was true. Don Enrique was considered one of the top legal authorities in Nicaragua, and he was now representing innumerable victims of this despotic regime, vainly attempting to bring legal pressure to bear on a government that ruled with an iron fist indifferent to the rule of law. His real office had been burned to the ground. His associates and he were now working out of the remnants of an open-air shack with a makeshift tarp to protect it from the omnipresent tropical sun and rainstorms. He had his desk and a chair, and all around his feet were piles of files in withered old folders, the caseloads of prisoners whose whereabouts were unknown, sentenced to punishments undetermined for crimes unclear, with every step adjudicated by ruthless tyrants. Yet this attorney soldiered on, making as public a statement as he could that the rule of law must be restored. Supporters milled about the shack, doing nothing, really. They were there perhaps because this man emitted a nobility and courage that were astounding. He was surrounded by doomed appeals, hoping against hope for success, and knowing that success, any success on his part, might lead to the crack-up of this despotic regime. His death sentence would come before they'd allow that.

Don Enrique was equally courageous in his interview, unambiguously denouncing the military regime while eloquently extolling his vision for the return to the rule of law. We asked him for a favor. Could he assemble some of the *madres de los desaparecidos* for us to interview? These were the mothers—and wives, and sisters, and children—of the men suffering underground, if not already dead. He balked at first and explained this could put them in real danger. Might he just approach them with our request? He agreed to make the inquiries but could make no promises. If he succeeded, he'd send a message with the time and location. But we'd have to wait, possibly days. We accepted the terms.

Our final interview that day was with the moral leader of the Nicaraguan people, Cardinal Miguel Obando y Bravo. A large man with piercing eyes and deep voice, Obando y Bravo projected the strength of a Catholic Church led by the Vicar of Christ who, as archbishop of Krakow, had led his people in Poland against an oppressive communist regime. Now as bishop of Rome he was rallying the world against Marxist totalitarianism. For his efforts he would come within a whisker of death by assassination, and for his godliness would become Saint John Paul II. Cardinal Obando y Bravo was his able lieutenant in Nicaragua, both a spiritual leader and the chief representative of the people.

Which is not to say that Obando had always been on the side of the angels. He was a fierce opponent of the Anastasio Somoza regime in the 1970s, largely considered corrupt. When the leftist Sandinistas launched an armed insurrection, he first served as an intermediary between the two camps and ultimately threw his weight behind the Sandinistas, becoming in the eyes of the Somoza regime, "Comandante Miguel."

A half decade later he was the moral face of the new opposition against this new dictatorship. His offices were simple, but compared to what we'd just been through, they were regal. He greeted us graciously. Compared to Don Enrique, he was more diplomatic. While also denouncing the ruling regime, the cardinal knew anything he said, once made public, could lead to unintended consequences in his ongoing negotiations with Ortega. He was careful but unequivocal. "We're suffering the consequence of maintaining our identity. We've lost seventeen priests. Our printing presses and radio stations are closed, and our efforts to aid the poor have been stopped." Then he brought it home. "Only those totally aligned with the Sandinistas have religious freedom. Ask the Christians in the United States to pray for us."

It was a helluva way to end a day's filming.

Dinner (probably awful), drinks (probably too many), and bedtime for the married guys. Carvelli was a free man, so into the night he went with Luis. They went to his house and then to a massive club where, within moments, "There were women all around us," Carvelli laughs. He befriended one, and eventually they made their way back to the InterContinental. They—ahem—became more acquainted in the lobby, then took the elevator to his floor. There were two soldiers in the hallway. "They were waiting for us. They had to be following us. They took her away."

Day three arrived, and we wanted a change of pace. We headed outside the capital in search of footage. We chose the town of Masaya for no particular reason other than it was close enough to Managua that, should bad things happen, we wouldn't be too far away from US embassy protection, but we'd also be far enough away that we might find a different, more countrified setting. It was almost a big mistake for a reason never anticipated.

The weather on this day was more oppressively hot and humid than ever. It was a good old jungle sweat box. It took over an hour for our driver to get us there, and by the time we arrived our throats were parched, which was okay since we needed only stick our heads in a bar except… nothing was open. It was around 10:30 a.m., and apparently the Sandinistas deemed that too early for drinking establishments or restaurants. We cruised up and down the dusty little streets all the while becoming ever thirstier. It was more than discomfort. We were seriously dehydrated. Finally, we were rescued. We asked an old man standing on the street if he could point us to some establishment that might *por favor* have a cerveza. He studied us carefully then turned, unlocked the door, and motioned us inside to his bar.

Cold beer never tasted better. We were thirsty enough that cold gasoline might have tasted good too, but Victoria beer, naturally a fine offering, was spectacular that day. One beer wasn't enough. We asked for and were served a second round, a third round, and still our bodies craved more relief. All we did was sweat it out in the jungle heat. "That day I drank twenty bottles and never took a piss," said Larry.

We sat around a large table, and the old man joined us, bringing a bottle of rum and a glass for himself. He poured a generous serving and asked what brought us to this jungle hellhole. He spoke only broken English so I translated again. We were careful at first. You just didn't know who to trust. It was obvious he was thinking the same thing, but after about an hour of rum drinking that wasn't sweating out, our friend became increasingly open about his opposition to the Sandinistas. Mark saw the opportunity and through me asked if he'd consent to an interview. The man was feeling courageous enough to agree.

Larry and John set the equipment up, and the interview began in Spanish. Actually, it was just a chat since it was spontaneous. As will happen with some, the more this man drank, the better his English became, or so he thought as he tested a sentence here, a phrase there. Ultimately, he changed languages altogether. The old man and I talked about his life—where he grew up, what kind of family he had, and so on. He continued drinking his rum and I my beer, but as we proceeded an angry tone began to emerge as he became increasingly critical of the government, decrying what it had done to his poor nation and to his own family. I pointed to the wall where he had tacked up postcards depicting famous American landmarks—the Bay Bridge, the Statue of Liberty, the US Capitol, the Grand Canyon, and the like. I asked him why they were there.

That did it. He erupted. Those, he declared, were sites he'd always wanted to visit someday, and would have succeeded, but then the goddamn Sandinistas came, and the goddamn Sandinistas destroyed his country. "We used to have everything here! Peace! Money! We used to live good. Now we have just rice and beans."

I didn't need to ask any more questions. Our guest was emptying his soul and speaking for millions of his countrymen, telling us what no other strangers would have the courage to say. But suddenly he stopped in midsentence. The color drained from his face. He realized he'd gone too far.

At once he was dead sober and terrified. He wanted the camera turned off. "I might lose my business and my life if I answer any more questions. It's very dangerous! I hope I'm not talking too much because I'll get me in trouble." Larry shut the camera off; John lowered the boom mic. I shut my mouth. The interview was over.

But we needed this footage. We reminded this kind man of our mission and how the only way those bastards were ever going to be replaced was through a successful revolution, or the ballot box, and neither option would ever materialize unless the United States forced the issue. Mark came up with the solution. A disguise. We would cover his face and distort his voice in the final product. I explained the procedure to the old man, and asked him permission to use his interview provided we do this. We both knew that he had to trust us at our word. I asked for that faith. He paused, then nodded his approval. We thanked this very special fellow, bought some cold beers for the road, and left.

We did as we promised. In the commercial his face was screened and his voice distorted, and both gave even greater gravitas to his words. It would have been the perfect interview except in our relaxed state it hadn't occurred to us to clear the table of the two dozen or so empty beer bottles. The gravitas was diminished a bit.

We were back in our rooms by midafternoon decompressing when the messenger arrived. Las madres de los desaparecidos were assembled in a hidden location. Our lawyer had come through. Our driver was given directions and off we went.

We meandered through depressing neighborhoods with depressing sameness, one after another, decrepit metal shacks or brick boxes with tin roofs on dirty lots. Eventually we came across a blue metal shack with a silver tin roof, some sort of empty storage shed. They were inside, waiting.

The sun was bright so when we entered this unlit shed we were immediately blinded. It took a few minutes for our eyes to adjust, helped by faint natural sunlight coming in from the uneven metal slats otherwise known as a roof. The room was perhaps twelve foot by twelve foot with a dirt floor. Along three sides there were wooden benches. Sitting on the benches were about twenty women with a dozen or so little children in tow. They had come not just from Managua but from surrounding villages, summoned clandestinely by our lawyer friend. None moved or spoke a word; they just looked at us. The peasant women were dressed in worn, colorless frocks and dusty slippers, their feet dirty and their long hair tied from behind. All had ruddy features, their faces worn and sad. Some of the mothers were middle-aged and still strong, though missing teeth; others were old and tired, the gaps between surviving teeth more pronounced, their faces more lined and stooped. All stared at us silently in the dark, hopefully but warily, clutching their children. Said John, "It was the most vivid demonstration of sadness and fear I've ever seen." But they'd been asked to tell their stories, and that's what they were here to do.

We interviewed about a half dozen of them. Every story was shocking and sad, but when told by the mother of a victim, the stories reached a level of unexpected horror. Some of the men hauled away most certainly were from the opposition and were perhaps linked directly to the Contras, but the madres were not about to say so, and for understandable reasons. Other men were not, and their mothers were emphatic about that point. It just made no difference. In most cases the men had just disappeared, hauled away for questioning and, presumably, torture, then cast into the prison below. Joseph Stalin would have been proud of his Latin comrades.

More than one of the mothers was there to talk about a family member who had been killed by these butchers. I called on one woman who seemed eager to talk. She didn't wait for a question. As soon as Larry announced tape was rolling, she began. Mind you, there's a near 100 percent certainty this peasant had never participated in an interview in her entire life. She did not speak; she orated. She looked not at me but directly into the camera, addressing the audience on the other side of the lens. She was holding what looked like a textbook. She opened it to a certain dog-eared page and showed it to the camera. It featured a series of oblong, pointy symbols being used to show a variety of formulas.

"My son was a student in correspondence school," she explained, pointing to the symbols. "The secret police accused him of being a Contra. They said these were secret codes for rockets. One night at midnight they dragged him outside of our house and murdered him." Off camera she told me they later returned her son's corpse to the house and threw it at her feet.

One after another the stories came out. These women were frightened, almost without hope except for that brave lawyer championing their cause.

But nothing could prepare me for what happened during one of the interviews. While I was asking a question I felt a tug at my jeans. I looked down and found this mother's little boy, maybe five years old, looking up at me. He had the most beautiful blue eyes I've ever seen. "Are you the man who is going to bring my papa home?" I can't remember how I answered that little angel. How do you answer a question like that?

Thankfully, there was one anecdote that offset that heartbreaking moment. In the midst of one interview a typical tropical storm hit, the kind that brings violent torrents of rain, but just for a few minutes, just to make everything just a tad more humid. The rain splatting the roof sounded like machine gun fire, and water poured through the tin roof openings, causing some to scatter. We had to pause our taping. That's when the giant rat fell through the ceiling and crashed to the ground. With lightning speed but without showing a lick of emotion, one of the peasant women grabbed a stick and dispatched the rodent with a series of violent whacks. All the while the women seated around her didn't budge an inch, nor utter a word. This was just another day at the office for them.

This would become perhaps the strongest element in the final product, a scene featuring a panoramic shot of the interior of the shack, with las madres seated on the benches; that innocent child with the beautiful blue eyes; a little girl looking at the camera, her face tragic in her sadness; and the defiant woman holding the tattered textbook, telling her story. But no rat.

We had all the footage we needed, and it was time to leave this unholy city. The following morning, we checked out of our hotel before dawn, but not before we received one final dollop of corruption from this wretched government. Two little men met us at the counter wearing matching trench coats to demonstrate they were government agents. They looked ridiculous, like the characters in the old "Spy vs. Spy" comic strip. Using an officious-sounding staccato voice, one goon announced we had to pay the hotel "exit fee" of fifteen dollars apiece, US cash only, and to them personally. As we were forking over the sixty dollars I asked sarcastically if they provided receipts. "Of course!" he replied, tearing four from a roll in his pocket. We paid our hotel bills and walked out through the revolving doors, only to be met by two other goons wearing the same trench coats. "Receipts, please!" they ordered. A couple of hours later we were on a plane headed for Tegucigalpa, Honduras, and a rendezvous with the Contras.

3. The Contras

The trip had been arranged through Contra political leader Adolfo Calero. We caught a taxi and gave the address we'd been provided. Where were we headed? A secret Batcave hideaway? A *Narcos*-style compound with heavily armed bodyguards wearing sunglasses with reflecting lenses? That's just Hollywood; this was reality. We were dropped off in front of a row of one-story nondescript houses on a nondescript street in the middle of town. The doors were solid and locked. There were no guards posted anywhere. We knocked, the door opened, and we walked right into the foyer with heavy camera bags no one bothered to examine. A few unarmed aides were milling about. But for a scattering of chairs and a desk in the lobby, it was empty. Very disappointing.

We stated our business. An aide casually pointed to the empty chairs and told us to wait. Calero might be the political leader of the Contras, but this was Central America. And so we waited—for over two hours. Finally others joined us, media types from various locations, and when all was set, we were led outside. Four cars were waiting, engines running. We piled in, and off we went.

We drove about a half hour south of Tegucigalpa on a presentable paved road before turning right on an unmarked dirt road which soon led into the jungle. Once we went under the canopy, everything changed. The dirt road became a dirt path, and the deeper into the jungle we traveled, the more primitive it became. It was now no more than a bumpy path carved out by some Caterpillar tractor. There were divots a foot deep and dangerous rocks protruding from the ground. There were felled trees we drove over, or around, if possible. It was hours of uncomfortable (and for those of us cursed with bad backs, painful) jostling, up and down as we banged into and over everything Mother Nature had to throw at us. Six hours after we left Tegucigalpa we came to the crest of the hill where the canopy opened. Armed soldiers were milling about. There were also a handful of other military, some fair skinned, some black. They were each a foot taller, and at least fifty pounds heavier than the others, all chiseled muscle. Mean sons of bitches. These were the American "advisors."

There were five thousand freedom fighters occupying the side of the mountain. There was everything from army tents to makeshift huts. More than one consisted of four branches stuck in the ground and a plastic tarp for cover. We were given a VIP tent. It had three cots and a hammock. Somehow I got stuck with the hammock.

We walked about looking for some camera shots. That's when disaster struck. The camera had somehow broken on the ride. Larry furtively tried meatball surgery but to no avail. With help from the Contras, he managed to reach a repair shop in San Diego, but that, too, ended in failure. A new part was required, and God only knew if it might be found anywhere in Central America. We were fairly certain UPS didn't deliver to war zones in the middle of the Honduran jungle. We were sunk.

That is, until Providence came to our rescue. A Venezuelan press team was part of the entourage and came over inquiring about our plight. We quickly learned each had what the other needed. They had the camera equipment essential to our mission, but they hadn't arranged any interviews for this trip, and our dance card was filled with those. As a value added proposition, we also had all that footage from Managua. A deal was struck. They'd lend us their equipment, and when we were finished we'd deliver the subsequent raw footage as well as what we'd already shot. Our work continued; they were now on vacation (of sorts).

Almost immediately we came upon a man seated on the ground, surrounded by soldiers and shaking from head to toe. He was wearing a Sandinista uniform: a prisoner. We knew instinctively we were not to tape this. Carvelli recalls his thoughts that day: "I couldn't stop staring… something was wrong and they were going to kill him and this was war."

We were led to a makeshift wooden structure serving as the headquarters. Soldiers guarding the building eyed us warily. On the wall there were two posters, one calling for *Ojo!* and the demand that soldiers keep their eyes open for any spies in their midst. The second was a large photograph of the dreaded Soviet Hind helicopter which had recently been put into play by the Sandinista forces and was wreaking havoc on the Contras. We learned that the base had come under attack the month before, and there'd been a fierce firefight before the Contras finally repelled it. The photograph pinpointed the vulnerable areas on the helicopter that needed to be the targets of return fire.

In due course *El General* appeared. He was short, with a bit of a paunch, but that's not what grabbed our attention. Whereas the Contra soldiers were wearing old, ill-fitting US Army-issued fatigues, or just simple peasant wear, this man was impeccable in his attire. His military uniform was crisp and fit perfectly. He wore a revolver around his waist, and aviator glasses shielded his eyes. All he needed was a corncob pipe, and he'd win a General MacArthur look-alike contest. He'd assigned himself a bizarre *nom de guerre*, "Comandante 380." His aides stood behind him in deference; his bodyguards continued glaring at us.

I'd met Bermúdez at a private function back in the States (which is what led to this interview). After attempting and failing to exchange some pleasantries with this no-nonsense general ("So how's the war coming?" "And the family?") it was down to business. The general wanted to stand for the interview and pointed to the spot a few feet away. Larry and John positioned the equipment, and we began. It was almost comical. No matter what I asked, the answer was formal and a dramatic, pure Hispanic macho. He denounced *los comunistas* and called on the world to support *los campesinos* pining for *la libertad!* The answers were canned and came too naturally. You had the sense he'd delivered these words a thousand times before. That was fine. It was what we needed.

Bermúdez's public relations team had the next interview prepared. A young boy sat on the stump of a felled tree. His name was Jaime, we were told. The lad was about fourteen years old, but there was nothing juvenile about him. He wore a military uniform. He had his weapon at his side. He said nothing. And the eyes! He looked, said one of our guys, "like a legit gang member. He had the dead eyes of a life of violence." He stared at us, through us, past us. We meant nothing to him.

The aide explained why they wanted us to talk to this boy. When Jaime was ten years old, living in a little village, his uncle joined the Contras, disappearing into the relative safety of the jungle. Jaime was tasked with delivering messages from his father to his uncle, which he did until he was caught by the Sandinistas. At that tender age he was conscripted into the Sandinista army and sent to war. He had recently been liberated by the Contras during a battle, one of eight in which he'd participated.

The equipment was set up, and I asked questions but received only clipped sentences void of all emotion in return. We were looking into the soul of a boy who had been destroyed. He confirmed the story and condemned his captors. His words ultimately would serve as the sound bite for the ad. I asked if he'd been in battles. He nodded his head. I asked him if he'd shot anyone. He gave me no response, just looked right in my eyes. I had my answer. When we huddled later, and I translated for my team the answers he'd given, we concluded unanimously that this poor child had told the truth.

We had some downtime and then rejoined our hosts for dinner.

Which was unforgettable. We sat on benches in an open-air pavilion, we being General Bermúdez and a dozen or so handpicked guests, including translators for my team. Dangling light bulbs illuminated our gazebo. These were the only bright lights on the side of the mountain. It felt like summer camp in New Hampshire, just hotter. Soldiers served the dinner, and at once we could tell the dire straits of the freedom fighters. The best they could muster up for their general and his foreign guests were eggs and rice. The plates were army-issued, as were the well-worn tin cups for coffee. On the plus side, it was by far the most delicious coffee I've ever tasted. And why not? It had been plucked right from that hillside. If they have meals in heaven, the coffee will be on the dessert menu.

I caught its shadow in the corner of my eye. Attracted by the light, a bug flew in from the darkness over my left shoulder. Whatever the hell it was, it was massive, as big as a bat, with ugly, angry wings propelling its gigantic body. The damn thing might have chosen to buzz about the gazebo to frighten everyone, but it had other plans. Apparently, it, too, enjoyed fresh Honduran jungle coffee. It headed right for my cup, and I watched in horror as it literally splashed into it. The hot liquid did not kill the creature. It flopped around, which made the scene that much more memorable. I called one of the soldiers over, pointed to this pterodactyl, and asked, "Please, might I get another cup?" Mistake. Big mistake. The soldier looked at me with sheer contempt, grabbed the fouled cup, flung the UFO over the side and slammed it right in front of me. "What you theenk thees ees?" he spat out. "Da Heelton?"

During dinner we were the interviewees. There was no jocularity. Their military situation was precarious, and the Contras wanted to know the political mood in Washington. We really weren't much help because, though we knew the mood in Washington, it was impossible to predict which side would prevail. The meal concluded, we went our separate ways, our guys toward our tent, Bermúdez and his aides in another direction. We were told that for security reasons he slept in a different tent every night. Back in ours we chatted until one by one my friends fell asleep. For whatever reason I couldn't. After a few restless hours I left the tent to have a smoke. I walked aimlessly around the cluttered tents enjoying the moonlit night when I turned a corner only to have the world's most vicious dog lunge straight for my throat. Thank God his chain caught him in mid-flight and yanked the monster down to earth. I knew where Bermúdez was bunking that night.

The following morning the general departed for some undisclosed location but left behind the Contra air force for our use, which is to say, the Lady Ellen. On this day it operated just fine. There were a half dozen soldiers accompanying us, the fellow next to me playfully jabbing his pet crab attached to a string tied to his rifle, for no reason.

We lifted off and thum-thumped over dense jungle carpeting for about fifteen minutes before the jungle opened, and we dropped into the bank alongside the Coco River. We were on the border. The river was perhaps fifty yards wide. On the southern side the jungle reached to the edge of the water. That was Nicaragua, and presumably there were Sandinistas lurking within. We stood on the hardened mud on the Honduran side. Behind us was a steep hill. It was fascinating. Throughout the next hour, we kept identifying one, then another Contra soldier expertly camouflaged on that hill, dead still, menacing. It was "Where's Waldo?" in a war zone. The more of them we found, the happier we became.

This would be our final interview. As stated earlier, the most lethal weapon in the Sandinista arsenal was the Soviet Hind helicopter. It was fitted with the twin-barrel GSh-23V 23 mm cannon capable of firing up to thirty-six hundred rounds a minute. If you watched *Rambo* I or II, you'll recognize the beast. It was invincible against troops on the ground until the Reagan administration managed to get some Redeye missiles into the freedom fighters' hands. The Contra soldier we were set to interview was the fellow who had stood in that very river and shot down the first Hind helicopter, thus proving the weapon's effectiveness and the Contras' shot at winning with, of course, adequate funding.

I asked the soldier, and he told me his rather blasé story. He had a Redeye. He heard the helicopter approaching. He stood in the river and fired, and it came down, and that was pretty much it. Back in our hotel later I confided to Mark that I sensed there was something wrong here. Mark quietly nodded in agreement. The four of us sat down to watch the tape. "Pay attention to his eyes." Mark had nailed it. Every time I asked a salient question—say, "How close were you to it?"—his eyes shifted nervously. He was lying. We decided to chuck that segment, and wisely so. A couple of weeks later he was to have been paraded by the Contras in front of an international press corps to repeat this story. Before it began, he excused himself to use the bathroom. Unfortunately for his minders, this poor fellow then bolted out the bathroom window and disappeared into the jungle.

One more job and we were done: an unscripted on-camera conclusion from me. Although I delivered it so poorly even my parents would be hard-pressed to praise it, we shot only one take and took off. This was not a place we wanted to hang around.

We posed for a picture I still have in my office. I have my arms around my friends. John and Larry are smiling broadly, well satisfied. Mark is just staring off toward nothing in particular as if refusing to engage in such frivolity while in the middle of a war zone. And yet that picture tells you all you will ever want to know about that impish, unpredictable, hilarious, and utterly unique fellow beloved by all who knew him: Mark is dressed in a Mickey Mouse T-shirt.

Time to wrap things up. Another six-hour bumper car ride through jungle hell, and we were back to Tegucigalpa, headed home.

4. The Commercials

Mark would have the commercials ready a couple of weeks later, one sixty seconds and the other cut down to thirty. Both included 800 phone numbers for contributions. There would also be a two-minute spot, this one elongated to include more voices, to be aired privately in the pursuit of major grants to help place as many of the others as possible. The sixty-second ad told the powerful story. The visuals we shot describe a narrator's words:

Nicaragua. A nation lays dying. Eight years after the Sandinista revolution, the dictators have reduced this once beautiful country to ruins. Poverty is rampant. Where once supermarkets were laden with food, the shelves are now empty or stocked with Marxist propaganda. Where once religious faith flourished, today it is persecuted. Beautiful churches lay in ruins while clergymen are expelled, imprisoned, or murdered. Where once opposing views were freely heard, today all independent media have been closed, replaced by arms of the communist propaganda regime.

Those who dare to speak out about the brutality of the Sandinista regime are routinely arrested, tortured and killed in prisons like El Chipote, one of the worst in a system with more political prisoners per capita than any nation in the world.

Against this formidable enemy stands a growing group of Nicaraguans fighting for the cause of freedom in Central America. These are the Contras, who stand alone against the Cuban and Soviet forces of aggression, the freedom fighters to whom President Reagan has pledged the means and the will to survive. But now, liberal sympathizers of the Sandinista communists are determined to abandon the freedom fighters. That is why your support is critical.

If you are committed to the cause of freedom, let President Reagan know now. Call the number on your screen—1-800-642-4000—and a letter in your name will be sent free of charge tomorrow to the President. That's 1-800-642-8000. The call and the letter are free, but your support is priceless.

They were good spots and might have had some impact, but in the political world anything can happen, and in the end they turned out not to be really necessary. First, the Iran-Contra mess badly hurt the cause. Then there was the Soviet Union death spiral. Its support for adventurism in Central America, including bankrolling its most treasured satellite, Cuba, was eroding and the threat to the Monroe Doctrine receding. Finally there was the war itself. Nicaraguans on both sides of the divide were tiring of it. In 1990 there would be a new presidential contest, this time not at the point of a gun. Daniel Ortega and his Sandinista Party would be thrown out of power. Seventeen years later he'd run again, and this time win democratically. He rules again with an iron fist.

I never saw any of the folks I met on this journey again, except for the occasional visit with Calero in Washington. But I did read about General Bermúdez in the papers. Not long after this trip there was a cease-fire, and several Contra leaders traveled to Managua to negotiate a peaceful resolution. Bermúdez was staying at the Hotel InterContinental. He stepped out the front door and a sniper's bullet blew his head off.

More Planes, Trains, and Automobiles

1. Why We Like Hoses

It's the fall of 1984. I'm working at NCPAC and several of us are returning from another gala we've held with Bob Hope, this time in Oklahoma City, with a bevy of celebrities in tow from comedienne Phyllis Diller to actor Fred MacMurray to boxing great Ken Norton. We are on a TWA flight headed back to Washington, DC, via St. Louis. Things are uneventful until we take off from St. Louis. Within minutes everyone hears a loud grinding in the fuselage. Passengers exchange "Can you hear it too?" looks. Finally it stops. The plane begins a lazy, wide turn to the left. The captain comes on the intercom to explain the situation. Apparently the hydraulic lines have parted, and we no longer have access to things such as, oh, landing gear.

That sound we heard was the copilot down below cranking that gear manually. So we are returning to St. Louis, he explains. The very good news is that Lambert International Airport has one of the longest runways in America. Further, that long, slow loop served a purpose.

He'd just emptied the fuel tanks over the city.

As we begin our final approach I look out the window. The runways are obviously closed. All manner of fire trucks, ambulances, and the rest are lined up awaiting us with their red cherries sparkling. All that's missing is George Kennedy and some snow, and we'd have our own *Airport '84*. We come in way too fast, unevenly lurching to and fro. We hit the ground and roll down the runway seemingly forever until we finally come to a stop. Most of the emergency vehicles depart as we're towed to our gate. Only then does the stewardess privately give a few of us some details the pilot omitted. When one loses his hydraulics, apparently other niceties are lost as well, things like flaps and brakes, and thrust reversers and flight controls.

After taking all our onboard belongings, we sit in the lobby for about an hour awaiting a new plane. But no. Comes the announcement over the loudspeaker that our old plane is now repaired and boarding will begin momentarily. Not a soul moves. There is no way on God's green earth that any of us is getting back on that damn plane. Finally the authorities relent. It's towed away. It exits stage right. About fifteen minutes later another TWA plane appears from our left. We embark and finish our voyage. But to this day I wonder if this was really a different plane or if they didn't they just roll the old one around the building and come out the other side, now with the "replacement."

2. Biggest Bump Award

Traveling to the Caribbean some years ago we hit massive, unexpected turbulence. The plane drops suddenly. Everyone is caught off guard. My orange juice cup goes flying out of my hand, travels across the aisle and dumps itself all over a passenger seated in the other window seat. She is not pleased.

3. Lift Off!

Norma and I are headed to Saint Martin, and as we travel down the Florida coast the plane slows down dramatically. The pilot tells us he's just learned NASA will be launching a rocket at any moment from Cape Canaveral, which is below us, and if we're lucky we'll get to see it. It happens. Passengers on the left side of the plane, soon joined by those on the right, preen out the window. There below, way down there, a golden glow! Lift-off! For a few moments there is nothing, then…here it comes. Ladies and gentlemen, there is nothing like watching a rocket ship *coming toward you*. It streaks past us and continues its ascent. At thirty-five thousand feet up, we can see it go into the darkness above and disappear.

4. You Gotta Be Kidding Me

I am on a TACA Airlines flight leaving San Salvador. Moments after liftoff we know there's a problem. The cabin air won't pressurize. The plane returns immediately to the airport. Rather than disembark, we are parked away from the traffic for on-the-spot repairs. A few minutes later I hear faint tapping on the side of the plane. I look out the window and see two mechanics below wearing trademark blue overalls. They are walking along- side the plane. One is holding a large screwdriver by the tip and tapping the handle against the fuselage. He's trying to *hear* the problem. Never has a passenger had less confidence in a repair job than on this day.

5. Corn on the Cob

It's 1991 and I'm an election observer in Guatemala, to monitor the voting in the first round of the presidential contest. Four of us are assigned a small twin-engine propeller plane, making drop-by inspections around the small country throughout the day. We are on our third leg. I am seated up front with the pilot. As he begins his descent I look down and see a very small village below—with no runway. *NO RUNWAY*. I try to act nonchalant as I ask the pilot, "Say, just wondering. Where do you suppose we are going to land?"

He points to a dirt path. "*Allí.*" And that's just what we do, like it's just another day at the office. We come to a stop in front of a corn field with tall, mature stalks. There are a couple of army jeeps with soldiers waiting to escort us into town. We walk around a bit, and seeing nothing, return to our trusty dirt path. The pilot walks that path, inspecting it, and returns with bad news.

There is a divot close enough that the plane cannot achieve liftoff before reaching it. The hole is so menacing that should we hit it, the plane could flip, which would not be a good thing. We are stranded, or so we stupid Americans think. Except we're in Central America, where all things are possible because there's no one to tell you they aren't. The pilot instructs everyone to help push the plane back into the cornfield. We do as we're told until the pilot tells us to stop, about fifty yards in. The crop has matured, and we are enveloped in it.

We are Children of the Corn. We board, he fires the puppy up, and turns on the propellers. They grind a few stalks as they gain strength. When they're at full throttle, off we go, into the green. We are now barreling through the field, mercilessly slicing corn stalks and sending them flying in every which direction. We burst out of the foliage, into the open, and lift off, with plenty of space between us and that divot ahead, leaving a devastated cornfield behind.

6. Security? What Security?

Ironically, it's the next (and final) stop that day. This time as we begin our descent we face the opposite prospect. There is no town below but there *is* a runway. A *paved* runway. An airfield! We are landing at the official Guatemalan Air Force base. After what we've just been through, this is Nirvana. There is an officer waiting for us outside our plane as we disembark. He greets us with Central American military formality. But something is amiss. I look around. He is the only soldier there. The only *thing* there. There is not a single aircraft in sight. Again it's time for some feigned nonchalance. "Excuse me, but where is, you know, your air force?" He shakes his head and points his thumb over his shoulder to the fence line about one hundred yards away. The jungle is on the other side. "*Muy peligroso. Guerrillas.*"

THE FINE ART OF MONITORING ELECTIONS IN DICTATORSHIPS

1. War or Peace?

I was back with the Contras two years later, this time with a different group and for a different purpose.

The public appetite for military aid to the freedom fighters was waning. The Iran-Contra scandal had cast a deep pall over the cause. Besides, this war had been ongoing for almost a decade and was in a deadlock. The Contras weren't making much progress, but the Sandinista dream of becoming a communist powerhouse was also dead. The country was in ruins.

So the Bush 41 administration put out the word that it was preparing to end its military support. That upset the hawks, and I was in that camp. Perhaps the most ardent in that camp was the late Howard Phillips, founder and leader of the Conservative Caucus, then still a powerhouse in the movement, albeit in decline. Howie decided to sponsor a fact-finding mission to the region so some of us could examine the situation firsthand. I joined him as did a few others including Representative Dan Burton of Indiana.

As before, we traveled to the Contra compound in Tegucigalpa followed by that endless creep through the jungles. As before, others had joined us so there were enough people for another four or five vehicles. Burton was given the luxury ride on the Lady Ellen. This trip saw a couple of ripples I'd not experienced the first time around. First, in the middle of nowhere we came across an unexpected makeshift checkpoint. A handful of soldiers demanded we stop and present passports and so forth. But who were they? Hondurans? Contras? Sandinistas? Bandits? Honduran and Contra soldiers wore US-issued military gear. The Sandinistas' camouflage uniforms had a slightly bluish tint, but they were known to wear US gear when causing trouble. We had no way of knowing who they were. Our guides did—or guessed correctly. They were Honduran, on the lookout for Sandinista infiltrators.

But that wasn't the fun part. About halfway through the trip we came across a small clearing with a slight bend back under the canopy. The lead car stopped, and the driver got out. I was in the second vehicle, and I heard him ask the driver, "*Preparado?*" Our driver nodded. I watched the lead guide approach the other drivers in the vehicles behind us with the same question. After the leader returned to his jeep our driver turned to us and admonished us to hold on. With that all drivers gunned their vehicles. We didn't travel more than twenty-five to thirty miles per hour, but we may as well have been doing the speed of sound. Up to this point we rarely hit ten miles per hour on that rutted path and now we were driving what can only be described as controlled road rage. Our heads crashed into ceilings, and our bodies lurched wildly in one direction and then the next as we banged into each other mercilessly. Once around that bend, maybe five hundred yards later, we returned to our crawl. We'd learn later that at that point, the trail had taken us directly to the edge of the Nicaraguan border, and reportedly there were several hundred Sandinista troops stationed over the crest of the hill. The preceding month they had opened fire on a convoy, killing a journalist. When we reached the camp we also were informed that when Burton flew overhead they had locked a surface-to-air missile on the Lady Ellen, presumably just to intimidate. (Mission accomplished.)

As we neared the base, the clouds unloaded their cargo on us. It was one of the hardest rains I've ever encountered. The rain lasted for a good hour, long enough to turn the mountainside into one big mudslide. We were no longer banging on the rutty road; we were now slogging through almost impassable guck. At one point the path was simply swept away. A crevasse had quickly widened to some five feet across and was deep enough that our vehicles couldn't maneuver through it. We waited as soaked Contras found enough logs to lay across the divide, then smaller ones to place across them. Each car inched along as those logs slid to and fro over the larger ones. But we made it.

As we climbed the final hill before entering the Contra camps we saw how desperate the situation had become for the freedom fighters. The soldiers were starving. We'd found ourselves behind a dump truck stacked to the hilt with literally hundreds, if not thousands, of heads of lettuce. That was the food supply. Given the slope and mud causing slippage, some of the heads rolled off the truck and right into the slime. I watched, horrified, as soldiers greedily yanked them out of the slop and without hesitation began to gnaw on them in the pouring rain, like dogs.

We entered the camp. Now there were fewer soldiers—attrition caused by the hopelessness of the situation, I imagine. Given the peace talks there was enough sense of security that some women had joined their husbands. This just made the situation that much more depressing. There was squalor everywhere. "Housing" was nonexistent; tents were a luxury. The noncombatants wore ragged clothing. The soldiers milled about aimlessly. We got out of our vehicles and were instantly drenched to the bone. We were escorted to the headquarters building and met with the leaders (such as they were). In short order they confirmed what our eyes had shown us. They were willing to keep fighting, but they were falling apart.

We were back in the States two days later and shortly thereafter I was invited as a part of a group of some ten conservative leaders to a meeting at the White House with National Security Advisor Robert Gates. He presented the position the administration was set to announce: there would be continued humanitarian aid to the Contras provided both sides agreed to a cease-fire while negotiations were underway. After his presentation he asked for endorsements. Everyone agreed to the idea except me. They were not privy to what I'd witnessed. To call what the Contras were receiving "humanitarian" was putting lipstick on a pig. I urged the administration either to provide real aid during the negotiations or just disband the Contras altogether. One way or another this war had to be resolved and the Contra cause decided.

2. Tripping Toward Elections

Fate took matters into her own hands. In short order the Soviet Union collapsed. With that, continued support from the Soviets or their Cuban proxies came to an end. The Sandinistas were losing control of the country, partly because of armed insurrection but also because its infrastructure had collapsed from the ravages of Marxism. The international community was demanding democratic elections, and the communists finally consented.

In 1987 I'd launched the World Freedom Foundation (a rather grandiose title, don't you think?). It was dedicated to combating communism wherever necessary. Two years later the Soviet Union fell. I took credit, declared unequivocal victory, and shut the foundation down. But we had accomplished one thing while the WFF was in existence, and it was important. When the decision to hold elections in Nicaragua was announced, I thought it was important to answer one question: Did they know what the hell they were doing?

Curtin ("Curt") Winsor was the ambassador to Costa Rica during the Reagan administration and more recently had joined the board of directors of the World Freedom Foundation. We had lunch to discuss this. It led to the idea: Why not form a commission to study the issue? With that, the Bipartisan Commission on Free and Fair Elections in Nicaragua was born.

But it had to be truly bipartisan for it to have traction. We recruited a fine group for the mission. Sergio Bendixen was a veteran consultant for various liberal Democratic senators and causes. Ambassador Alan Keyes had held several positions in the Reagan administration. Elaine Kamarck was another Democratic consultant at both the congressional and presidential levels. Vic Gold was Bush's speechwriter and worked for Spiro Agnew and enough said. Winsor would serve as cochairman, but who on the left to cohabit with him? Someone suggested Senator Gaylord Nelson. I thought it an odd choice. The founder of Earth Day was one of the most liberal members of Congress. Surely he was just too biased for this role, but we rolled the dice and prayed I was wrong. I was wrong. We could not have asked for better.

For three days the commission questioned twenty-six witnesses, each knowledgeable about some aspect of the process. Some came from Capitol Hill, led by Kansas senator Bob Dole. There were international election and human rights organizations like Amnesty International, unions like the AFL-CIO, public policy groups like the American Enterprise Institute, representatives of the Bush administration such as national security adviser Peter Rodman, religious leaders such as exiled Nicaraguan bishop Pablo Vega, and even a Sandinista representative, Major Roger Miranda. Because his command of the English language was insufficient, I volunteered to serve as his translator. There's nothing quite like translating bold-faced lies with a straight face. By the end of the proceedings it was apparent to all that this forthcoming election was going to be a farce, either through incompetency or theft or both unless there were international observers on the scene to monitor and report on the situation on the ground.

Overnight there were more than a dozen parties established across the spectrum, but only two mattered. Daniel Ortega and his Sandinista regime were on one side; Violeta Barrios de Chamorro, from the National Opposition Union (Unión Nacional Opositor: UNO), stood on the other. The Chamorro family was prominent in Nicaragua. Emiliano Chamorro Vargas was the thirty-ninth president of the country during the 1920s. His great-grandson Pedro Joaquín Chamorro Cardenal was the editor of *La Prensa*, which was by then owned by the Chamorro family. In 1950 Chamorro married Violeta Barrios Torres, also of wealthy stock. Anastasio Somoza, whose family ruled Nicaragua with an iron fist for forty-three years, was then running the country. *La Prensa* was powerful, and Chamorro was becoming increasingly critical of the Somoza regime. In 1978 Chamorro died in a hail of shotgun blasts. The Somozas blamed the anti-Catholic

Sandinistas; the Sandinistas pointed fingers at Somoza. The Chamorro family agreed with the Sandinistas. So, too, had the victim. Chamorro had written a letter three years previously to Somoza: "I am waiting, with a clear conscience, and a soul at peace, for the blow you are to deliver."

Central America is home to some strange politics. Some twenty years later Violeta Chamorro was now challenging the communist regime that had overthrown the Somoza dictatorship that had murdered her husband. She was an anti-Sandinista, which made her welcomed in conservative circles back home, but she was also rejecting the cause of the Contras. She wanted peace and preached reconciliation at every turn.

Three organizations were formed to attempt to monitor the elections. The first one came from the Organization of American States, a rather bland international body committed to the democratic process, and at times outspoken in its criticism of despots, but it did nothing more. Second, Jimmy Carter's Carter Center. Now that was a useless exercise. Carter clearly leaned in favor of the Sandinistas. Time and again his organization took a pass when a condemnation of that communist regime was in order.

Third was the National Endowment for Democracy, founded by Allen Weinstein, a veteran of the Reagan administration. I'd crossed paths with him and his assistant Caleb McCarry here and there and knew them to be both decent and committed to the cause of liberty. What I would learn soon enough was that they were also courageous as hell.

Caleb proposed a fact-finding trip to Nicaragua to examine conditions and determine if there could be an honest election. He chose a GOP/conservative delegation led by Republican National Committee Chairman Lee Atwater on one side and a Democratic/liberal delegation headed by Democratic National Committee Finance Chairman Peter Kelly on the other. Atwater recruited Peter Flaherty from the National Legal and Policy Center and me to serve as his lieutenants. Kelly chose Walter Mondale's presidential campaign manager Bob Beckel and Wally Chambers, a well-respected CBS producer. But almost immediately the State Department intervened. The situation down there was still dangerous and considered too risky for Atwater, given his position during a Republican administration. He pulled out, and his assistant Mary Matalin was assigned to take his place. (Yes, digest that one for a moment.)

The day of our departure I arrived early at Dulles International Airport and found Beckel at the bar, drinking heavily. Beckel would later write about his struggles with alcoholism, but this was worse. Beckel suffered from acute aerophobia. He told me as he gulped his liquor that every treatment he'd tried had failed, and he was down to drinking himself stupid to make a flight.

He failed. Our delegation boarded and the plane taxied down the runway. Every time it hit the slightest bump Beckel screamed from the back, frightened and now dead sober. On the way back it would be even worse. He was terrified as we descended toward our landing, moaning loudly, almost crying in front of everyone. As we made touchdown, this gruff, tough guy lay in a fetal position, his head on Mary's lap, whimpering and shaking like a baby.

The flight was noteworthy in another respect. The Democrats viewed the Contras as nothing more than contract killers doing the bidding of evil Reaganites. The Sandinistas, well, they were misunderstood and deserved support because they were of and for the people and blah, blah, blah. We saw things the other way around and pushed back strongly. There was real tension. When Flaherty delivered a wholly unprovoked oral bitch slap, the boil was lanced, and poisonous invective flowed from both sides. We were not getting along.

We were in our rooms at the InterContinental by early afternoon the following day. We had an office of sorts, with fax machines and phones, but other than that, not much was shared. The two camps kept to themselves. We set out immediately for a series of meetings with our American embassy contacts, UN representatives, Sandinista officials, and election observers from the OAS.

Our final order of business was dinner that night with political leaders to get their views on the campaign. The restaurant had been selected by the American embassy. It stood at the edge of the city and as with so much down there, it had no name, at least none that you could see. The parking lot was barely lit, the omnipresent weeds all about, and no one was there but us. Every car arrived at once, naturally dented or damaged some other way. The candidates entered the restaurant, most of them nervously since none of them had ever campaigned before. In fact, tonight might be the night some were first introduced as such.

We were placed in the dining room at a large rectangular table. The election observers sat at the head and the candidates and their aides along the other sides. From the start it was a circus. Every time a candidate was recognized, he or she gave a short presentation, predictably denouncing the election process as a sham, accusing the Sandinistas of foul play, and sometimes even violent foul play. But when he or she concluded his or her remarks, and I mean every time each mercifully short speech was over, the leader of the Communist Party, a diminutive, prematurely balding middle-aged gnome would jump to his feet to condemn *"Los Yanquis!"* And, *"Los capitalistas!"* And, *"Los imperialistas!"* He did this all the while extolling the virtues of *"La justicia!"* And *"El pueblo!"* And *"Los obreros!"* Workers of the world unite and all that. No matter how many times this pest was told to cut it out, Little Commie refused to comply, yelling, fist waving for dramatic emphasis, extolling everyone to join him in the condemnation of all things not communist.

We finished dinner, finally. I'm not sure what was accomplished. We learned little except that communists can be loud mouths, but by our presence alone our message to our guests carried tremendous importance: The United States was serious about these elections. As we climbed back into our dilapidated vehicles, we heard a roar coming from behind the building. Someone had parked his car there. It came around the corner and shot by us, a shiny brand new bright red Mercedes-Benz driven by— you guessed it—Little Commie. That was Friday.

Saturday morning we were told that Violeta Chamorro was holding a rally in the town of Masatepe, about thirty miles south of Managua.

There being nothing else of importance on the calendar, we decided to head there.

3. Masatepe

Sunday morning at the airport I penned an article that would appear in the *National Review* a couple of weeks later.

Murder in Masatepe

By L. Brent Bozell III

Masatepe, Nicaragua—"The People of Masatepe Repulse UNO's Terrorism," declared La Barricada. Both Sandinista-controlled newspapers carried the report: On Sunday, December 10, a mob organized by remnants of the hated National Guard and dispatched by the National Opposition Union (UNO) launched a vicious attack on peasants in the village during a sparsely attended opposition rally, killing one bystander, injuring 17 others, and destroying two houses. One headline read, "International Observers Witnessed Their Acts."

I was one of those observers. What we saw—and nearly fell victim to—was far different: a well-planned, murderous attempt by the Sandinistas to strike terror in the hearts of their popular opposition in the presidential election scheduled for February 25.

The Center for Democracy (CFD) had invited various delegations to gauge the prospects for a free and fair election. This group is composed of American political activists. The Democrats are led by CFD Chairman and former Democratic National Committee Finance Chairman Peter Kelly, the Republicans by RNC Chief of Staff Mary Matalin. We arrive in Managua Saturday and spend the day visiting with opposition leaders, the American embassy's chargé d'affaires, representatives of the Organization of American States (OAS) Observer Team, and Sandinista officials. Opposition spokesmen complain about increasing violence perpetrated at UNO rallies by the turbas divinas (the Sandinista-sponsored "divine mobs"). Foreign Ministry official Manuel Cordero dismisses the charges as "minor."

Sunday, we will briefly visit an UNO rally in Masatepe, a small town thirty miles south of Managua, then proceed deeper into the countryside to Matagalpa, where more tensions have been reported. As it turns out, we will never reach Matagalpa.

At about 11:30 am, we enter Masatepe, a typical Nicaraguan village whose ten thousand inhabitants live in (also typical) wretched poverty. We work our way toward the center of town, past idle bystanders, then growing groups of peasants, then—pandemonium. People are running to and from the square, where about two hundred UNO supporters are screaming and hurling stones. Several see our three jeeps approaching and run toward us crying "¡Las turbas! ¡Las turbas! ¡Están aquí las turbas!"—The Sandinista thugs are here.

A small hut on the western end of the square is surrounded by UNO supporters bombarding its sides and tin roof with heavy rocks, shattering windows. Up a short flight of stairs, in front of the village cathedral on the eastern end of the square, stand turbas raining down a rock bombardment of their own. No police or military officials are present to stop this, though we see one military truck drive past.

As we slowly make our way between them, both groups stop. We leave our jeeps, don our official blue and white election-observer caps and begin to question both sides. We are told that when the UNO rally began, the turbas began throwing rocks at the jeep carrying Dona Violeta Chamorro, UNO's presidential candidate. The turbas were chased to the square, where several were trapped in the shed and the rest regrouped in front of the cathedral.

As we talk, the stoning of the shed resumes; the Sandinista agitators burst out, cross the street, and jump into a party office. The others begin to taunt the crowd with insults. Fifty UNO marchers move toward them, but UNO organizers and OAS observers convince them to rejoin the rally, about four blocks west of the square.

We follow, through a crowd of UNO supporters packing the streets, the rooftops, even the make-shift stage. Homemade banners wave as vice-presidential candidate Dr. Virgilio Godoy and then "Dona Violeta" speak. The crowd of between 7,500 and 15,000 roars "UNO! UNO! UNO!"—interrupting speeches which can barely be heard through the primitive P.A. system. Then a new cry is heard: "Vienen las turbas!"

Some UNO supporters march peacefully up the street and are met by turbas, now armed with rocks, nail-studded clubs, and machetes. An argument breaks out. A thug charges forward and swings a machete into the UNO crowd. UNO supporters respond, some with their own machetes. Rocks fly. Peter Kelly, caught between two forces drives over a wall and watches as UNO forces drive back the turbas, but at a cost: a UNO bus comes up the street to carry off a woman. Her left arm has been chopped off by a turba machete.

We retreat down another street, then realize it is the route of the UNO march; Mrs. Chamorro's jeep is directly behind us, and thousands of supporters are behind her. Our group has split up. I am with former DNC Chief of Staff Wally Chalmers, Mary Matalin, and others; Robert Beckel (former Mondale for President campaign manager) and a friend are about 15 feet ahead. In a sudden commotion—running, shouting, shoving—Beckel disappears, enveloped by the crowd. Knocked to the ground, he manages to grab a little girl and shield her with his body, then looks up to witness a turba rip his machete into a UNO supporter, opening a wound from his left shoulder to his right hip. The man will soon be dead.

Still there is no sign of the police. The turbas have blocked off the intersection and are going to attack Mrs. Chamorro's jeep, but the peasants form a wall to protect her. Her jeep slowly backs up and retreats through side streets to the main road, and back to Managua.

Skirmishes erupt all over. Word goes out that one or more of the machete-wielders are hiding in a nearby Sandinista Front campaign office. One hundred angry UNO marchers rain a barrage of rocks through its windows, tear down and burn a Sandinista flag, and overturn and stone a UNO jeep parked in front. Rumors circulate: A man with a gun has been spotted inside. Yes, he has a gun at the head of a hostage. A new call rings out: There are children inside. CFD President Allen Weinstein and his assistant, Caleb McCarry, courageously plead with the UNO mob for the lives of the children. After several minutes, the stoning pauses as a frightened mother hugging her infant daughter comes out the front, then resumes with greater ferocity. An explosion rings out and black smoke fills the street: the jeep has been set afire.

It's a full-fledged riot now. Two and a half hours have gone by without sign of the police or army. We travel the four blocks to the police station and are told the chief of police "is in a meeting." Weinstein, insistent, gets him out of his "meeting" and demands to know why nothing is being done to stop the riot. The chief responds that his understanding was there was an argument going on "between two women."

After further pleas, he reluctantly agrees to investigate, accompanied by Weinstein, McCarry, an OAS representative, and a UNO official. But when they come within twenty feet of the houses under siege, two bursts of semiautomatic fire erupt from the vicinity of the buildings. As the crowd dives for cover, the gunman escapes. Several soldiers finally arrive, and the peasants disperse without further incident. We return to Managua, shaken by what we've witnessed, prayerful for the dead and wounded. Grateful to be alive.

In the next 24 hours we learn that the turbas returned to Masatepe and surrounding towns that evening—this time wearing masks. They machine gunned several UNO homes, dousing two with gasoline, beat up one UNO official, and spared the life of another only because of the tearful pleas of his children. They also took the body of the dead UNO supporter, proclaimed him a victim of UNO terrorism, and buried him in a Sandinista Front ceremony.

There's more. The night before the rally all electricity to Masatepe had been cut so as to bring in, under the cover of darkness, the truckloads of turbas. On the morning of the rally, Sandinista officials tried to disrupt it by ordering local school children and parents to a special meeting. The Sandinista campaign manager inadvertently admitted to being in radio contact with the Masatepe chief of police all afternoon, documenting conclusively the collusion between the local police and the Sandinista Front. Right and Left, we left Nicaragua convinced that under present circumstances there is no chance of a fair election.

There was another element to the story, kept out because of space limitation. It spoke to the successful manipulation of a gullible press clearly supportive of the Sandinista regime. The townsfolk had dispersed, but not immediately. After the jeep was set on fire, they remained, furiously screaming their contempt for all things Sandinista—the regime, the hired thugs, the police, everything—while they hurled rocks. The moment was perfect, clearly timed by the Sandinista police. A convoy of press rolled into town accompanied by Sandinista minders. *Look!* They pointed at the melee, the black smoke and flames shooting into the air. *Look!* They pointed to the mob attempting to destroy the UNO office. *Look what the terrorists are doing!* Camcorders rolled, cameras snapped, and reporters furiously jotted notes. The Sandinista goons had not only threatened Chamorro's life; they were turning her cause into a public relations nightmare on the world stage. From start to finish this had been orchestrated.

We knew the trouble this trumped-up story could cause the Chamorro campaign. We were witnesses to the truth, and we had to tell the story. We headed back directly to the InterContinental. It was decided that the conservatives would reach out to their media contacts, and the liberals theirs. It took our side about five minutes to reach our entire media universe—the *Washington Times*. The liberal contingent was far busier with their faxing efforts. At some point we realized (I forget how) our faxes were being intercepted. We made our way to the safety of the American embassy and continued our work there.

After dark we headed to the home of Violeta Chamorro to check on her. I was struck by the simplicity of her residence. I expected her to live in one of the few ornate villas, given her lineage and standing. Maybe for that war-torn country it was luxurious; in ours it would be considered no more than an ordinary suburban home. More amazing, there was no security present. There was no outside lighting. In the darkness by the trees there was an old man lurking, looking more like a gardener than a hired gun. Were an assassination attempted, she wouldn't stand a chance.

We were ushered inside by a maid and presented with an extraordinary sight on the large slate patio. In the middle of it a black shotgun-pellet-riddled limousine, maybe from the early sixties, sat on display. It was her husband's death car. On the wall, glass-enclosed, was her husband's blood-stained shirt. Perhaps this is why Violeta remained so calm, to the point of serenity, when she greeted us. All things in this war-torn country needed to be put in their proper perspective. We chatted for a while, promised we'd do our level best to testify to the truth, and that we'd call for her protection. Bidding this remarkable woman farewell, we returned to our hotel.

At some point that evening a new plot was hatched. We had Mary Matalin's VHS tape recording. It held the evidence, the American embassy knew it, and they, too, wanted the world to see it.

We were up before dawn the following morning, headed back to the airport. A funny thing happened there as I typed up my report on my lap. I spotted our very own Inspector Clouseau. Dressed in an iconic raincoat and wearing an equally ridiculous hat—indoors—and pretending to read a newspaper, he could not have looked more out of place. Nor was it the first time I'd seen him. I'd first spotted the fellow in the lobby of the hotel the day we'd arrived, seated and reading a paper (probably the same one). Later in the evening, when I got off the elevator at my floor and turned to my left toward my room, he just happened to be in the hallway on the other side of the elevator. When our eyes met for a moment, he turned and walked away, making it more apparent than ever he was our token spy, just not a very good one. And another thing. He wasn't waiting for a flight. There was no scheduled flight.

Instead, we were escorted onto the tarmac where a small, unmarked airplane awaited us. Don't ask, don't tell. We knew this had been arranged by the embassy, and that's all we knew. We boarded and took off. An hour later we touched down in San José, Costa Rica, where a large black van awaited us on that tarmac. No passport check. Off we went.

Óscar Arias, the socialist president of this scandal-ridden country, saw himself as some sort of Central American Solomon, convening irregular meetings of the five Central American nations in pursuit of his leftist foreign policy agenda. At least he did until he was ultimately embroiled in his own alleged crimes, ranging from personal corruption to sexual assault. The heads of those five nations—which included Ortega—were presently in San José meeting at the presidential palace to discuss the peace process in Nicaragua, with legions of international media present. Many there knew about Masatepe, and most had ignored it or had fallen for the Sandinista ruse.

Our plan was to hold a press conference inside the palace to provide the assembled media with the evidence of the Sandinista attack. God bless her, Mary had taped everything from the rock-throwing melee that greeted us to the machete attacks to the confrontation at the UNO headquarters. The tape gave the alpha and omega. On top of that we were six witnesses, official election observers all, from opposite sides of the political divide, yet unanimously in agreement over the guilt of the communist regime.

A few minutes away from the palace, our hosts—one Can Imagine At which agency they were assigned—were on walkie-talkies communicating with officials at the palace, providing logistics and such. But as we approached the entrance things changed abruptly. We were informed that a directive had just been issued, presumably by the president, now forbidding our presence inside the palace.

What to do? We were there, outside the gates. We exited the van and declared loudly we were holding a press conference right then and there. Word made its way inside the palace, and in short order reporters poured out. They'd been told we had video of the attack, and they wanted to see it. Someone found a way to rig some equipment to create a portable screen of sorts. We began.

We had to select a spokesman. If a conservative is a liberal who's been mugged, then a right-wing nut job is a liberal who just survived a communist machete attack. Our side enthusiastically agreed that Beckel should represent us. Bob was who Bob is: sharp, unequivocal, and passionate. He denounced the Sandinistas in no uncertain terms, laid the blame directly at their feet, and demanded that they pledge to protect Violeta Chamorro from any future attacks. The peace conference was formally disrupted. Numerous media outlets in the United States, from the *Washington Post* to the *New York Times*, finally filed stories about the video evidence; some video outlets like CNN and a broadcast network or two carried the footage. Presumably it received similar coverage in other countries as well.

4. Aftermath

We returned to the United States and made contact with the White House, which eagerly invited Beckel to give President George Bush 43 a briefing, which translated into another opportunity to affect the news cycle denouncing the Sandinistas. The communist regime continued to deny responsibility but to no avail. Ultimately they ate crow and promised Chamorro safe passage for her rallies.

But they didn't stop spinning. After promising Chamorro protection, the Sandinistas tried their level best to undermine the credibility of those involved in the election process. Several observers, both from our delegation and others, were denounced and forbidden reentry because of what the communists stated were attempts to overthrow the government. Former Ambassador to Costa Rica Curt Winsor was accused of restarting the war from the south. I was charged with restarting the war from the north. Curt was, and is still a member of the Board of Directors of the Media Research Center. At our next board meeting, Curt and I discussed this and pledged that in the future, when one of us was starting a war, he'd notify the other.

The Sandinistas still had their fellow travelers on the American left well placed in the worlds of policy and politics and in the media as well. Facts and footage meant nothing to them.

United Press International (UPI) would blandly file a story a month after the attack at Masatepe regarding an order by the Sandinistas' pompously-named "Supreme Electoral Council," and would subtly suggest Chamorro was to blame. According to the wire service, the order was "meant to prevent the kind of violence that occurred on December 10 when the opposition rally erupted into a melee that left one person dead and more than a dozen wounded." Nowhere was it stated that the Sandinistas were the ones responsible for the violence they were now allegedly preventing.

UPI turned to the one man whose feigned impartiality would best advance the Sandinista cause, Jimmy Carter himself. In reality, the Carter Commission could not monitor a school board election fairly let alone a violent election subverted by communists. What caused the attack in Masatepe? Who were the culprits and who the victims? Carter had the answer: "It would probably never be certain who started the violence." But there was one thing about which our former president Carter was certain. The UPI continued: "At a news conference in Managua, Carter praised the work of the Supreme Electoral Council, saying 'their actions have been without blemish, they have done a perfect job.'"

The campaign entered its final week with surveys showing the Sandinistas enjoying a twenty-plus point lead. On the eve of the election, I was asked to participate in a press conference to make my predictions. My three fellow panelists declared that the Sandinistas would win and win big. I picked Chamorro and credited columnist Ben Wattenberg for having convinced me of that. In a recent piece he'd opined that this was a referendum, not an election, and the unspoken question on the ballot was: "Do you want to starve?" Besides, he said, how else would you expect someone to respond to a Sandinista pollster?

Pretty much the way Trump supporters respond to pollsters here.

Two days later, in the most closely monitored election in the history of Central America, Violeta Chamorro won the presidency with 54.7 percent of the vote.

Even after the elections the left continued to shill for the Sandinistas. The February 25, 1990, edition of the *Los Angeles Times* focused on the observers recruited by Allen Weinstein and the Center for Democracy. The *Times* left unchallenged a quote from the Sandinistas suggesting Weinstein's crew corrupted the election. The Sandinista quote set the article's tone:

> We felt that to be an observer here, a person must be open-minded and objective," said Foreign Ministry spokesman Alejandro Bendana. "You don't have to be an admirer of the Sandinistas, but you have to want free and fair elections. That is not necessarily the case with some of the people Weinstein wanted to bring.

The *Times* took it from there. "The Sandinistas' distrust of the group began after the campaign clash in Masatepe on Dec. 10 that left one person dead. The center blamed the Sandinistas for the violence and flew observers to a meeting of the five Central American presidents in Costa Rica to denounce the Nicaraguan government. The OAS said it could not pinpoint the blame."

In the *Washington Post* on March 4, left-wing apologist Robert Pastor penned his recap—never acknowledging he was part of the Carter team— and in it dismissed the violence of Masatepe as of debatable importance:

> The U.S. debate on the contras and also on the elections was infected by this polarization. During the campaign, some conservatives in the United States dismissed the registration process as a sham, and interpreted the campaign violence in Masatepe to mean that the Sandinistas did not intend to permit a free election and viewed the delay on the release of U.S. funds as Sandinista skulduggery. At the same time, Ortega opened the system because he was confident of victory and wanted the election to be certified as fair.

THE STEWARDESS

Okay, one final airport story. It's about three weeks after 9/11. The country is still very much on edge, particularly those who are flying. Reports emerge about strange events taking place on flights around the country with Middle Eastern passengers abruptly standing up or causing other distractions that are deliberately upsetting passengers. Some are detained, but none (that I know of) is charged. There is speculation these are bad people testing security procedures or just trying to keep the country rattled. There are just too many of these reports to dismiss. Worse yet, one wonders how many other times it's happened, and it wasn't reported.

This is one such example.

It's a Saturday morning, September 22, and I'm leaving Grand Rapids, Michigan, after visiting with Amway founder Rich DeVos the day before. The airport is mostly empty except for the police and military presence that's everywhere. Most are carrying long arms. We board the American Airlines flight to Washington. It's one of those criminally small MD-80 puddle jumpers. I have little tolerance for these planes, but on a relatively short hop from a small city like Grand Rapids, it is what is expected. The rows are two by two, and the passengers are squished side by side. There is no first class. I'm seated in the second row on the left side, by the window. There is no one around me except two passengers seated in the first row on the right, behind the bulkhead. We are separated by no more than five feet. The man by their window is tall and looks Middle Eastern. The fellow seated next to him is shorter, heavyset, and black.

Given their size, they look uncomfortable squeezed together. I note casually that they are saying nothing. They just look straight ahead. The stewardess gets on the public address system and tells us that because of the light passenger load, anyone who likes can move to another seat and stretch out. I fully expect these two men to take advantage of the offer, just as everyone else sharing a row is doing. And yet, as everyone spreads out, the two men don't budge. They continue staring straight ahead in their cramped space.

The hatch has been closed going on twenty minutes, which is odd since there's so little air traffic post-September 11. Yet we don't move from the gate. Suddenly it flies open, and here they come. At least six very large men pour into the plane, and in seconds they are enveloping the two men. They are identified by their jackets as FBI and DEA and who knows what else. I know because they're just feet away from me. One agent is actually standing awkwardly on the seat next to mine. They all have their weapons drawn, pointed at these two men's heads, and they're screaming for them to sit perfectly still.

Now stop a moment. If you were an innocent man, and in their shoes, how would you react? For starters, you'd be startled out of those shoes, and you'd jump instinctively. You'd then protest—loudly, either in anger, or fear, or…something. But not these two. They *still* don't budge, not one inch. They say nothing. They continue to stare straight ahead at the bulk-head wall in front of them. They clearly have been expecting this. The authorities grab them and hustle them out immediately.

The captain comes out of his cabin and gets on the PA system to explain what had transpired. The stewardess had spoken with him during the boarding process and registered her concern about these two men behaving so oddly, especially after they declined to separate once given the chance. The captain explains that we'd been made to wait at the gate while authorities inside conducted background checks on the men. Neither man had any record that they could find, but no matter. The pilot insisted they be removed anyway. He is unapologetic with us. "I just didn't trust them."

He states that if the men were innocent, no harm would come to them. If they were not innocent, no potential harm was going to have come to anyone on board.

"I am the captain," he concludes in a firm voice, "and this is my ship." And that is that. The forty or so passengers burst into applause. The captain and the stewardess—a very pretty stewardess by the way—stand at the front, silently accepting the gratitude. There is something striking about the moment. There is no sense of fear. Or relief. Or even joy. It is a simple resolve.

No, you don't. Not again. Never again.

It is a very pleasant flight back to our nation's capital.

But I retell that story for another reason.

Note that I used the term "stewardess" three times. I did so deliberately. Did that sound somewhat awkward, maybe old-fashioned? And to insist on calling that stewardess "pretty"—did that ding you for just a second as just a wee bit inappropriate? If not, congratulations. You're normal.

Others won't see it that way.

"Stewardess" will strike some as retrograde, but for me it is a salient metaphor, a useful commentary on the present cultural condition. Once upon a time, the women who ran the cabin were indeed "stewardesses." But at some point it was deemed that this title was inappropriate because somehow it hinted at the sexist. It was *too* feminine. So just as the "actress" became an "actor," so, too, should the "stewardess" become…but that just didn't work. So the word was ditched and replaced by the asexual "flight attendant." In recent days that term has also come under scrutiny. Again there's something wrong. On a growing number of airlines "flight attendant" has been determined to be too formal, too suggestive of servitude. "'Flight attendants' is too vague and belittling for my taste," writes George Hobica of Airfarewatchdog.com. "*Merriam-Webster* defines 'attendant' as a 'servant' and I think that demeans and…" blah, blah, blah. So in a world where all things are now equal, the stewardesses are introduced as simply "Becky," or "Maggie," or if male, "Tyrone." Once the airplane was commandeered by Captain Michael Smith. Today it's "our captain, Mike."

Any flight attendant can pour coffee, but not every one of today's flight attendants could be a stewardess, certainly not the male ones (I think). It wasn't too long ago, a stewardess *had* to be attractive, young, single, pleasant, competent, and, of course, female. At TWA a stewardess retired at thirty-five or at marriage, whichever came first. It was a glamour job in a glamorous profession. Young women aspired to be one, and airlines could afford to be picky. The supply exceeded the demand.

Not too long ago we appreciated beauty, the beauty in architecture, in music, in art, in language, and in airline stewardesses. We demanded excellence of ourselves primarily, but—and this is important—of all around us as well, and that included our stewardesses. We believed in societal standards because they served a baseline purpose. If you didn't have what it took to be a stewardess, company execs didn't change the job description. They allowed a deserving candidate to take the position instead. And the captain? He was Captain Michael Smith—period. He called the shots—period. And you paid him that respect.

Today, the word "flight attendant" has no more meaning than "happy holidays" or "Indigenous People's Day" or "marriage equality." Language is far more insipid than most realize. In stripping us of our language, the left strips us of our history, of our culture, of our values. We cannot reflect on "better days" because we are no longer allowed to think of them as better. Those days, we are told, were not enlightened, not "woke," and how I hate that word! We cannot pass judgments on others' truths, never mind that it's a nonsensical proposition to believe every individual is entitled to a truth. We cannot place women on a pedestal because to do so is discriminatory, which it most certainly is, but good luck explaining that this is a good thing. There is no glamour, no beauty, no chivalry, because sameness forbids it.

It's a world gone mad. The cancel culture is very real. Just as the Taliban destroyed all statues depicting Afghanistan's pre-Islamic past, so, too, are the radicals attempting to destroy the cultural statuary that has defined America as well. The militant left has successfully co-opted liberalism and effectively intimidated everyone in its path. Society has turned its back on common sense. The Jacobins live to loathe but in so doing will ultimately self-destruct because in loathing everything they loathe themselves as well. But how much harm will they inflict on the world before it comes to its senses?

They rush to rid us of terms like "stewardess" because somehow they offend womankind. "The study of sexism has suggested that the solution to gender inequity is in changing sexist culture and institutions," lectures *Britannica*. "To overcome patriarchy in society is, then, to dismantle sexism in society." And so with a very straight face a member of Congress delivers the opening prayer of the 117th Congress and closes it with, "Amen and a-woman."

But how much do those who proclaim their solidarity with women's rights actually know about women? There is no greater example of courage than Saint Joan of Arc. There is no greater example of charity than Mother Teresa. Few could match the political spunk of Margaret Thatcher. And then there's the woman chosen to be the mother of the Son of God. The enlightened have turned their back on all these women, most especially Our Lady.

It's not just radical feminism, of course. Over the past half century liberalism has morphed from (mostly) innocent idealism to deadly Maoism. Fifty years ago liberalism had intellectual heft and political firepower but it lacked broad public support. Yes, there was a vibrant anti-war sentiment, and yes, some angrily marched against "Amerika," but they were the outliers. Most liberals gave all that a nod, and not much more. They disagreed with the basic tenets of free enterprise, ordered society, and American exceptionalism, but coexistence was mandated, love was free, and acid was dropped.

The '80s seemed to change all that. Liberalism was marching through the institutions and planting its flag on one hill after the next. The hippies of the '60s were now America's educators and in becoming so had sobered, with a seriousness of purpose. Hollywood was no different. The Waynes, Hestons, Stewarts, and Reagans were gone, replaced by Fondas, Baldwins, Redfords, and Streisands. Radical liberalism was becoming mainstream and the message unapologetic. Cohabitation was impossible. Western civilization was repressive. American exceptionalism was unjust. The free enterprise system was immoral. Religion must go.

It seems to have worked with a significant portion of the American people. It isn't the violence of Antifa and Black Lives Matter that concerns me. It is the lack of concern for the violence of Antifa and Black Lives Matter. When we allow the left to dictate change without conscience or consent, we have opened the door to a form of totalitarianism never before seen in this country. Their leaders declare themselves to be in Marxist communion with Mao, Stalin, and Kim. America no longer needs to be improved. She must be destroyed. We are no longer made in the likeness of God. We are God.

I am not of their world, but they aren't of mine either. They'll never understand this book I've written. They'll never comprehend an upbringing centered on faith embraced by ten children devoted to devilish misbehavior. The very concept of ten children is alien. They'll never appreciate how a father could send his boys thousands of miles from home by themselves, to fend for themselves not because it was the price of a superior academic education but because he wanted his children to live in a traditionalist Christian culture. They'll never feel the sensation of being pulled into the nobility of the Middle Ages while walking through castles and monasteries. They'll never fathom the joy derived in working for a man who derived such joy from removing liberals from office because he had no use for them. They'll never grasp the proposition that true social justice cannot be attained until *they* are destroyed. They'll never embrace the rejection of victimhood as a necessary imperative for happiness. I don't know that they can feel true happiness at all.

On that flight, on that day, our stewardess was on my side and I on hers. She rejected all of today's insane mandates and prohibitions and made a cold calculation based on common sense and experience. She did not like the way these two men looked, and so she profiled them. She felt a threat, and so she took preemptive action. She saw evil intention, and so she passed moral judgment. The captain trusted her judgment, agreed with her assessment, and acted on her recommendation. But here's the interesting thing. On board that plane that day there were surely some, perhaps many liberals, and a few hardened leftists to boot. At that moment not a one saw the world through the lens of the cancel culture. It was not they who were under attack, it was America under attack and America was worth defending because America is exceptional.

There surely will be another 9/11, and when it does happen, where will America look for safety? BLM and Antifa? Sanders, AOC and her Squad? The Southern Poverty Law Center and the ACLU? The National Council of Catholic Bishops and Nuns on the Bus? Planned Parenthood and Death with Dignity? Cuomo and Cuomo? De Niro and Clooney?

Or will they turn to that stewardess?

I've got my money on her.

ACKNOWLEDGMENTS

It is quite easy to go "woke" on the world. You simply declare everything is "my truth" and it's like donning an epistemological Superman outfit: all charges of inaccuracy simply bounce off you. I made every effort to avoid errors in fact but the written record from which to draw for this book is limited, so it was necessary to lean on the collective memory banks of quite a cast.

I thank my siblings—Chris (and Mary), Kathy (and Cy), Michael, Maureen, Johnny (and Carmen), Aloise, Patricia, Willie, and Jamie (and Julie)—for their unwavering patience as I lobbed several hundred emails at them, asking them to clarify this point or validate that anecdote. I needed guidance with the history of NCPAC and turned to dear friends with whom I've shared many political foxholes over the years: Craig Shirley, Greg Mueller, and Leif Noren. It was true joy becoming reacquainted with Larry Cushman and John Carvelli in conversations to recreate our adventure in Nicaragua more than thirty years ago, and thank God for them both as they remembered so much I'd forgotten. Thanks, Jack Fowler, for locating that long lost article in *National Review*.

What a professional machine you are, Post Hill Press! It starts with its Publisher, Anthony Ziccardi, who invited this book. Senior Managing Editor Madeline Sturgeon has the patience of Job, and was helpful on countless fronts. The gratitude continues, to Rachel Hoge, Production Editor; to Alana Mills, Production Manager; to Holly Layman, Editor, and to Mary Cantor, Proofreader.

Jack Cashill was the perfect guide as development editor, which is why I asked him to pen the foreword. Alex Hoyt, agent extraordinaire, arranged the marriage. Ed Molchany, Vice President for Programs at the Media Research Center, handled all business details. And my ever-suffering assistant Melissa Lopez was forced to slog through a half dozen drafts yet again. I heap buckets of praise on all of you.

Finally, and most importantly, to my bride for her boundless patience. In the immortal words of Ralph Kramden, Norma, you're the greatest.

If any inaccuracy managed to break through, I declare it to be my truth and take any criticism as an act of micro-aggression.

ABOUT THE AUTHOR

Lecturer, syndicated columnist, television commentator, debater, marketer, businessman, author, publisher, and activist, L. Brent Bozell III is one of the most outspoken and effective national leaders in the conservative movement today.

Founder and president of the Media Research Center, Mr. Bozell runs the largest media watchdog organization in America. Since its launch in 1987, the MRC has developed the largest video archive in the world; the popular NewsBusters.org blog site; the CNSNews.com internet news service; MRC Business; MRC Culture; MRCTV; MRC Latino; and most recently, Free Speech America. The MRC has nearly 650,000 members nationwide, with over 12 million fans on Facebook and over 7 million video views per week online.

In 2010, Mr. Bozell founded ForAmerica, an organization committed to restoring America to its founding principles. ForAmerica has grown to over 7 million Facebook followers with the most engaged social media army in the conservative movement. Twice, ForAmerica has registered as the most engaged group on Facebook's entire platform. In 1998, Mr. Bozell founded and was the first president of the Parents Television Council, the largest group in America dedicated to restoring decency to Hollywood. He founded the Conservative Victory Committee PAC in 1987. Before founding the MRC, Mr. Bozell was the finance director and later the president of the National Conservative Political Action Committee and the National Conservative Foundation.

Mr. Bozell's bi-weekly column (with Tim Graham) was syndicated by Creators Syndicate to over fifty media outlets nationwide. His writings have also appeared in numerous other outlets including the *Wall Street Journal*, *The Washington Post*, FoxNews.com and *USA Today*. He is the author of five books, including *And That's the Way It Is(n't)* (with Brent Baker), *Weapons of Mass Distortion*, *Collusion: How the Media Stole the 2012 Election* (with Tim Graham), *Whitewash* (with Tim Graham), and *Unmasked: Big Media's War Against Trump* (with Tim Graham).

He has been a guest on numerous television programs, including the *O'Reilly Factor*, *Nightline*, *The Today Show*, and *Good Morning America*. He appeared weekly on the "Media Mas" segment of *Hannity* on Fox News, and has appeared regularly on *The Kelly File*, *Your World with Neil Cavuto*, and *Varney & Co.*

Named the 1998 Pew Memorial Lecturer by Grove City College, Mr. Bozell is a frequent speaker on school campuses and for civic and political organizations around the country. Mr. Bozell serves on numerous boards of public policy, religious, and artistic organizations

Mr. Bozell received his B.A. in History from the University of Dallas, where he was named the 1998 Alumnus of the Year. In 2015, he received an honorary PhD from UD. He is married with five children and fourteen grandchildren.